ILLUSTRATED GUIDE
TO SHEFFIELD
AND NEIGHBOURHOOD

PAWSON & BRAILSFORD'S

ILLUSTRATED GUIDE
TO SHEFFIELD

AND NEIGHBOURHOOD

WITH A NEW FOREWORD BY
MARY WALTON

Republished S.R. Publishers Ltd., 1971
First published Pawson & Brailsford, Sheffield, 1862

© 1971 S.R. Publishers Limited,
East Ardsley, Wakefield,
Yorkshire, England.

ISBN 0 85409 671 X

Printed by Scolar Press Ltd.,
Menston, Yorkshire, U.K.

FOREWORD

To the 1971 Edition

This Guide was offered by its publishers in 1862 as a publication which "had long been wanted". It is, therefore, of particular interest as being one of the first results of a new business venture, and it is likely that the idea had for some time been in the mind of one or other of the partners. It must have taken some time to prepare, and it was only in 1859 that Henry Pawson and Joseph Brailsford set up in business together as printers. Pawson, who was an accurate and civilised reporter on the *Sheffield Times*, showed in his articles on the Sheffield exhibits at the Great Exhibition of 1851 a style and approach which makes it possible that the idea of reporting Sheffield more generally was his idea.

The careers of both partners were among those which illustrate the very close connection in Sheffield of the history of the printing trade and of journalism. Henry Pawson was born in Makerfield in 1820, and after apprenticeship to Nicholls, a well-known printer, he worked on the *Leeds Intelligencer* (now the *Yorkshire Post*). He came to Sheffield as a reporter for the *Sheffield Times*, and about 1853 went into partnership with Samuel Harrison to buy the paper from William Willott; he broke this connection in 1857 and turned his thoughts to independent printing.

Joseph Brailsford was of Sheffield parentage and born in 1824. He was taken as a trainee on to the staff of the *Sheffield and Rotherham Independent* in 1844 through the interest of the editor Robert Leader, and had a successful career with the paper until 1859, when he joined Pawson.

The two acquired a works in Mulberry Street, and established a shop and works at the Church Gates (shown as a discreet advertisement in the picture of the parish church on page 35). On this site they built a new works in 1884. A later journalist, catching the "Guide's" heavily romantic style, called the building a "stately and elegant pile", and its architect seems vaguely to have had in mind the Tudor foundations at Cambridge. After the deaths of Brailsford in 1891 and Pawson in 1907, their sons withdrew from the High Street building, which is now occupied by the National Westminster Bank. The firm continued at Mulberry Street until 1965, when a new works was built in Fitzwilliam Street. It is now, sadly, coming to an end.

In its heyday the firm produced much fine coloured work, of which the best known is the illustrated book by Henry Seebohm, "Coloured figures of the eggs of British birds". They employed artists and engravers most of whom will probably, but for happy accident, now remain anonymous. There is no clue in the "Guide" as to who produced the engravings which are its most valuable feature, but they were almost certainly both drawn (many copied on a smaller scale from earlier pictures) and engraved by the staff.

The "Guide", a hundred years after its first production, has become a standard work of reference in local history. The editor acknowledges his huge debt to Joseph Hunter, and his other acknowledgments are to writers whose names are a guarantee of reliability. But its main value lies not so much in the historical and topographical notes as in the wide and detailed coverage of contemporary industrial and commercial life. It is easy to pick out such unfamiliar items as the manufacture of crinolines (infinitely flexible structures of steel, cotton and dress material), the slightly alarming account of the goings-on at the sweet factory

(v)

of G. Bassett & Co., the note on the patent gas meters produced at Benjamin Vickers's Atlas Brass Works—matters for which there is not much easily accessible evidence.

On the whole, for the modern reader the "Guide" establishes an interesting picture of a Sheffield in a state half familiar, half very strange, and perhaps a little absurd. The style is often too florid for the subject, and it is easy to smile at the writers' pride in small attempts at elegance and improvement. But in fact these attempts were made at the cost of a good deal of really benevolent effort.

It is a good thing to be reminded for instance, that some quite charming open spaces had already been preserved in an environment to which the nineteenth century was at least as sensitive as the twentieth. The hospitals may have been "tasteful", but they were also efficient. Nowadays, the use of half a page for describing drinking fountains "munificently provided" may seem odd, but it should be a sobering thought that in those days there were many people so poor that when, literally without the price of the cheapest meal, they faced a long weary walk to wherever there might be a gleam of hope, a free drink of cold water did at least save them from the anguish of thirst. People born in the twentieth century can still remember the ragged children eagerly using those fountains.

Although the "Guide" was revised and re-issued more than once many of the illustrations and some of the letterpress were omitted. This, the first edition has thus been chosen for facsimile reprint in order to make available once again the original material in its entirety.

February 1971   MARY WALTON

PAWSON & BRAILSFORD'S

ILLUSTRATED GUIDE

TO

SHEFFIELD AND NEIGHBOURHOOD,

INCLUDING

THE EARLY HISTORY OF THE TOWN, AN ACCOUNT OF THE
PUBLIC BODIES, AND THE PUBLIC, RELIGIOUS, AND
OTHER EDIFICES, A DESCRIPTION OF THE
MANUFACTURES, SKETCHES OF THE
SURROUNDING SCENERY,
&c., &c.

ILLUSTRATED WITH ONE HUNDRED ENGRAVINGS.

SHEFFIELD:

PAWSON AND BRAILSFORD, PRINTERS, HIGH STREET, (CHURCH-GATES), AND CASTLE-STREET.

INTRODUCTION.

A few words will suffice to explain the specific nature and objects of this work. It is intended primarily to provide for the visitor a guide to whatever may be considered interesting in Sheffield and the neighbourhood. This being so, it is obvious that much of what has been written will prove familiar to residents ; but it is believed that, even to these, the volume will be acceptable as furnishing what has long been wanted—a hand-book and record of such things as are worth knowing in connection with the town. There are many subjects of interest—the olden history of the town, the beautiful scenery in the neighbourhood, the lives of eminent men who have flourished here, the facts relating to our public buildings, the progress of the manufactures that have made Sheffield celebrated—in respect to which it is impossible for the mind to retain everything that is desired. All these matters have been fully dealt with, though in a popular manner, and so as not to fall into the region of mere technicality. Disclaiming all credit for original research in regard to the early history of the town, it is only right to say that this part of the volume is mainly an embodiment of the leading facts of what must inevitably be the groundwork of every history of this neighbourhood—Hunter's great work on Hallamshire. In the other portions of the Guide many new facts will be found ; and it may be generally stated that all the subjects within the range of personal inquiry have been carefully verified when necessary, while great pains have been taken to render the volume thoroughly accurate and trustworthy. Amongst the other works from which facts have been obtained, may be mentioned two essays by Mr. Samuel Mitchell, referred to in the body of the Guide ; Mr. John Holland's Memoir of Chantrey; the article on Sheffield in the Encyclopædia Britannica, by Mr. Leader ; an essay on the Manufacture of Steel, by Mr. Charles Sanderson, &c. &c. It is also a duty to acknowledge the valuable information communicated personally by the Rev. Charles Collier, M.A., of Winchester, Mr. John Holland, Mr. Samuel Mitchell, Mr. William Swift, Mr. John Wilson, and others.

Any corrections or suggestions for a future edition will be received by the publishers with thanks, and shall have careful consideration.

INDEX.

6 INDEX.

INDEX TO ENGRAVINGS.

SUBURBAN SCENERY.

ERRATA.

Page 32, " The Highway Board." Since this was written, the offices of the Sheffield Highway Board have been removed to Bower-spring.

Page 73, first line of last paragraph, for " on closing St. Philip's *Church*," read " closing St. Philip's *Churchyard*."

Page 136, in line above engraving, for " description," read " *delineation*."

THE SHEFFIELD GUIDE.

ALTHOUGH Sheffield is of course in its manufacturing parts not more clean or less smoky than other similar centres of industry, there is perhaps no large town in the kingdom situated in the midst of so charming and picturesque a district. In whatever direction we go beyond the outskirts of the town, a beautiful view is sure to meet the eye; and if the walk is extended four or five miles, delightful combinations of hill and valley, wood and stream, will be found, not to be surpassed except by the most lovely spots of Derbyshire or Cumberland. The town of Sheffield is situated in a natural amphitheatre of hills, the site of the town itself being also of a very undulating character, to such an extent that some of the streets are even precipitous. This characteristic makes the town healthy, and supplies an almost natural system of drainage. It used to be a sort of boast that there was no street in the town from which the country could not be seen; and though this is no longer literally true, there are still few localities from which glimpses of the hillsides may not be observed between the tall chimneys and above the spacious manufactories. The very spot on which Sheffield stands must originally have been one of the most lovely of the whole of this very beautiful district; and some of the names of thoroughfares which remain are highly suggestive of those primitive days when the birds warbled and the wild flowers grew on what are now the most densely populated parts of the town. "Barker's-pool," "Bower-spring," and "Balm-green," are significant in this way, but hardly so much as "Daisy-walk" and "Pea-croft,"—twin localities where neither pea nor croft flourishes, and where there are about as many daisies as in the streets of Manchester. There are some other names which are suggestive, though in a different view. "Lady's-bridge" carries with it a pleasant smack of the olden days; and "Spital-hill" has distinct reminiscences connected with it, the latest of which date as far back as Henry VIII. "Figtree-lane," "Sheffield-moor," and "Castle-green," also strike the ear with a suggestive sound. All these localities still exist; but there are some which are no longer to be found by their ancient titles. "Lady's-walk" is now not a promenade for ladies either in fact or in name. " True Lover's Gutter" no longer runs; and "Pudding-lane" is changed into the more euphonic and ambitious King-street. "Bull-stake" has altogether disappeared, along with the brutal sport which obviously gave birth to the title.

B

Sheffield is situated in the south of the West Riding of Yorkshire, on the borders of Derbyshire, and is about equidistant from the eastern and western coasts. It is on the eastern side of the range of hills running southward from Westmoreland into Staffordshire. The town is intersected by rivers, which add greatly to the natural beauty of the place, and also assisted in its early development as the great seat of the cutlery manufacture. There are five rivers, which unite at the town—the Porter, the Rivelin, the Loxley, the Don, and the Sheaf. From this last it is generally supposed the town derives its name, though other and more recondite sources of origin have been suggested. None of these rivers are large. The most considerable is the Don, over which the traveller crosses by means of Lady's-bridge, when entering the town from the present station of the Midland Railway.

HALLAMSHIRE.

The town of Sheffield is the great centre of a locality the name of which has no doubt puzzled the stranger, as furnishing a " shire" unknown to his early geographical studies. " Hallamshire" is the title of a district the exact limits of which are not defined. Originally, it comprehended the parishes of Sheffield, Ecclesfield, and Handsworth ; but it must now be taken as embracing the whole of the neighbouring villages in which cutlery work is carried on. In the Cutlers' Company's Act of James I., the ancient confines of Hallamshire are extended by a compass of six miles, so as to include the whole cutlery district. It is a name to which are attached associations derived from a remote antiquity. It is still commonly used in Sheffield, and is very popular, as is strikingly shown by the fact that the " Hallamshire Volunteer Rifles" is the title of the first of the Volunteer bodies established in Sheffield in connection with the recent movement. It is believed that there was once the hall of a Saxon thane, and perhaps a city, which gave its name to the district ; but of neither is there the slightest trace remaining. There is, however, a tradition which very distinctly asserts that on the sloping banks of the Rivelin—one of the most lovely of the many charming walks around the town—there was in the time of the Saxons a flourishing and populous city of Hallam, which was one of those razed to the ground by the Norman William. Some colour was given to the legend by the discovery, in the neighbourhood of the Rivelin, of two plates of copper bearing an inscription supposed to signify the manumission of three Roman soldiers. It is conjectured that these plates were given to the soldiers as a token of their admission into Roman citizenship, and (in pursuance of the known policy of some of the Emperors) to induce them to settle in the colony they had helped to conquer; that they betook themselves to the rising community which afterwards became the city of Hallam ; and that the plates, which had of course been carefully preserved, were eventually buried in the ruins of the destroyed buildings. These are mere conjectures ; but, combined with the tradition, they are not without a show of probability.

The title Hallamshire is by some connected with a popular distich in a way which, though not very apparent at first sight, gives a distinct meaning to a saying otherwise not very intelligible. Hull, Hallamshire, and Halifax were, it is said, three of the districts which during the middle ages existed in this country as small independent States, something like the petty duchies of Germany in the present day. The lords, who had arbitrary control in these districts, were some of them very rapacious and cruel—in Hull, Hallam, and Halifax peculiarly so, if we are to believe the interpretation put upon the " Hull, Hell (Hallam), and Halifax," from which people pray to be " delivered."

EARLY HISTORY OF SHEFFIELD.

There are in the immediate neighbourhood of Sheffield distinct remains of an encampment which is supposed to have been formed by the Brigantes, one of the native tribes which opposed the Romans in their invasion of Britain. The remains of the camp are thus described by Mr. S. Mitchell :*—" There is a third and most important barrier of defence, which displays the great skill and strategetical talent of the warlike Brigantes, more than any other which I can ascribe to that people, and which seems to have been constructed on a sudden emergency and on an occasion of urgent necessity. I allude to the fine camp on the summit of Wincobank, and the fortified earthworks which are connected with it both eastward and westward. This British fortress occupies the crown of a beautifully wooded hill, about two miles east from Sheffield, commanding most extensive views of the country on all sides, and being itself a most prominent object from every quarter. It has evidently been raised by the great throw or fault which here occurs in the coal formation. The form of the camp is nearly circular, enclosing, with its immense vallum and ditch, with internal covered way, an area of several acres. On its north-west side, where the ground descends very abruptly, the vallum is imperfectly raised. Proceeding from this point to the eastward runs an immense bank, partly natural from the coal throw already named, of which the British have taken advantage, and artificial wherever the works required additional strength. An outward ditch of considerable depth has been excavated on the south side of this immense vallum. The antiquity of this rampart may be partially gathered from its being the boundary of the two parishes of Sheffield and Ecclesfield for about a mile, till it crosses the Blackburn, where it enters the parish of Rotherham. Its course is then prominently visible to Kimberworth, Greasbro', the Upper Haugh (in

* In his Essay on the Early British Defences in the North.

Rawmarsh), Swinton Potteries, and across the Dearne and Dove Canal and the Midland Railway to Mexbrough, where it terminates in some rude earthworks, or loses itself in the marshes, which eighteen hundred years ago would extend thence to the foot of Conisbro' Cliffs. It is now traceable at intervals the whole of the distance of five or six miles, but in many parts of its course, especially in the meadow lands, the plough has so far obliterated it that an eye unpractised in such matters would fail to discover its site. Its continuity for five or six miles cannot, however, be doubted. To the westward of the Winco-camp a similar rampart is visible, after the almost precipitous declivity to Grimesthorpe; it is prominent to the westward of the small brook which runs through Grimesthorpe, ascending the hill to a wood now called ' Wilkinson Spring,' where the vallum and ditch are almost as perfect as when they were first formed. At the back of a house called Woodside, the fortified bank takes a sharp turn towards Sheffield (still adopting the line of the coal throw), and crowning the hill, having the military advantage of the most perfect view of the whole valley of the Don from Sheffield to Rotherham. The line of defence then follows the present course of the well-known Occupation-road [in the suburbs of Sheffield,] which is in fact the ditch of the rampart; while the fields to the rear of the barrier yet show (despite of ploughing) that they have been excavated with the double purpose of elevating the already sharp natural ridge, and to form a sort of covered way in the interior of the defensive earthworks. These works would follow the course of the present road, behind Hall Carr, across the Burngreave-road, along Tomcross-lane, to the ford at Bridgehouses, where it crossed the Don, to and by the Millsands to Sheffield Castle."

Mr. Mitchell gives the following ingenious hypothesis to account for the origin of these ancient works (which have been attributed by various antiquarians to several different sources):—" About the year 60, when the southern part of our island had been subdued, and pretty comfortably settled into the form of a Roman province, under the name of Flavia Cæsariensis, the resolute Italians resolved to penetrate the land till they attained the ' Ultima Thule.' The territory of the Brigantes stretched from sea to sea. They must be subjugated. They were quite aware of the fate of their southern compatriots, with whom they were yet in constant warlike broils. The Romans approach: they are determined to make the most vigorous stand, not aware that skill and discipline will always conquer reckless, disunited, though determined valour. They see their enemy on the southern banks of the Don, ready to cross at the only favourable point. To stem this inroad they fortify the northern banks, taking all the advantages which the geological character of the country, and the woods and morasses (such as the Red Marsh or the Raw Marsh) presented to them, to impede their southern enemies; for it is a matter of the greatest importance to observe that all these works indicate incontestibly that it was against a southern foe only that they were intended, or could be at all made operative. These works were no doubt provided for the retreat of the native Brigantes, who were appointed to dispute the fords of Temple-brough and Mexbrough, from which they were at last dislodged by the Roman invincibles, 'the Legio Sexta Virtrix,' who for three centuries afterwards had their head-quarters at York. This was the last great contest for their original freedom which the Brigantes attempted."

Traces of another encampment, upon a smaller scale, exist in the Great Roe Wood, between Wincobank and Wilkinson Spring. There are also some very interesting remains of a fortress (probably Saxon) at Bradfield, a village about seven miles from Sheffield.

There is a tradition that there was once a Roman camp on the site of the present graveyard of the Sheffield Parish Church. Some colour is given to the legend by the fact that Roman funeral remains have been dug up in Bank-street, a spot close at hand, and also by the circumstance that one of the thoroughfares immediately adjoining the graveyard is still called "Campo-lane." But there is no means of deciding the truth of this tradition.

Even when we descend to later times, the history of the locality is still to a large extent merely legendary. There were, however, without doubt, a manor of Hallam and a series of Saxon lords of it, the last of whom, Earl Waltheof, was a man of great note in his day. Some interest attaches to him as the son of the Siward who commanded the English army sent to Scotland against Macbeth. He headed a conspiracy against William the Conqueror, and was defeated and executed.

In Doomsday Book the district is found to be in the possession of Roger de Busli; but by the time of Henry I. it had changed to the De Lovetots. The Lovetots were a powerful family, and their arms are now in the Parish Church as amongst the early patrons of that edifice. From the De Lovetots the estates of Hallamshire were transmitted to the noble family of Furnival; and there is a tradition that during the life of Gerard de Furnival King John once visited him at Sheffield Castle. This seems not unlikely to be true, as King John was at war with his nobles, and Gerard was one of his most powerful friends. The date assigned to this visit is 1215. A tradition which asserts that a subsequent visit was paid by the King to Sheffield itself seems less likely. On this second occasion, it is stated, John merely stayed a night in passing through the town on his way to York; but it is said that he was so pleased with his entertainment that he granted various privileges to the inhabitants. Though no date is handed down, tradition is extremely precise on the subject, the very house in which John is said to have lodged in High-street having been pointed out, till it was pulled down not many years since. It is only right to say that this legend is quite contrary to probability, and not borne out by the records which exist of the journeys of the King.

The last of the male Furnivals died in 1406, and the estates passed by marriage to the Shrewsburys, one of the most powerful amongst all our ancient noble families. From this time forward for a lengthened

period the early history of Sheffield is intimately connected with that
of the house of Talbot. It would be out of place here to give even
an outline of the general history of the Earls of Shrewsbury, seven of
whom enjoyed the Hallamshire estates. There are, however, some
facts connected with them which are especially interesting in regard
to this locality.

John, the first Earl of Shrewsbury, was killed with his son gal-
lantly fighting in the French wars in 1453.   There is a very interesting
legend connecting Sheffield with these wars. It is said that a large
part of the Earl's army was composed of Hallamshire men, and that
" so greatly did they suffer while fighting round the Earl as he lay
bleeding on the field of battle, that there was not a family nor a house
in all Hallamshire that did not lose either a father, or a brother, or a
husband, or a son, on that fatal day."

George, the fourth Earl of Shrewsbury, was for a short time the
custodian of the great Cardinal Wolsey in his disgrace, the Earl enter-
taining him with great courtesy at Sheffield Manor. Wolsey's gentleman usher, Cavendish, has left us very minute details of his master's
last days, from which we extract the following account of the sojourn
at Sheffield, merely modernizing the spelling for the reader's convenience :—" And the next day we removed and rode to Sheffield Park,
where my Lord of Shrewsbury lay within the Lodge [the Manor], the
people all the way thitherward lamenting him. And when we came
into the Park of Sheffield, nigh to the Lodge, my Lord of Shrewsbury, with my Lady of Shrewsbury, and a train of gentlewomen, and
all other his gentlemen and servants, stood without the gates to attend
my Lord's coming to receive him. At whose alighting the Earl received him with much honour, and embraced my Lord, saying these
words, ' My Lord,' quoth he, ' your grace is most heartily welcome
unto me, and I am glad to see you here in my poor Lodge, where I
have long desired to see you, and much more gladder if ye had come
after another sort.' ' Ah, my gentle Lord of Shrewsbury,' quoth my
Lord, ' I heartily thank you.   And although I have cause to lament,
yet as a faithful heart may, I do rejoice that my chance is to come
into the custody of so noble a person, whose approved honour and
wisdom hath always been right well known to all noble estates. And,
sir, howsoever my accusers have used their accusations against me,
this I know, and so before your Lordship and all the world I do pro-
test, that my demeanour and proceeding have always been both just
and loyal towards my sovereign and liege lord, and of whose usage
in his grace's affairs your Lordship hath had good experience. And
even according to my truth, so I beseech God help me.' ' I doubt
not,' quoth my Lord of Shrewsbury, ' of your truth ; therefore my
Lord be of good cheer and fear not, for I am nothing sorry, but yet I
have not wherewith to entertain you according to my good will and
to your honour ; but such as I have you shall be welcome to it, for I
will not receive you as a prisoner but as my good Lord, and the

King's true and faithful subject. And, sir, here is my wife come to salute you;' whom my Lord kissed with his cap in his hand, bare headed, and all the other gentlewomen, and took the Earl's servants by the hand, as well gentlemen as yeomen. This done these two Lords went into the Lodge arm in arm, and so conducted my Lord to a fair gallery, where was in the further end thereof a goodly tower with lodging where my Lord was lodged. There was also in the midst of the same gallery a travers of sarcenet drawn, so that the one end thereof was preserved for my Lord and the other for the Earl. Then departed from my Lord all the great number of gentlemen and others that conducted him thither. And my Lord being thus with my Lord of Shrewsbury continued there eighteen days after, upon whom my Lord of Shrewsbury appointed divers worthy gentlemen to attend continually to foresee that he should lack nothing that he should desire, being served in his own chamber at dinner and supper as honourably and with as many dainty dishes as he had in his own house commonly, being at liberty. And once every day my Lord of Shrewsbury would repair in to him, and commune with him, sitting upon a bench in a great window in the gallery. And although that my said Earl of Shrewsbury would right heartily comfort him, yet would he lament so piteously that it would make my Lord of Shrewsbury to be very heavy for his grief."

Wolsey remained at Sheffield Manor eighteen days. Shortly before he left a very severe attack of dysentery set in, which the physician said would be fatal; but he was hurried away on a mule to undergo his trial. On the third night after his departure from Sheffield he reached Leicester Abbey, to the abbot of which he exclaimed, " Father Abbot, I come hither to leave my bones among you." Two days afterwards he died.

MARY QUEEN OF SCOTS AT SHEFFIELD.

We now come to the most interesting event in the ancient history of Sheffield, that of the imprisonment of the beautiful but ill-fated Mary Queen of Scots in the Castle here. Mary must have been very familiar with the beautiful natural scenery which was at this time visible all through the neighbourhood, for she was imprisoned at Sheffield no less than twelve years out of the nineteen which she altogether passed in England. It was to George, the sixth Earl of Shrewsbury, that the custody of the unfortunate Queen was confided at Sheffield. Mary escaped from Lochleven, and landed at Workington, Cumberland, in May, 1568, throwing herself with generous confidence on the protection of Elizabeth. The English Queen repaid the confidence by placing her in confinement, first entrusting her to Lord Scrope, and afterwards to the Earl of Shrewsbury. The Shrewsburys were immensely rich, and had several residences in various parts of the kingdom; but Sheffield, from its great natural beauty, seems always to have been the favourite one. It was to one of the other of these mansions—Tutbury Castle, in Staffordshire—that Mary was first taken upon being received into the care of the Earl of Shrewsbury. From Tutbury Queen Mary was removed to Coventry, on account of an attempt which was being organized by her friends to rescue her ; but she only remained there a short time, and was taken back to Tutbury. In the summer of 1570 she was removed to Chatsworth, and before Christmas of that year she had entered the walls at Sheffield which were destined to form the scene of her longest and most dreary confinement.

The task of guarding the Scottish Queen seems to have been an irksome one to the Earl from the very outset; but the imperious will of Elizabeth left him no alternative. The unpleasantness inseparable from such a duty was increased by the severity with which Elizabeth required it to be carried out. To this policy of the English Queen, Shrewsbury seems, however, eventually to have very fully lent himself. Nor can this be much wondered at. The Earl, when once entered on the task, would naturally incline to strictness, because he was responsible for the safe-keeping of his captive ; and there were continual plots for her rescue. Mary's own personal attendants when she entered Sheffield Castle numbered thirty. The Earl selected forty of the most trusty of his dependants to form a guard over her ; and these men watched the Castle day and night. The following regulations issued by the Earl for the management of his household during the imprisonment of the Queen show the extreme rigour with which she was guarded, and furnish incidentally a graphic picture of the times :—

" To the Master of the Scotts Queenes household, Mr. Beton.

" First,—That all your people which appertayneth to the Quene shall depart from the Queen's chamber or chambers to their own lodging at IX. of the clock at night, winter and summer, whatsoever he or she ; either to their lodging within the house or without in the towne, and there to remain till the next day at VI. of the clock.

" Item,—That none of the Queen's people shall at no time wear his sword neither within the house, nor when her Grace rydeth or goeth abroad : unless the Master of the Household himself to weare a sword and no more without my special license.

" Item,—That there shall none of the Queen's people carry any bow or shaftes, at no tyme, neither to the field nor to the butts, unless it be foure or fyve, and no more being in the Queen's companye.

" Item,—That none of the Queen's people shall ryde or go at no tyme abroad out of the house or towne without my special license ; and if he or they so doth, they or he shall come no more in at the gates, neither in the towne, whatsoever he or she or they be."

" Item,—That you or some of the Queen's chamber, when her Grace will walke abroad, shall advertyse the officiar of my warde, who shall declare the messuage to me one houer before she goeth forth.

" Item,—That none of the Queen's people, whatsoever he or they be, not once offer at no tyme to come forth of their chamber or lodging when anie alarum is given by night or daie, whether they be in the Queen's chamber or in their chambers within the house or without in the towne. And yf he or they keepe not their chambers or lodgings wheresoever that be, he or they shall stande at their perill for deathe.

" At Shefeild the 26th daie of April 1571, per me

" SHREWSBURIE."

A letter written by the Earl of Shrewsbury to Lord Burghley, in December, 1571, also shows how strict was the seclusion in which the unhappy Mary was kept. In this document the Earl states that Mary has complained of sickness, but that he thinks it is only a trick to get liberty to go outside the gates, which he is determined not to consent to, as he sees " no small peril therein." And he adds, complacently, " I do suffer her to walk upon the leads here in open ayre and in my large dining chamber, and also in this court yard, so as both I myself or my wife be alwaies in her company, for avoiding all others talk either to her self or any of hers." The temper of the Earl, whose harshness seems to have grown with the duration of his office and to have degenerated into sheer brutality, is further shown by a letter of his to Queen Elizabeth, intended to assure her Majesty that none of the plots which were afloat could succeed. In this letter he in fact announces his intention to kill his captive rather than let her escape. " I have hur sure inoughe," he writes, " and shall keep hur forthe comyng at your Majesty's commandment, ether quyke or ded, what soever she or anny for hur inventes for the contrary ; and as I have no doute at all of hur stelynge away from me, so if any forsabull attempts be gyven for hur, the gretest perell is sure to be hur's."

We cannot wonder that poor Mary, accustomed as she had been to all the gaieties of a French court, should suffer both in mind and body during such an imprisonment. Accordingly we find the Earl, who, it is evident, was not likely to exaggerate the distress of his royal prisoner, writing thus of her :—" She is within a few dayes become more malincholy than of long before, and complenes of hur wronges and imprisonments. I am sure hur malyncholy and grefe is grattar than she in words uttars ; and yett, rather than contynew this imprisonment, she styckes not to saye she wyll gyve hur boddy, hur sonne and cuntry for lyberty."

At the time these last two letters were written, the severity with which Mary was watched had very greatly increased, owing in the first instance to the news of the Massacre of St. Bartholomew, which created a sort of panic throughout the Protestant countries of Europe, and caused Shrewsbury to add thirty soldiers to the guard which watched his castle. The neighbouring woods, and every place where it was possible for friends of the captive Queen to be secreted, were vigilantly searched. In the autumn of 1572, the Earl had intended to remove Mary for a few days to the Manor, in order to have the Castle cleansed.   The news of the massacre put an end to this project for a time; but in the spring of the following year she was taken to the Manor, where she remained a few days.   During this change of residence there were rumours of a plot to rescue her from the Manor; but, though there is a tradition connected with the building that she actually escaped from one of the windows, there does not seem to have been any attempt made either by herself or her friends.   Indeed it would have been a most difficult task to rescue her, looking at the manner in which she was watched, as we incidentally gather from a letter written by one of the sons of the Earl of Shrewsbury. The letter states:—"Good numbers of men, continually armed, watched hir day and nyght, and both under hir windows, over hir chamber, and of every syde hir; so that, unless she could transform hirself to a flee or a mouse, it was impossible she should scape."

The health of the royal prisoner at length gave way, and in the autumn of 1573, by the mediation of the French ambassador with the English Queen, Mary was permitted to pay a visit to Buxton, in Derbyshire, which was as celebrated for its medicinal waters at that distant time as it is now.   The same precautions were taken as at Sheffield for Mary's safe keeping, and no strangers were allowed to be at Buxton during her stay there.   After leaving Buxton she spent a short time at Chatsworth, and returned to Sheffield Castle in November.

So matters went on till 1575, without anything locally interesting in the history of the captive Queen.   On the 26th of February in that year, the walls of the Castle were severely shaken by an earthquake. It was more particularly felt in the chamber occupied by Mary, so much so that Shrewsbury says, quaintly, "I doubted more hur faleng than hur goinge."   According to the Earl, her room was "sunke" by the shock.   Mary was greatly alarmed, of course; and the Earl writes, "God be thanked, she is forth cumyng, and grante it may be a forwarnyng unto hur."   The friends of Mary, on the contrary, considered it a judgment upon *him*.   In the same year there were transactions of national importance at the Castle which seem a sad mockery, considering the abject state of captivity in which the Queen was kept.   Commissioners waited upon her from the French Court, and with them she negociated an exchange of the Duchy of Touraine, which belonged to her, for the county of Vermandaise and some other territories.   In a letter dated from Sheffield Castle in August of the same year, and addressed to a dignitary of the Romish Church, she expresses her firm determination to restore the Catholic religion in England, if it ever should be in her power.   It was about this time that a friend of Cousin, the Jesuit, had interviews with Mary at the Sheffield Castle, and was so carried away by her beauty and fascinating manners that he declared it was " impossible to see this excellent Queen without rapture and celestial joy."

During the ensuing years Mary was kept in still greater seclusion. Even the members of Lord Shrewsbury's family were not allowed access to her. She spent her time principally upon needlework. Another short period was passed at Buxton, in the spring of 1576. A will of Queen Mary's is dated at Sheffield Manor, August, 1577. Another visit to Buxton, in 1580, was unfortunate for Mary, as in mounting her horse she fell and injured her back. During the year 1581 Mary suffered much from sickness. She had been so weakened by want of fresh air and exercise, that she had to be carried from one room to another. In November of this year, she had to transact business in bed, and she touchingly exclaimed that "though she was not old in years she found herself old in body, that her hair was turned gray, and that she should soon have another husband." The unfortunate Queen, at this time only thirty-eight, found her anticipated "husband" at the hand of the executioner, perhaps sooner than she anticipated; but there must have been something of relief, considering the extreme wretchedness of her condition, even in the terrible fate she had to endure.

After temporary sojourns, at intervals, at Buxton, Worksop, &c., the Queen was, at the earnest entreaty of the Earl of Shrewsbury, removed from his custody; and on the 3rd September, 1584, she left Sheffield Castle, never to re-enter its walls. She was placed under the care of Sir Ralph Sadler and Sir John Somers, and was taken to Winfield. The ill-fated Queen, after being removed to one or two other places, met her fate at Fotheringay, where she was executed on the 8th of February, 1587.

THE CIVIL WARS.

There is nothing more of local interest until we come to the time of those commotions in the seventeenth century which have left their destructive traces in so many parts of the country. The Earls of Shrewsbury, it is true, took a prominent part in several events which have become historical; but none of these are directly connected with Sheffield like the history of Queen Mary. The male branch of the Talbot family becoming extinct, the Sheffield estates were absorbed by marriage in the property of the noble house of Howard. In their possession these estates still remain, the Duke of Norfolk being now the owner of them; and owing to the demand for land for the purposes of trade, they have become enormously enhanced in value.

The first distinct movement at Sheffield in connection with the great conflict between Charles I. and his people was in 1642. There seems to have been a strong Parliamentarian party in Sheffield; and in the summer of the above year they co-operated with Sir John Gell, who was in command of a force in the neighbourhood, and obtained possession of the Castle, which they garrisoned. They threw entrenchments round both the Castle and town, which at that time was not so large as to present much difficulty in the way of such an undertaking. The Earl of Newcastle, who had the command of the King's forces in the North, entered Yorkshire in the ensuing autumn with about 8,000 men. He found the people generally so much opposed to the King that most of the Royalists had retired for safety to York. Leeds and Wakefield surrendered to the Earl, who advanced with a large party of his troops to reduce Rotherham and Sheffield. This took place in April, 1643. The Rotherham people proved stout-hearted. The place was garrisoned and fortified, and they refused to surrender. After a cannonade the Earl entered the town by storm. In the course of two or three days he followed up his success by marching to Sheffield. The Earl's prowess at Rotherham had struck a panic into the undisciplined forces at Sheffield Castle; and when they heard of Newcastle's approach they fled into Derbyshire and left the town to the mercy of the Earl. He thoroughly fortified the Castle, put a garrison in it, and left it under the command of Sir William Saville. Newcastle, moreover, made use of the iron and steel works which he found in the neighbourhood, by causing their proprietors to construct for his army cannon and other munitions of war. Sir William was shortly afterwards put in a higher command, and was replaced by Major Beaumont.

The Castle was attacked by the Parliamentarians on the 4th August, 1644. The commander of the attacking party, Major General Crawford, announced his intentions in the following courteous missive :—" Sir, I am sent by the Earl of Manchester to reduce this place you hold, and therefore send you yet a summons, though my trumpett was shott att, against the lawes of armes, the other day. You may easily perceive I desire not the effusion of blood, otherwise I should have spared myself this labour. If you think good to surrender it, you may expect all fair respects befitting a gentleman and souldiers : otherwise you must expect those extremities which they have that refuse mercy. I desire your answere within one houre, and rest your servant, L. CRAWFORD."

What answer the Royalist commander, Major Beaumont, sent, is not recorded ; but he did not yield without a struggle. The shooting at the " trumpett," referred to by General Crawford, seems to have been rather a barbarous proceeding. Upon first coming up to the Castle, Crawford fired three shots into it, and then sent a trumpeter to sound a parley with the inmates. The defenders, irritated at the attack, instead of consenting to a parley, fired three times at the trumpeter, "two of which came very neer, and barely missed him," says the chronicler ; " and they, flourishing their swords, cried out, 'they would have no other parley.' " The attacking party consisted of a regiment of cavalry and about twelve hundred foot soldiers. In the Castle there were only about two hundred infantry and a troop of horse. It was, however, pretty strongly fortified. There was around it a broad trench filled with water eighteen feet deep, a strong pallisaded breastwork, and a wall two yards thick. It also contained eight pieces of ordnance and two mortars.

Finding no chance of a surrender, Crawford proceeded to offensive operations. He constructed two batteries sixty yards from the out-works of the Castle, and from these he battered the walls with such guns as he possessed. He had but three, however, and these not large. After plying them for about twenty-four hours, he sent to Lord Fairfax for the "Queen's pocket pistoll, and a whole culverin." When this ordnance arrived, a practicable breach was soon made in the Castle walls, and the General prepared to enter by storm. However, he first tried the efficacy of another summons to surrender, and this time it was successful. It was agreed that the garrison should march out with all the honours of war, and without any of them becoming prisoners. A special provision was made for the protection of Lady Saville, widow of the former governor of the Castle. This lady, who was in the Castle during the siege, behaved with great heroism. Though the attacking party refused to allow a midwife, whom she had sent for, to pass into the Castle, she was far from begging the commander to surrender on her account. On the contrary, she de-clared she would rather perish than be the cause of the Castle being given up. It is said, however, that the soldiers, moved with pity for her, mutinied and compelled the governor to surrender. This noble-minded lady, in the midst of her sorrow and peril, had a child born to her the night after the Castle was given up.

The Parliamentarians took possession of the munitions of war in the Castle, comprising the cannon already mentioned, four hundred small arms, twelve barrels of powder, and twenty tons of iron shot. The estates surrounding the Castle were confiscated by Parliament; but in 1648 they were restored to their former owner, the Earl of Arundel, on his paying £6,000.

SHEFFIELD CASTLE AND MANOR, &c.

We have no longer any incidents worth describing in the history of Sheffield, except such as are connected with its rise as a manufacturing community; and before proceeding to these we will give some par-ticulars of the Castle and Manor around which such a romantic halo is cast by their connection with Queen Mary.

Without entering into the question as to where the hall of the Saxon lords of the manor was located, and whether it was taken possession of and adapted to the wants of the Norman conquerors who overran the country, it is quite clear that a Castle existed at a very remote period. Mr. Mitchell, in his erudite little "History of the Burgery of Sheffield," conjectures with considerable show of probability that a Castle existed anterior to the time of Henry III. That monarch, in the 54th year of his reign, granted a charter to Thomas de Furnival, to construct and embattle a Castle at Sheffield. There seems little

question that during the wars of that period, Sheffield was burnt to
the ground by John D'Eyvill, a leader of the barons. The charter
granted by King Henry was about six years subsequent to this act
of violence. Mr. Mitchell conjectures that the Castle was burnt with
the town, and that the permission granted by the King was to recon-
struct it and make it more powerful. At all events, there can be no
doubt that from the period of Henry III. there was a very strong
Castle at Sheffield, and that it was the head of the barony held by
the De Furnivals. It is said that at the demolition of the Castle in
the time of Cromwell, a large flat stone was found, attesting the
building of the structure in the following quaint rhyme :—

> " I Lord Furnibal,
> I built this Castle Hall,
> And under this wall
> Within this tomb was my burial."

The building must have been a large one, Not even a ruin now
remains ; but an idea of its actual site may easily be obtained. The
course of the Don and Sheaf at their confluence near Waingate would,
from the natural protection they afforded, obviously form the boundary
on that side ; while it probably filled up the whole space between
Waingate and Dixon-lane on the other. After the Castle was taken
by the Parliamentarians in the Civil Wars, it was decided to destroy
it, and in 1648 the work of demolition was carried out. When the
estates were restored to the Earl of Arundel and Surrey, he began to
rebuild it ; but the work was never prosecuted with vigour, and was
soon abandoned.

The Manor was comparatively a modern edifice, having been built
by the fourth Earl of Shrewsbury and completed early in the reign
of Henry VIII. It was about two miles from the Castle, and was
intended as a country residence. It must have been a very handsome
building, and have formed a mansion worthy of the noble house by
whom it was raised. It continued to be habitable for some fifty years
after the Castle was destroyed. It was dismantled in 1706. It was
in the centre of Sheffield Park. The Park remains, but in name
only, a large portion of the district still so called being a densely populated part of the town. Of the Manor House itself little now exists ;
and what there is, is fast crumbling away before the hand of time.
One of the outer walls of the mansion remains, with the stone
framework of two fine old windows and a handsome chimney ; but
this wall is now used to form part of some hovels in which labouring
people dwell. Part of the external walls which surrounded the grounds
also remain, close without one of which may be heard the hiss of
the engine which works a coalpit. Yet even with all these unromantic
adjuncts, it is impossible to survey the spot without having the mind
carried back to the times when the ambitious Wolsey, stricken down

with disappointment and pain, took counsel of the lord of the Manor within its picturesque walls, and when the beautiful Mary, pale and worn with captivity, sat listless at her embroidery and looked out with moistened eyes over the green hills which still beautify the neighbourhood.

There is one very interesting relic of the Castle remaining, if it be only genuine. Adjoining the ruins of the Manor there is a stone trough. This trough, it is said, was the coffin in which was buried the founder of the Castle, Thomas de Furnival. It was found at the demolition of the Castle, and on the stone forming the lid of it, it is said, was the inscription already mentioned; but this cover is not now to be found. The trough has all the appearance of having been originally intended for a coffin. Not far from the ruins is the Queen's Tower, a residence built by the late Mr. Samuel Roberts. This building has no connection with the unfortunate Mary, except by name; but on the grounds there is a small structure, styled " Queen Mary's Bower," which is of some interest as being built entirely from the ruins of the Manor.

It would seem as if, since the house of Talbot became dispossessed of the Sheffield estates, this locality, beautiful as it still is, were fated never again to be the favourite residence of a noble family. This continues, in a remarkable way, down to the present moment. When the late Duke of Norfolk died in November, 1860, a handsome residence had just been finished for the family, and it was the intention of his Grace to spend in it a portion of every year. The untimely death of the Duke, however, prevented his desire from being fulfilled; and the furniture of the mansion, almost immediately after it had been collected, was dispersed by sale.

Lady's-bridge, in the immediate vicinity of the site of the Castle, is a very ancient structure, having been beyond doubt in existence in the time of Henry II. It was, however, rebuilt during the reign of Henry VII. Its name was derived from a small chapel dedicated to " Our Lady," which formerly stood at the west end of the bridge, under the Castle wall.

RISE AND PROGRESS OF THE TOWN.

The cutlery trade is throughout the whole world associated with the name of Sheffield. The celebrity of the town for these wares is not merely a modern one. Perhaps no town in England can trace its connection with any trade back to so remote a period. There are, indeed, traditions that the steel workers at Sheffield manufactured arrows for some of the ancient British tribes who opposed the Roman legions. This is mere legend; but there are authentic records of Sheffield having obtained a celebrity for its steel manufactures at a very early period. The first reliable intimation of the existence of the iron

trade in this neighbourhood, is in a grant made by Richard de
Builli, in the reign of Henry II., to the monks of Kirkstead, and
which included four forges for smelting and working iron. Though
this does not apply to Sheffield itself, the Monastery being situated at
Kimberworth, some miles distant from the town, it shows that the
iron trade was cultivated in the locality at that early period. There
can be no reasonable doubt that at the time when this grant was
made, the inhabitants of Sheffield were busy with their steel wares.
Before the fifteenth century the town had become thoroughly celebrated for its cutlery manufactures. This is proved from the fact
that the old poet Chaucer writes thus of one of the characters in the
"Canterbury Tales"—

> " A Shefeld thwytel bare he in his hose."

The "thwytel" or "whittle"—for which, in the days of Chaucer, it
is thus evident, Sheffield had become as noted as it now is for files,
saws, and all kinds of cutlery—was a knife formerly carried for purposes of defence in place of a sword. It answered precisely, in fact
(in everything but shape) to the American bowie knife, which is still
largely made here. It is curious, too, that not only the weapon but
the former name of it, which have both become nearly obsolete in
England, have been revived in America, where "whittling" is quite a
national characteristic.

Though this incidental notice by Chaucer fixes a period when Sheffield
had without doubt become known throughout the country for its manufactures, the commencement of its prosperity as a town dates at a much
earlier period. It began with the De Lovetots, who became extinct
about the period when the grant of Richard de Builli was given to the
monks of Kirkstead. The De Lovetots made Sheffield their chief residence, and laboured to promote its prosperity. So much did the
importance of Sheffield increase, that the manor of Hallam, formerly
the principal one, became merged in that of Sheffield. The De Lovetots seem to have been a family who, in the midst of a rude feudal
age, when almost absolute power was possessed by them, exercised
their rule mercifully and with justice. They founded a hospital for
the sick on a spot the name of which still revives recollections of the
ancient charity, though every other trace of it has long been swept
away. The De Lovetots' hospital was on the locality still known as Spital
Hill. The building itself was destroyed in the reign of Henry VIII.
A church was also founded by this munificent family. A mill, and a
bridge over the Don, had been added to the convenience of the inhabitants at this period. There is no doubt, therefore, that the community
had attained a position qualifying it to be reckoned as a budding town,
though its actual extent and the number of its inhabitants are matters
of pure conjecture.

The prosperity of Sheffield continued to grow under the succeeding
lords of the manor, the De Furnivals. The charter for the weekly

market, on Tuesdays, was obtained by Thomas de Furnival in 1296; and further privileges were granted to the inhabitants, greatly tending to the growth of its trade. Down to the passing of the estates from the Shrewsburys to the house of Howard, Sheffield enjoyed all the advantages which followed from being the favourite residence of a powerful lord. During the feudal ages this was a great benefit; and the protection was not withdrawn until a period when trade had become so vigorous that any such patronage would rather have hindered than forwarded its progress.

To recur to the history of the trade itself. There are some incidental historical notices which show that the steel workers of Sheffield progressed with the times, even in the middle ages. In these days of Armstrong guns and Whitworth rifles, it is amusing to read of a great improvement in the arrows made at Sheffield, this weapon being one of the staple manufactures of the town. At the battle of Bosworth, it is said, the Earl of Richmond's men used arrows from Sheffield, of a very superior make, being longer, sharper, better ground, and more highly polished, than those previously manufactured. The town, however, did not retain the arrow trade long after this period, as in less than half a century muskets were given to the soldiers; and even the rude fire-arms of that period were found to be far superior to the arrow.

In 1575, we find that the Earl of Shrewsbury presented to Lord Burghley a case of Hallamshire whittles, " being such fruictes as his poor country afforded with fame therefrom."

It would seem that the trade of Sheffield benefited, indirectly, from the cruel persecution of the Netherlanders by the Duke of Alva. Many of the most skilled Dutch artizans left their country, and, very naturally, fled for refuge to Protestant England. They were kindly received by Queen Elizabeth, who settled them in various parts of the country, according to their trades. The workers in iron and steel were sent to Sheffield, where they were protected by the Earl of Shrewsbury, and greatly assisted in the development of the local trade.

The commercial prosperity of Sheffield does not, however, seem to have made great progress at this period, as is proved by the following curious document:—

" By a survaie of the towne of Sheffield made the second daie of Januarie, 1615, by twenty-four of the most sufficient inhabitants there, it appeareth that there are in the towne of Sheffield 2,207 people : of which there are 725 which are not able to live without the charity of their neighbours. These are all begging poore. 100 householders which relieve others. These (though the best sorte) are but poor artificers : among them there is not one which can keep a teame on his own land, and not above tenn who have grounds of their owne that will keep a cow. 160 householders, not able to relieve others. These are such (though they beg not) as are not able to abide the storme of one fortnight's sickness, but would be thereby driven to beggary. 1,222 children of the said householders, the greatest part of which are such

c

as live of small wages, and are constrained to worke sore, to provide
them necessaries."

One great cause of the small increase in the trade may doubtless be
traced to the absurd restrictions which in those days were imposed
upon the cutlery workers in common with all other branches of manufacture.   Juries of cutlers were periodically empanelled to manage
the trade and carry out these restrictive regulations, some of which
were so strange as to be scarcely credible.   One of them, for instance,
was that no person engaged in the cutlery manufacture, master, workman, or apprentice, should do any work appertaining to the " said
scyence or mystere of cutlers" for twenty-eight days next following
after the 8th of August in each year, nor from Christmas to the 23rd
of January, under penalty of twenty shillings.   A fine of forty shillings
was inflicted upon any person allowing work to be done on his premises during the prescribed periods.   There was a fine of six and eight-
pence for selling knife blades to any person not dwelling within the
district.   And there were many other regulations equally stringent and
absurd.   The powers possessed were eventually found to be quite inadequate to the management of the trade, and an Act of Parliament
was obtained incorporating the Cutlers' Company. Of this body we treat
elsewhere.

From this time the trade of the town extended more surely, though
still not very rapidly.   At the commencement of the eighteenth century, the number of those actually engaged in the cutlery trade is
estimated at 6,000 ; and it is supposed that there were several thousands more in Sheffield and the neighbourhood, employed as smiths,
anvil makers, &c.   The goods manufactured amounted yearly to about
£100,000 in value.   But the spirit of enterprise which has since been
so signally manifested in the town, had not yet exhibited itself.
Transit was difficult.   There were no merchants in the town.   Great
timidity was felt in extending trade beyond the old and limited cha-
nels.   The position of the town at this period is thus described by a
writer at the end of the eighteenth century :—

" During a considerable part of this century the Sheffield manufacturers discovered more labour than ingenuity ; the workmen durst not
exert themselves for fear of being overstocked with goods ; their trade
was inconsiderable, confined, and precarious.   None presumed to extend their limits beyound the bounds of the island.   The chief produce of the manufactories was carried weekly by a few of Mr. Newsom's
pack-horses, to the Metropolis, the inhabitants viewing their passage
up the Park-hill with much pleasure."

We may add that in 1776, the whole of the manufactured goods
which left Sheffield for Birmingham was about two tons a week.   At
the present time about 1,500 tons leave Sheffield for that town by
railway alone.*

    * Communicated by Mr. Henry Jackson in a paper read to the Literary and
Philosophical Society.

These figures do not furnish an exaggerated idea of the general growth of the town. The increase has been enormous during the last century, and the ratio of progress has enlarged rather than diminished up to the date of the latest authentic records. We find from the last census-taking, in 1861, that the population of Sheffield had increased at a greater rate than that of any other town in England. The total population of the borough, was 185,157. The only other town of larger population in Yorkshire is Leeds ; and Sheffield has so far gained upon Leeds that if the two towns continue to increase in the same proportionate rate for twenty years more, Sheffield will be the larger of the two. The vast increase of population during the last century and a quarter, and especially since the commencement of the present century, is strikingly shown by the following table :—

YEAR.	TOTAL POPULATION.
1736	14,105
1801	45,755
1821	65,275
1841	110,891
1851	135,307
1861	185,157

The wealth of the inhabitants, and the value of the property in the town, have increased in a proportionate degree. In 1849, the rateable property was assessed at £270,816 ; at the present time, (1862), it is £446,864.

Formerly the great motive power in the manufactories was the water abounding in the numerous streams of the neighbourhood. This power is still fully used ; but in addition, it is computed that there are 406 steam engines in use, furnishing 6,286 horse-power. From a mere inland traffic, the trade of Sheffield has become world-wide. Directly, or through the merchants of this and other towns, the products of Sheffield are sent to the northern and southern continents of America, to the whole of the nations of Europe, to India, Australia, Africa, and even to China. The branches of trade cultivated have expanded in a similar degree. Though Sheffield is still popularly known as the world's cutlery mart, the wares by which it has gained this celebrity are now only a considerable part of her staple industries. Of these manufactures we treat in detail in another place.

Sheffield is far from being an unhealthy town. Although there are of course densely-populated districts where disease is rife, and which increase the general total of mortality in the borough, a comparison with other large towns is favourable to Sheffield. Thus, in Birmingham the average of deaths is 26 in the thousand ; in Newcastle, 27 ; in Wolverhampton, 27 ; in Wigan, 28 ; in Bristol, 29 ; in Leeds, 30 ; in Hull, 31 ; in Manchester, 33 ; in Liverpool, 36 ; and in Sheffield, 27.*

* Mr. Alderman Saunders made the following remarkable statement at a meeting of the Sheffield Town Council, in February, 1862, the figures being obtained from returns made by the local Government registrars of births and deaths :—" Since 1857,

The town is generally well lighted and paved. The central streets show some very handsome shop fronts. Still more attractive are the villa residences and mansions which have sprung up in the suburbs of the town. Especially in the Broomhall, Broomhill, and Sharrow districts, the visitor will be struck by the beauty of the dwellings, the attractions of which are greatly enhanced by the natural scenery, and are hardly to be surpassed by the suburbs of any town in the kingdom. Even more pleasing, in a moral point of view, is the spectacle presented at Walkley and other of the out-districts. There are several localities where estates have been purchased and partitioned out by means of the Freehold Land Societies; but Walkley is peculiarly the region for these allotments. The hill sides are dotted in every direction with houses, almost all of them obtained by working men through the instrumentality of Freehold Land or Building Societies. Nothing can furnish a more striking and demonstrative illustration of the thrift of at least a considerable part of the Sheffield artizans.

Sheffield returns two representatives to the House of Commons, under the Reform Act of 1832. The present members are Mr. J. A. Roebuck and Mr. George Hadfield. It was also incorporated under the Municipal Act. The limits of the borough are very large, being more than ten miles in length, while the average breadth is about three miles. It comprises the townships of Sheffield, Ecclesall Bierlow, Nether Hallam, Upper Hallam, Brightside Bierlow, and Attercliffe-cum-Darnall.

GOVERNING AND PUBLIC BODIES, &c.

The most ancient of all the distinctively local public bodies in Sheffield are

THE TOWN TRUSTEES.

The origin of the corporate body now known as the Town Trustees dates back as far as 1297, when a charter was granted to the inhabitants by Thomas, the third Lord Furnival. The original document is still in the possession of the Trustees. The funds of the Trust were increased by many benefactors besides its first founders. They were principally appropriated to public uses, such as keeping in repair the bridges, the town armour, the pillory, the "cuck-stool," &c. At the Reformation, about two-thirds of the funds were appropriated to the

there have been about 25,000 souls added to the population of the town, and yet during that time the death rate has been decreasing. In the quarter ending December 31, 1857, there were 999 deaths in Sheffield; in the same quarter of 1858, there were 972; in 1859 there were 801; in 1860, 857; whilst in the same period of 1861 there were only 788 deaths. The difference between the first and last of those returns gives a decrease of 211 deaths, although the population has increased by 25,000.

maintenance of the three priests who assisted the Vicar. Afterwards the whole of the property was confiscated, but eventually it was restored, the two-thirds being devoted to the support of the priests mentioned, and the remaining third being vested in a body of the principal inhabitants. Under the name of "The Town Trustees," this body still exists, and now numbers twelve. Vacancies are filled up by public election amongst the freeholders of the township of Sheffield. The Town Trustees are of great public service, as, by the terms of their charter, they are allowed to spend their funds on "any charitable and public uses," so that they frequently carry out, or materially assist in carrying out, valuable projects for the improvement of the town. In 1565, the property belonging to the Trust realized £7 7s. a year ; it now amounts to upwards of £2,000 per annum. Mr. W. Butcher is the head of the Trust, being called the Town Collector ; Mr. H. Vickers, Bank street, is Law Clerk ; and Mr. T. J. Flockton, East Parade, Surveyor.

THE CHURCH BURGESSES.

The Church Burgesses, as they are now called, are also a very ancient body. The Capital Burgesses and Commonalty were incorporated in 1554, by a charter granted by Queen Mary ; but the circumstances attending the origin of the body take us to a much earlier period. It seems that the " voluntary principle" existed largely in Sheffield even in the middle ages ; for the inhabitants maintained three priests to assist the Vicar in his duties. The violent changes in the time of Henry VIII. caused a failure of the contributions by which these ministers were maintained, and part of the funds mentioned in our account of the Town Trust were diverted to their support. This continued till the reign of Edward VI., when the lands by which they were maintained were seized and confiscated for the Crown. On the accession of Mary the inhabitants petitioned for the lands to be restored for the maintenance of the three priests, and the Queen granted the prayer by the charter already mentioned. By this deed the inhabitants of Sheffield were constituted a corporate body, entitled the "Twelve Capital Burgesses and Commonalty of the town and parish of Sheffield." According to the terms of the charter, twelve resident gentlemen were appointed as the executive body. By vote of their own members, they have continued to fill up the vacancies which have occurred ; and the twelve Capital Burgesses still constitute a local corporate body of considerable influence and utility. The object of the Burgesses, as declared by the charter, was to maintain three ministers to assist the Vicar ; to repair the Parish Church, bridges, and common ways ; and to assist the poor and needy inhabitants. Almost the whole of the revenues, however, became devoted to ecclesiastical purposes. Three ministers are still maintained to assist the Vicar. They are called chaplains. The funds are also devoted to the payment of sums for the chaplain at the Infirmary, the sexton and organist at the Parish Church,

&c. A gradual extension of the benefits of the funds is provided for by an order of Chancery obtained in 1854. In the time of Henry VIII. the estates realized £17 a year, which was divided amongst the three priests, one receiving £7 and the others £5 each. Now the estates are worth about £2,200 a year ; and the chaplains are paid £400 a year each. The head of the body, called the Capital Burgess, is Mr. S. Roberts ; and the Law Clerk is Mr. J. J. Wheat, solicitor, Paradise-square.

THE CUTLERS' COMPANY.

This body was incorporated by Act of Parliament, passed in 1624, entitled " An Act for the good order and government of the makers of knives, sickles, shears, scissors, and other cutlery wares in Hallamshire, in the county of York, and parts near adjoining." The cause of the application for the Act we have already mentioned—namely, that the juries which were empanelled had not sufficient powers to regulate the trade. Accordingly, we find the preamble of the Act declaring that many of the cutlery workers refused to submit to the ordinances of the trade ; that they persisted in taking as many apprentices, and for such a term of years, as they chose, whereby it was feared that the calling would be "overthrown ;" and that the workmen, owing to the absence of proper authority, " are thereby emboldened and do make such deceitful, unworkmanlike wares, and sell the same in divers parts of the kingdom, to the great deceit of his Majesty's subjects and scandal of the cutlers of Hallamshire, and disgrace and hindrance of the sale of cutlery and iron and steel wares there made, and to the great impoverishment, ruin, and overthrow of multitudes of poor people."' The Act provided that the cutlery manufacturers of Hallamshire and six miles round, should form a body corporate, to consist of a Master, two wardens, six searchers, and twenty-four assistant searchers. These were the executive of the body, the rest of the manufacturers being included under the term " commonalty." Power was given to these officers to make such regulations as they thought proper for the management of the trade, and to inflict fines for the breaking of them. The Act directed that all persons engaged in the trade should make the edges of their goods only of steel, and that they should stamp them only with such marks as might be assigned by the Company. Such were some of the principal provisions of the Cutlers' Company, as originally constituted. It seems to have been popular, for 360 manufacturers at once joined it. The Company passed regulations to a considerable extent more stringent than those formerly enforced by the juries. The " searchers" were empowered to enter houses for the purpose of seizing the " deceitful, unworkmanlike wares" which were so bitterly complained of. Rules for the restriction of the trade, so as to prevent it from being " overthrown" by the multitude of workmen, were rigidly carried out. The privilege of working at the cutlery business was strictly confined to freemen, of whom for a long time an average of only about thirty new ones a year were admitted. Various modifications were afterwards made by Act of Parliament; but no radical change was effected till 1814, when the system of freemen was found to check the progress of the trade to such an extent that an Act of Parliament was obtained rescinding it. By that Act the trade was thrown open to every one who might choose to engage in it. All the other powers of the Company, except that of granting and protecting marks, were taken away. This continues to be the only privilege practically possessed by the Cutlers' Company; but it is still of great importance, and has materially assisted in aiding the growth of the large Sheffield firms which have obtained a world-wide reputation for their wares. By an Act obtained in 1860 the Company has been still further popularized, the benefits of it having been extended to steel manufacturers and makers of all goods with a "cutting edge." The income of the company is not very large, being about £800 a year. It has arisen principally from the fees for granting marks. Out of their funds, however, the Company have built their handsome Hall (which is described amongst the public buildings).

The annual festivity of the Cutlers' Company is well known. The "Cutlers' Feast" is noted not in Sheffield merely, but throughout the country, as an occasion on which members of the nobility are frequently present, and on which some of the most distinguished politicians of the country find an opportunity of expressing a public opinion on current events. We find that the Cutlers' Feast had become an important social gathering at an early period, for in 1682 several peers attended, while in 1771 there were present the Dukes of Norfolk, Devonshire, and Leeds, the Marquis of Rockingham, and the Earls of Holderness, Scarborough, Effingham, Bute, and Stafford, with several other peers and baronets. The dinner is given by the Master Cutler upon his installation in office, and the Company provide him with £105 towards the expense; but it costs a large sum besides, the "Feast," which may more properly be called a banquet, being in every respect of the most sumptuous and *recherché* description. The following curious document of the "settling up" of the Feast in 1749, shows in a remarkable manner the change in the social habits of Sheffield, in common with the rest of the community, during the last hundred years :—" Expenses of the Cutler's Feast : Rump of Beef, 3s. 4d. ; six Fowls, 2s. 8d.; ham, 3s ; pies and puddings, 2s. 6d. ; hare, 1s. 6d. ; loin of veal, 1s. 10d. ; bread, 1s.; butter, 2s.; roots, 4d.; ale and punch, 20s. 7d. ; dressing, 4s ; Total, £2 2s. 9d. Collected by the Company, 21s ; paid out of stock, 21s. 9d. Received contents in full by WILLIAM DIXON."

The Master Cutler at the present time is Mr. George Wilkinson, cutlery manufacturer, New Church-street; but the office is only held for a year, the election taking place in August. The Law Clerk is Mr. James Wilson, solicitor, East Parade.

LIGHTING AND CLEANSING COMMISSIONERS.

This body is popularly known as the "Police Commissioners," or the "Improvement Commissioners;" but both these titles are now misnomers, as they have no such powers as these names imply. The Commissioners were established in 1818 by Act of Parliament, there being up to that time no corporate body vested with authority to raise money to light and cleanse the town, which were done by the Town Trustees. The Commissioners still retain the power of lighting and cleansing; but the control of the constabulary which they formerly possessed has been transferred to the Town Council. Mr. John Jackson is Surveyor to the Commissioners; his offices are at the Town Hall. The Law Clerk is Mr. W. Smith, jun., solicitor, Campo-lane.

THE MUNICIPAL CORPORATION.

Though of modern origin, the Municipal Corporation is of course the most influential body in the borough. Sheffield was incorporated by royal charter in 1843. The Town Council is composed of a mayor, fourteen aldermen, and forty-two councillors. The borough is divided into nine wards, St. Peter's, St. George's, St. Philip's, Ecclesall, and Park, each of which returns six councillors, and Nether Hallam, Upper Hallam, Brightside, and Attercliffe, each of which sends three. The Town Council has no property like some old Corporations, and the whole of its expenses have to be raised by rate. The total sum expended yearly is about £14,000. Mr. John Brown (of the Atlas Iron and Steel Works) is Mayor. The Town Clerk is Mr. John Yeomans, whose offices are in Bank-street.

THE HIGHWAY BOARDS.

The Board for the repair of the roads in the township of Sheffield is elected annually, by the ratepayers. The offices are in Queen street. Mr. J. Wheatley is Clerk, and Mr. R. Chapman Surveyor. There are also separate Boards for the townships of Ecclesall, Nether Hallam, Upper Hallam, Brightside, and Attercliffe.

THE LAW COURTS.

The sittings of the Bankruptcy Court are held in one of the rooms at the Council Hall, usually before Mr. Commissioner West or Mr. Registrar Payne. The official Assignee is Mr. George Young, whose offices are in St. James's-street.

The County Court possesses commodious buildings in Bank-street, which have been built specially for the administration of this branch of justice. There are a handsome and spacious court room and very convenient offices. The Judge is Mr. William Walker; the Registrars, Messrs. W. Wake and T. W. Rodgers; and the High Bailiff, Mr. Smilter, who has separate offices in Bank street.

Sheffield not possessing a Recorder and separate Quarter Sessions, its prisoners are tried at the West Riding Sessions, which are held by rotation, (about twice a quarter), at Sheffield, Rotherham, and other places in the West Riding. The Court of Quarter Sessions is, in Sheffield, held at the Town Hall, where also the local Magistrates sit daily in Petty Sessions. The Clerk to the Magistrates is Mr. Albert Smith, Castle-street.

THE POLICE FORCE,

Under the management of an energetic Watch Committee and a most intelligent Chief Constable, has become a well-trained and thoroughly efficient body. Besides the Chief Constable (Mr. John Jackson), there are a warrant officer, five detective officers, two inspectors, five sub-inspectors, eleven sergeants, and 162 constables. The principal Police Office is at the Town Hall. There is also a station in Tenter-street. The annual cost of the police force is about £11,000.

GUARDIANS OF THE POOR, AND WORKHOUSES.

The systematic method of relieving the poor which, under the New Poor Law, was adopted in place of the loose and unsatisfactory system formerly in use, has taken shape in this borough in the formation of two Unions, those of Sheffield and Ecclesall Bierlow. Though comprising parishes or townships situated mainly within the borough, both Unions comprise a rural population. The Sheffield Union contains the townships of Sheffield, Brightside, and Attercliffe, within the borough, and Handsworth without. The Workhouse of the Sheffield Union, with the board-room for the Guardians, &c., is situated in Kelham street. The buildings, which were originally used for a cotton mill, and were altered for Workhouse purposes, are situated in the heart of the town. A few years since, when the accommodation was found to be getting too scanty, a project was mooted for building a new Workhouse outside the town, and land was purchased at Darnall for that purpose. A public agitation was aroused, however, in opposition to the scheme, principally on account of its expense ; the land was re-sold, and the existing Workhouse was altered and enlarged, at an expense of about £5,900. There are separate buildings for the children at Pitsmoor. There is also another establishment belonging to the Union, of a somewhat peculiar character. In 1849 the Guardians leased from the Duke of Norfolk about fifty acres of moorland, at Hollow Meadows, about six miles from the town, with a view of reclaiming it by pauper labour. Nearly the whole of the land has been brought under cultivation, and sub-let to farm tenants. The Farm, as it is called, is still retained by the Guardians, and a number of the able-bodied men who require relief in times of bad trade are sent to labour at it. The undertaking has been so successful that at the time we write, (February, 1862,) the Guardians are in negociation for the leasing of further land.

Ecclesall Bierlow Union is more agricultural than Sheffield, though even in this the larger part is urban. It comprises the townships

of Ecclesall Bierlow, Nether Hallam, and Upper Hallam, within the
borough, with Norton, Totley, Dore, and Beauchief, in Derbyshire.
The Workhouse is a handsome structure at Cherry-tree Hill, about two
miles from Sheffield. It has cost altogether about £15,000.

The total expenditure of the Sheffield Union in the year ending
March, 1857, was about £33,000. In the year 1861-2, (when there had
been a winter of great commercial depression) the expenditure reached
about £50,000. But in order to calculate the entire expenditure on
the poor in the borough this year it is necessary to take into account
the sum spent in the Ecclesall Union. In the same year more than
£16,000 was expended in the Ecclesall Union, and, deducting £2,200
for the rural districts in the two Unions, this leaves £13,800 to be
added to the sum expended in the Sheffield Union, making a total of
more than £63,800 spent during the year on the poor of the borough.
The sum spent in 1784 was £3,223.

The Clerk to the Sheffield Guardians is Mr. J. Spencer, whose
offices are in Kelham-street. The Clerk to the Ecclesall Guardians is
Mr. T. Smith, and his offices are at the Workhouse at Cherry-tree.

RELIGIOUS EDIFICES.

CHURCH OF ENGLAND.

Sheffield has benefited largely by the legislation of late years providing for the sub-division of over-populous parishes. In 1719 the
large increase of the inhabitants forced upon the attention of the town
the necessity of providing a place of worship in addition to the existing
Parish Church; and the object was accomplished by the erection of
St. Paul's, notwithstanding the legal difficulties at that time attending
such a project. But in 1845, church extension in the town was promoted by its division into twenty-five parochial districts, each to
have a church and an incumbent.

PARISH CHURCH.

By far the most ancient and most interesting building in Sheffield
is the handsome structure still commonly known as the Parish Church.
The De Lovetots, amongst their other munificent acts, founded a
church at Sheffield, and it seems probable that it was originated by the
first of these lords, in the reign of Henry I. This nobleman, who
seems to have been of a most pious and munificent disposition, also
founded and endowed a monastery at Worksop. The church has been
variously styled. It is now usually called St. Peter's. In certain
documents, the earliest of which dates in 1556, it is styled "St. Peter's
and St. Paul's." It has also borne the appellation of Holy Trinity, and
is said to have so been dedicated originally.

PARISH CHURCH, SHEFFIELD.

The Parish Church is rectangular in shape, with a crocketed tower and spire near the centre. Hunter gives the following conjectures as to its present form and construction :—" Originally, like most of our churches that were erected for the use of a considerable population, it was in the form of a cross, the tower and spire rising at the intersection of the two limbs. In the original design were included side aisles, both on the north and south, above which rose the nave, with a range of clerestory windows. Perhaps the first change in its form was produced by the erection of the Shrewsbury Chapel, which now forms the south-east angle of the building. Since that period there have been many changes and many re-edifications, till nothing remains of the original fabric except the massy pillars that support the tower, and the whole has assumed a form which never belonged to the ancient churches of this country—a parallelogram contained by walls of equal altitude."

The early editions of Hunter are quite incorrect as to the dimensions of the church. A recent admeasurement gives them as—inside, nave 64 feet, tower 29 feet, and chancel 45 feet, giving a total length of 138 feet, while the width is 66 feet. Outside the length is 143 feet, and the width 72 feet. Another recent admeasurement varies very little, making the length outside 150 feet and the width 75 feet. The great defect of the building, architecturally, is that there is no perfect style about it. Nevertheless, it is a handsome edifice, and, inside, has a very pleasing appearance. The most prominent style in the building is the perpendicular; the chancel is decorated. The most important alterations which have been recently made were carried out in 1856, under the superintendence of Messrs. Flockton and Son, of Sheffield. The interior of the edifice was to a large extent re-constructed, and its whole internal appearance was vastly improved. The most prominent change was the taking down of an unsightly screen which separated the nave from the chancel. Various other improvements have since been made; and there are now few parish churches, (however superior in architectural beauty they may be,) which, internally, have so solemn and pleasing an aspect. There is a north and a south aisle, and the nave is divided into five bays, with stone pillars and arches. It accommodates 2,200 persons.

There are some handsome ornamental windows. That at the west end is a fine work of art in the flamboyant style, given by the Rev. Dr. Sale in 1857. It contains the arms and seals of the Church Burgesses, the Town Trustees, and the Cutler's Company, the Corporation, the Vicar, and the Archbishop of York. There are also in the tracery lights emblems of the Evangelists. There is a handsome window on each side of the principal one. The central east window was erected in 1858 in memory of James Montgomery the Poet, being the gift of Mr. J. N. Mappin. It is in the same style as the west window. It is 23 feet high and 12 feet wide. There are four lower lights, on which are depicted some of the principal personages of the Old and New Testament. The left centre light contains the figure of Moses with the tables of the law and the rod; and on the right centre light is the figure of David. Of the two outer lights, the one on the left contains a figure of St. Matthew holding the pen and book illustrat:ve of his inspired authorship, while that on the right has a representation of the beloved disciple, John. Below these last two figures are the following inscriptions:—"In memory of James Montgomery, died 1854," and "The gift of John Newton Mappin, churchwarden, 1857." In the upper part of the four principal lights are depicted representations of the baptism of the Saviour, His transfiguration, crucifixion, and ascension. Above these, surrounded by foliage, are the figures of two angels, containing on one the words, "We praise Thee, O God!" and on the other, "We acknowledge Thee to be the Lord!" Over all is the figure of a hovering dove. The upper window contains figures of St. Paul with a sword and St. Peter with the keys. Above are the arms of the donor of the window. In March, 1862, the Mayor, (Mr. John Brown,) placed in the chancel a beautifully designed and executed memorial window, in memory of his parents. The subject is the history of Joseph. On the top of the window are representations of six angels, two of which are bearing scrolls, on one of which is inscribed, "Lift up your heads O ye gates," and on the other, "And be lift up ye everlasting doors." The centre scene is that of two angels bearing a scroll on which is inscribed the fifth commandment, and the remaining parts are scenes connected with the life of Joseph. Beneath the whole is inscribed, "John Brown, Esq., Mayor of Sheffield, erected this window A.D. 1862, to the memory of his parents. Samuel Brown, his father, died April 27, 1861; Ann Brown, his mother, died April 12, 1856; and both are interred in Ecclesall Churchyard." There are also the Mayor's arms.

Under the clerestory windows there are eight coats-of-arms. Looking towards the west end of the church, the arms are in the following order:—On the right are those of four of the principal Lords of the Manor, viz., the De Lovetots, the De Furnivals, the Talbots, and the Howards. On the left are the arms of four of the proprietors of the advowson since the Reformation—viz., the Swyfts, the Jessops, the Gells, and the Lawsons.

THE SHREWSBURY CHAPEL.—FROM AN ENGRAVING IN HUNTER'S HALLAMSHIRE.

In the south-east corner of the church is the Shrewsbury Chapel, which contains sepulchral monuments of great beauty.* This struc-

* A copy of Hunter's "Hallamshire" had been annotated by the author before his death; and it, with the copyright of the work, have been purchased with a view to the publication of a new edition by Messrs. Pawson and Brailsford. It contains the following note on the Shrewsbury Chapel:—"I regard the monuments in this chapel as among the finest in the kingdom."

ture and its contents are sufficient of themselves to prove the high regard in which Sheffield was held by the house of Talbot, for it was evidently intended as the great resting place for the members of the family, and the spot on which were to be recorded, by the sculptor's art, the deeds of the succeeding inheritors of the title. The chapel was founded in the reign of Henry VIII., by the fourth Earl of Shrewsbury. The chapel is about 25 feet long and 17 feet wide. On the north side there is a beautiful stone arch, beneath which stands the monument of the Earl who built this edifice. The monument consists of an altar tomb. At each corner is a spiral column; and on the sides were once the heraldic quarterings of the Earl. There were originally ten of these; but only two are now left. On the top of the tomb are recumbent marble figures of the Earl and his two Countesses, Ann and Elizabeth. The figure of the Earl is garbed in the robes of the Order of the Garter and has the peer's coronet, the feet resting on a talbot. On the vest underneath the robes are visible the principal quarterings of the Earl, the same as are on the sides of the tomb. The dresses of the Countesses are also decorated with heraldic devices. At the feet of each is the figure of an angel supporting a shield without device. The hands of the Earl and of his wives are joined in supplication, as is frequent in sepulchral effigies. A ledge of brass running round the tomb contains a Latin inscription stating that the bodies of the Earl and of the Ladies Ann and Elizabeth lie below; but this is not entirely correct, for the latter lady had a choice of her own, and, surviving the Earl, was buried at Erith, in Kent.

About the centre of the chapel there is another altar tomb without figures or inscription. Hunter conjectures, from the shields of arms on the sides, (which are still in good preservation,) that this "might be the first design of the sixth Earl for a monument for himself, abandoned for one of an entirely different form and structure, or perhaps intended by him as a memorial of his son and heir-apparent, Francis Lord Talbot, who was interred at Sheffield, in September, 1585."

The monument of the sixth Earl above referred to, is placed against the south wall, and was erected during his lifetime. The effigy of the Earl is represented in plate armour, lying on a sarcophagus, with the helmet placed above the head. There was formerly a truncheon in the hand, but it has been broken off. The features, before they were injured, were no doubt a good likeness; but the portraiture has been partially destroyed by the adding of new portions to the face where it had been mutilated. Still the features retain sufficient of their original outline to have enabled Miss Strickland, the historian, to recognize them as corresponding with those of an authentic likeness of the Earl of Shrewsbury who was present at the execution of Mary,—this being the Earl who had the custody of the unfortunate Queen, and who was amongst the persons that saw her beheaded. On a slab of marble above the effigy is a very long inscription in Latin, which has been restored and is in good preservation. Surrounding the inscription there is a border of military trophies and shields of arms. The long inscription derives some interest from its having been composed by worthy old Fox, whose unctuous descriptions of the sufferings of the martyrs so terrified us all in our childish days. A copy of the inscription, in Fox's own writing, is still preserved in the Harleian Library.

Amongst the other monuments in the church are two by Chantrey. One of these is peculiarly interesting, as being the first work executed in marble by the great sculptor. It is located in the chancel. It is a simple bust representing the Rev. James Wilkinson, one of the former Vicars, who died in 1805. Mr. Wilkinson was so much respected, that a subscription was raised for a monument to his memory. Young Chantrey was entrusted with the commission. He undertook it, though at that time very diffident of his untried powers. He was thoroughly successful, however; and although of course this piece of sculpture will not bear comparison with Chantrey's more ambitious and matured conceptions, it is nevertheless an excellent work of art and an admirable likeness. The other monument, which is near to that already described, is a work of considerably greater pretension, and possesses many beauties. It is to the memory of Mr. Thomas Harrison, of Weston, and Elizabeth his wife, the former of whom died in 1818, and the latter in 1823. There is a sorrowing figure, life size, leaning over a tomb, on which are medallion portraits of the persons in whose memory the monument is raised.

The vaults under the Shrewsbury Chapel have considerable interest attached to them. Hunter makes out a list of eighteen persons buried there. He gives the following account of a visit he paid these vaults in 1809 :—" By eight or nine steps from the chancel we descended to an upright door, which we found so decayed that it fell from its bolt and hinges on a very slight force being applied to it. We were then admitted into a room about 10 feet square and six feet in height, its stone roof supported by a rough hewn pillar, rising in the centre. We found only two coffins lying on tressels."

The vaults were again entered in May, 1858, for the purpose of making a search in connection with the celebrated Shrewsbury peerage case, then pending in the House of Lords. The following particulars were given in a local paper at the time :—A list had been made of seventeen members of the noble family buried in the vaults, beginning with Ann, Countess of Shrewsbury and daughter of Lord Hastings, early in the 16th century, and ending with Henry Howard Esq., 1787. In the open part of the vault were found two coffins, one of Gilbert, Earl of Shrewsbury, who died in 1616, and the other of Mr. Henry Howard. The wooden coffin of the Earl has been several times renewed, and in 1774 a brass plate was put upon it, containing the inscription found upon the lead in which the body was enveloped. On opening the coffin it was found that the lead covering of the body was not in the form of a coffin, but was wrapped about it after the manner of the envelopes of an Egyptian mummy. The lead bore an inscription containing the full titles of the Earl. Mr. Hunter had supposed that other coffins were walled up on the north side of the vault, under the tomb of George the fourth Earl, and the founder of the chapel; and in order to find them an excavation was made in that direction. After this had been prosecuted for about four feet, it was found that it had reached the original foundation of the church. No trace of a vault or of any human remains was found. Search was then made under the floor of the vault. Here was found a body encased in lead. The lead tore like coarse paper, and, being removed from over the face, it disclosed the skull, evidently of a male person, on which there still remained some reddish gray hair. There was, however, no inscription. Two coffins were found *under* this, one containing the body of John Sherburne, gentleman, and the other of Ruth, his widow. There were also the remains of an empty wooden coffin, without date or name. A great number of loose bones were found, with no traces of coffins. The conclusion was, that at some period the vault had been ransacked, the lead stolen, and the contents buried here. After excavating the floor for about six feet, the labourers found themselves stopped by the solid rock.

Within the chancel of the Parish Church was buried a man named William Walker, respecting whom a very interesting tradition exists. There was formerly a brass on the south wall of the chancel, commemorating his burial underneath in November, 1700. Walker is supposed to have been the executioner of Charles I. His native place was Darnall, a village about three miles from Sheffield; and here he returned and spent the remainder of his days after the restoration of Charles II. Walker was a man of literary tastes; but, living a secluded life, and being known to have taken an active share in political affairs during the Commonwealth, it seems not extraordinary that rumours of this kind should have been associated with his name amongst the villagers. On the other hand, it is known that he was a person of high standing in the neighbourhood, for in 1681 the honorary freedom of the Cutlers' Company was conferred on him. Still there is distinct evidence, though very much of a hearsay character, which tends to fix the deed upon Walker. This evidence, which was published in the 37th and 38th volumes of the "Gentleman's Magazine," seemed so conclusive to Archdeacon Blackburn, that, writing on the subject, he expressed his opinion that there is a stronger case against this Walker than against any one else who has been suspected. The evidence consists for the most part of recollections, sometimes second and third-hand, of what Walker is alleged to have done and said. It is stated, for instance, that he "died very hard," and that he said he "could not leave the world without confessing that he was the King's executioner." A warrant is said to have been sent for his apprehension, and he concealed himself for a time at Handsworth Woodhouse, a neighbouring village. One of the writers in the "Gentleman's Magazine," after stating the date of Walker's baptism (September, 1621) adds, "By which it appears that he was a young man in the flower of his life when he beheaded the King; and by the report of ancient people who knew him, he was a lusty, strong-boned, tall man, even in his old age."

Amongst the monumental works in the church is an excellent one, on the north wall of the chancel, to the memory of various members of the Jessops—a local family of note. The artist is not known. Between the communion table and the vestry there is a fine marble bust by the late Mr. Edward Law (a local sculptor), in memory of Mr. Thomas Watson. Over the chancel door there is a striking monument to a member of the Bamforth family. There are several other monuments to departed local worthies, and also various monumental brasses, very interesting, and in a beautiful state of preservation. Amongst them is one which was formerly fixed in the floor, but has been taken up and placed against the wall just outside the Shrewsbury Chapel. The following is the inscription:—" Here lyeth Elizabeth, Doughter of Thomas Erle of Ormonde, and of Lore, his wyf, sometyme wyf to the Lorde Mountioye, wiche Elizabeth deceased the xx day of February the yeare of our Lord MCCCCCX, on whose soule Jhu have mercy. Men."

An interesting relic of ancient times still remains in the church. This consists of the wooden stalls for three persons, in which the priest and his two assistants used to sit at the celebration of the mass, before the Reformation. These seats are in a perfect state of preservation, and are still used by the ministers of the church. There is a piscina in the Shrewsbury Chapel, and the old altar stone with its crosses forms one of the flags of the church floor.

The organ in this church is a very fine instrument built, by Mr. G. P. England in the early part of the present century. It has three rows of keys and an effective pedal organ, the latter portion being the work of Messrs Kirtland and Jerdine, of Manchester, who made this addition with other improvements to the organ about four years ago. Mr. G. H. Smith is the organist.

The Rev. Canon Sale, D.D., is Vicar of the Parish Church, and rural dean. The vicarage is valued at about £500. It is in the alternate gift of Mrs. Thornhill, of Stanton Park, near Bakewell, and Mr. A. Lawson of Boroughbridge.

ST. PAUL'S.

This church, which is in Norfolk-street, is in the Grecian style of architecture. It ranks next in antiquity to the Parish Church, though it is, comparatively, quite a modern structure. As already intimated, the undertaking for its erection by public subscription was commenced in 1719, but it was not actually opened till 1740, when it was made a

ST. PAUL'S CHURCH.

chapel-of-ease to the Parish Church. The dome was added in 1769. It is a spacious building; and improvements have been recently made which greatly add both to the beauty of the interior of the edifice and the comfort of the congregation. The organ is by the celebrated builder Snetzler. It is one of his best productions, and was built one hundred and five years ago. Since its erection it has, however, been considerably modernized, but the original portion still bears its distinctive excellence. The latest additions have been made by Mr. Brindley, of this town, who supplied the pedal organ and several new stops to other portions of the instrument, and also equalized the whole. It has three manuals and a pedal organ. The organist is Mr. J. C. Walker. About 40 years ago, performances of sacred music on a grand scale were given in this church, Madame Malibran and other distinguished vocalists singing within its walls. There is a mural monument by Chantrey in St. Paul's Church, not unworthy of the great sculptor's celebrity. It is erected to the memory of the Rev. Alexander Mackenzie, one of the incumbents of the church, who died in 1816. The work is thus described by Mr. John Holland, in his life of Chantrey:—"It consists of a plain square plinth, an entablature with sacerdotal emblems, and, between these, three slabs. That in the middle contains the inscription; the lateral ones, figures in low relief of Faith with a cross, and Mourning with hands on the face; the whole surmounted by a marble bust, in which the sculptor has done justice to the fine head and face of the deceased." The Rev.

J. E. Blakeney, M.A., is the perpetual curate of St. Paul's. The living is in the gift of the Vicar of Sheffield.

ST. JAMES'S.

This building is at the end of St. James's-street, not far from the Parish Church. It was consecrated in 1789. The cost of the building was rather over £3,000, which was raised in £50 shares, each share entitling the holder to a pew as his freehold. In the east window there is a painting by Peckitt, executed in 1797, and representing the Crucifixion. The perpetual curacy, which is in gift of the Vicar of Sheffield, is held by the Rev. Thomas Best, M.A.

ST. GEORGE'S.

This edifice, together with St. Mary's and St Philip's, was amongst those built at the cost of the nation. It is situated at the top of Broad-lane and Portobello-street. It was finished in 1825, at the cost of £14,819. There are 2,000 sittings, 1000 of which are free. Over the communion table there is a painting, by Paris, of Christ blessing little children. The living is a perpetual curacy, in the patronage of the Vicar, and is now held by the Rev. William Mercer, M.A. (compiler of the "Church Psalter and Hymn Book.")

ST. PHILIP'S.

St. Philip's Church stands at the junction of the Infirmary and Penistone roads, on a site given by the late Mr. Philip Gell, of Hopton. It was completed in 1828, at a cost of £13,000. There is accommodation for 2,000 worshippers. It has a fine east window. The organ is a very noble instrument of three rows of keys, and pedals, built by the celebrated makers, Messrs. Hill & Sons, London. Mr. George Lee is the organist. The cathedral-like character of the building within, and the possession of so fine an organ, have led to the adoption of the choral service, and the establishment of a choir which for many years has maintained a well-earned celebrity.

Connected with St. Philip's is the chapel school, at Walkley, on a site given by the Incumbent, and completed about the beginning of 1862, at a cost of £1,100. This is used as a church on Sundays, and as a school in connection with the National Society on week days, until funds can be obtained for erecting a substantial school-house and completing the present structure, hereafter to be consecrated as St. Mary's Church. Measures are also in progress for the like provision for the populous and rapidly-increasing village of Owlerton, where an eligible site for a church has been offered by Mr. Montagu George Burgoyne. The living is a perpetual curacy, in the gift of the Vicar, and held by the Rev. John Livesey, M.A.

ST. MARY'S.

This church was consecrated in 1830. It cost £12,649. It is a large and handsome Gothic building, in Bramall-lane. The perpetual

curacy is in the gift of the Vicar, and is held by the Rev. William
Wilkinson, M.A.

ST. JOHN'S.

This church, situated in the Park district, is a modern erection, in
the early English style. It has a tower 50 feet high, surmounted by
a spire of the same height. It stands on a bold eminence overlooking
the town. It was erected in the years 1836-37, at a cost of £3,500,
raised by subscription. It will accommodate about 1,000 persons,
and all the sittings are free. Around the church is a fine open burial
ground of several acres, which, with the site of the parsonage-house,
was given by the late Duke of Norfolk. The living is a perpetual
curacy, in the gift of trustees, and in the incumbency of the Rev. R.
Heslop.

TRINITY CHURCH.

This building is situated in Nursery-street. It is in the early
English style, and was built in 1847-8 for the Wicker district, entirely
at the expense of the Misses Harrison, of Weston Hall. There are
1,000 sittings, of which 333 are free. There is a handsome east
window of stained glass. The living, which is a perpetual curacy, is
in the gift of Miss Harrison. The Rev. John Aldous is incumbent.

ST. JUDE'S, ELDON.

The site of this edifice was given by Mr. Samuel Younge, of Brincliffe Edge. The style of the building is early English. The cost was
£2,200, £500 being contributed by the Church Building and Incorporated Societies. The date of its consecration was June 16th, 1849.
There is accommodation for 730 persons. The Rev. George Sandford,
M.A., is the incumbent. The living is in the gift of the Crown and
the Archbishop of York alternately.

ST. JUDE'S, MOORFIELDS.

This church, which is for the Moorfields district, is in a very dis-
advantageous situation, being completely built up with houses. The
entrance is from Gibraltar-street. It was commenced in 1849; but in
1852, when it was nearly finished, the whole of the tower fell, owing to
some defect in the foundations, and had to be entirely reconstructed.
The building was completed in 1855. It is in the early English style,
and is a neat structure. It cost about £2,400. The late Mr. John
Gaunt, of Darnall, gave the site and £1,000, the Incorporated Society
£550, and the Ecclesiastical Commissioners £350. There are 900
sittings, the whole of which are free. The Rev. Greville J. Chester,
B.A., is the incumbent. The perpetual curacy is in the gift of the
Crown and the Archbishop of York alternately.

CHRIST CHURCH, PITSMOOR.

This church, which is in the early decorated style, was built in
1855. The cost was about £2,500. This sum was raised by sub-

scription, except £500 given by the Ecclesiastical Commissioners and the Incorporated Society. There are 800 sittings, of which 529 are free. The Rev. Henry Barlow, M.A,., is perpetual curate. The living is in the alternate gift of the Crown and the Archbishop.

ST. MATTHEW'S.

This church, which is in Carver-street, was consecrated in 1855. It is a neat building, with a graceful spire. It has 731 sittings, of which 458 are free. The building of the church, including £600 paid for the site, cost nearly £4,000. Mr. Henry Wilson, of Westbrook, subscribed £1020. The Ecclesiastical Commissioners granted £200, and the Incorporated Church Building Society granted £250. The rest was raised by the Incumbent. The living is a perpetual curacy in the alternate gift of the Crown and the Archbishop of York. The Rev J. F. Witty holds the incumbency.

ST. STEPHEN'S.

This church, which is in Fawcett-street, St. Philip's-road, is for the Netherthorpe district. The style is decorated early English, and the shape is cruciform without aisles. In the interior the tower is supported by four handsome arches. In each transept there is a gallery and one at the end of the nave. An organ chapel opens into the church by an arch in the chancel and another in the south transept. The roof is open timbered. There is a fine five-light east window. The font is handsome, and embellished by some graceful stone carving about the arches. The exterior of the building is ornamented by a fine tower. Accomodation is provided for 480 adults and 190 children. The entire site and building are the gift of Mr. Henry Wilson, of Westbrook. The cost of the building was between £4,000 and £5,000. The total amount expended, including site, building, and endowment, was nearly £10,000. Incumbent, the Rev. John Burbidge.

ST. SIMON'S.

This church, which is for the Porter-street parish, is situated at the corner of Eyre-street and Duke-street. It is a brick building, which was originally used as a Baptist Chapel, but in 1857 it was purchased and adapted to its present use at a cost of £2,200. The appointment is in the gift of the Vicar, and the curacy is held by the Rev. J. Battersby.

ST. MARK'S.

This edifice, popularly known as the "Iron Church," from its peculiar structure, was erected in 1859 for the Broomhall district. It is in the Glossop-road. The land belongs to Mr. W. Butcher, and the building was erected by the Vicar, Mr. W. Butcher, Mr. S. Butcher, Mr. J. N. Mappin, and Mr. H. Rodgers, at a cost of about £1,500, to be repaid out of the pew rents. It is a simple but neat structure of wood and iron. There are 625 sittings. Service is performed by the Vicar of the Parish Church and his assistant ministers. The wants of the district being urgent, this building was erected for immediate use ; but it is intended ultimately to build a larger and more handsome fabric in place of it.

ST. LUKE'S.

St. Luke's Church is a neat structure, opened in 1861, for the Hollis-croft district. It is situated in Solly-street. The cost was about £3,500. There are 800 sittings. The Rev. R. H. Deane, M.A., is the incumbent. The living is in the gift of the Crown and the Archbishop alternately.

GILCAR AND DYER'S-HILL DISTRICTS.

For both of these districts (which are within the town) it is contemplated to build churches ; but at present divine worship is celebrated in temporary buildings. The Rev. John Harrison holds the curacy of the Gilcar district, and service is performed in the new National Schools, in Hodgson-street, which have been built recently by voluntary subscription. For Dyer's-hill district commodious schools have been built in Granville-street, Park, at a cost of about £1,800, and service is held on Sundays in this building. The Rev. W. Hall, M.A., holds the incumbency.

This concludes a list of the churches actually within the town. Those which remain to be described are all outside, though included amongst those of the twenty-five districts already referred to into which the parish of Sheffield has been divided.

ECCLESALL.

Ecclesall Church, which is about two miles from the town, was consecrated by the Archbishop in 1789. The church contains 700 sittings, of which 120 are free. The building underwent great alterations about twenty years ago, by which its appearance was much improved, and in 1860 two acres of land were added to the burial ground. The excellent parsonage (which is said to be one of the prettiest in England), together with the schools, was erected in the year 1834. New schools were erected in 1861. When the present church was built in 1789, it replaced a small fabric which was originally used by the monks of Beauchief. The Vicar of Sheffield has the perpetual curacy in his gift. It is held by the Rev. Edward Newman, M.A.

ATTERCLIFFE.

There is a handsome church at Attercliffe, which is about two miles from the centre of the town, on the Doncaster-road. Formerly Attercliffe was a detached village, but now it is practically a busy manufacturing suburb of Sheffield. The church is dedicated to Christ. It was opened in 1826, having been built by means of a Parliamentary grant, at the cost of £14,000. It is a Gothic building, with lancet windows and a handsome groined roof. It will accomodate from 1,100 to 1,200 persons. The incumbency is held by the Rev. C. T. Wilkinson, M.A., and is in the gift of the Vicar of Sheffield.

FULWOOD.

Christ Church, Fulwood, is in the Upper Hallam district, adjoining the town. It is a handsome Gothic building, with a tower. It was built and endowed by the late Miss Phœbe Silcock, at a cost of £2,200. It was opened in 1838. It will accommodate about 300 persons. The benefice is in the gift of trustees, and is held by the Rev E. B. Chalmer, M.A.

CROOKES.

Crookes Church, just without the suburbs of the town, was built and endowed by subscription. It was consecrated in 1840. It cost £1,500, inclusive of site and burial ground. It was enlarged in 1857, and now accommodates about 700. It is dedicated to St. Thomas. The patronage is vested in trustees. The Rev. C. G. Coombe, M.A., is the incumbent.

DARNALL.

Darnall Church is about three miles east from Sheffield, the village being on the Manchester, Sheffield, and Lincolnshire Railway. The church was built by subscription, at the cost of £2,800, and was opened in 1848. It is dedicated to Holy Trinity. The perpetual curacy, which is in the gift of trustees, is held by the Rev. W. L. Gibson, M.A.

HEELEY.

This church, dedicated to Christ, was consecrated in 1848. It is a small cruciform structure in the early English style, and has a short tower rising from the south transept. The cost of erection was about £2,690, raised by subscription, aided by a grant from the Incorporated Society. It is calculated to accommodate 450 persons, and can have galleries added when required. The living is a perpetual curacy, in the alternate patronage of the Crown and Archbishop of York. The incumbent is the Rev. H. D. Jones, B.A.

BRIGHTSIDE.

There is a small church at Brightside, which is a district immediately adjoining Attercliffe, and which is increasing in population most rapidly, owing to the new manufactories which have been and are being built on the Midland Railway. The church, which is dedicated to St. Thomas, is erected within an acre of land given by the late Earl Fitzwilliam. It was opened in 1854, having been built by subscription at a cost of £1,600. It is a neat Gothic building, with tower and spire. There is a parsonage-house adjoining, erected in 1855, at a cost of £500. The Rev. Thomas Hulme holds the living.

THE METHODIST BODIES.

WESLEYAN METHODISTS.

The Wesleyan Methodists are a numerous and influential body in Sheffield. Their early history here is very interesting. The following account of it is abridged from a sketch of their first progress in the town, written by Mr. George B. Cocking:—"In the year 1741, David Taylor visited Sheffield, and preached. His converts erected a chapel in Cheney-square. An outrageous persecution was soon commenced against them, and the populace, finding that they were not to be intimidated by stones, mud, rotten eggs, and other similar materials, concluded that the most effectual method would be to demolish the building in which they worshipped. Accordingly, on the 25th of May, 1743, a grand meeting of the rioters took place, and having undermined as much of the building as would admit of it standing, they, by means of ropes and long poles, levelled the entire structure to the ground. The Methodists being destitute of a place of worship, they erected another building larger than the previous one near to the same place. It was several times attacked by the rioters, but survived their fury. They were, however, obliged to leave, and got a third place of worship near to what is now called Burgess-street. That place during the six days ending February 14th, 1746, was a scene of nightly tumult and confusion, the result being its entire destruction. The chapel which succeeded this appears to have been situated in West-street, and to have been occupied by both the Methodists and Calvinists, Calvinism being probably preached in the morning and Arminianism in the evening. This of course could not last. The Methodists, being driven out of doors, began to provide for themselves. They procured a building in Mulberry-street, which they converted into a place of worship, measuring about twelve yards by ten, the walls though whitewashed being unplastered. This building was afterwards enlarged.* From this time the society appears to have made rapid progress, as in 1780 a more commodious chapel was erected in Norfolk-street, and shortly afterwards one built by the Independents in Garden-street was purchased by the Wesleyans, who occupied it until the erection of the one in Carver-street, the foundation stone of which was laid by Mr. Thos. Holy, March 1st, 1804. The foundation stone bore the following inscription:—' On March 1st, 1804, in the 44th year of the reign of George the Third, the father of his people, and the protector of religious liberty—at a time when the nation was engaged in an expensive war, and threatened with extermination by a haughty usurper—here was laid the first stone of a Methodist chapel, as an act of faith towards God.' "

* John Wesley, in his " Journal," mentions having preached in this chapel in Mulberry-street.

BRUNSWICK CHAPEL.

In 1832, Sheffield was found to have become so large that it was
necessary to divide it into two circuits : these are known as the east
and the west.   In the East Circuit there are five regular ministers
stationed by the Conference, and 47 local preachers; and in the West
Circuit there are six regular ministers, and 43 local preachers.   In
each of the circuits there are three places of worship, and there is also
a chapel at Wesley College.   Those in the East Circuit are Norfolk-
street, Brunswick, and Park.   The NORFOLK STREET CHAPEL was
opened in 1780; it accommodates about 1,500.   The organ in this
chapel contains all the modern improvements, and is in every respect
a most complete instrument.   It has three rows of keys, and a pedal
organ down to the 16-feet open pipe.   Mr. Charles Brindley was the
builder, and Mr. T. B. Brittain is the organist.   The BRUNSWICK
CHAPEL was opened in 1834; it accommodates about 1,700.   The
PARK CHAPEL was opened in 1830; it will accommodate about 1,000.
The chapels in the West Circuit are Carver-street, Ebenezer, and
Bridgehouses, and also that at Wesley College.   The CARVER STREET
CHAPEL was opened in 1805 :   it accommodates nearly 2,000.
EBENEZER CHAPEL was opened in 1823;   it accommodates about
1,100.   BRIDGEHOUSES CHAPEL was opened in 1808;   it accommo-
dates about 700.   The chapel at Wesley College accommodates
about 600.

WESLEYAN REFORMERS.

The Wesleyan Reformers in Sheffield have 24 chapels and preaching places, supplied entirely by the voluntary and gratuitous labours of the preachers belonging to the body, who number more than fifty. WESTON STREET CHAPEL (St. Philip's-road) is a neat and commodious stone building, erected at a cost of £1,200 in a very populous neighbourhood. This chapel was opened September, 1861, by Lord Teynham. WATERY STREET CHAPEL is also a stone building, recently enlarged, capable of accommodating about 800, with good school premises and class-rooms for 500 children. PHILADELPHIA CHAPEL is a stone structure, situated a little beyond the General Infirmary. It is in contemplation either to enlarge this chapel or build a more commodious one, and appropriate the present building for the purposes of the Sabbath school. MOUNT GERIZIM CHAPEL is in Duke-street, Sheffield Park, and was erected in 1861 at a cost of about £1,000. It is a commodious building. GOWER STREET CHAPEL is in a very populous part of the town, adjacent to the Midland line of Railway. The Wesleyan Reformers have chapels also at Attercliffe, Grimesthorpe, Abbeydale, Owlerton, Oughtibridge, Richmond, Holmsfield, Coal Aston, Hampden View, &c.

THE METHODIST NEW CONNEXION.

This body has at present three town chapels, viz.:—SCOTLAND STREET, erected 1764 and rebuilt in 1829. It will accommodate 700 persons. SOUTH STREET CHAPEL was built in 1828, and will seat 800. TALBOT STREET CHAPEL was erected in 1851, and will seat about 500. At Broomhill an eligible site of land has been secured for a commodious chapel and school, at a cost, exclusive of land, of not less than £2,500. Also, at Walkley, a plot of land has been given by Mr. Henry Wilson for the erection of a chapel to accommodate 500 persons, with school and vestry to hold about 300 scholars, at a cost of £1,000.

PRIMITIVE METHODISTS.

There are chapels belonging to this body in Coalpit-lane, Stanley-street, and at Walkley. They have also opened a chapel in Jericho-street, erected in 1861, at a cost of £1,200. It is a handsome building, of stone, and will hold about 700 persons.

UNITED METHODIST FREE CHURCH.

HANOVER CHAPEL is situated at the intersection of Hanover-street and Broom Spring-lane, and was opened for public worship in 1860. The site comprises an area of 2,600 square yards. The chapel, which is one of the largest places of worship in the town, is a lofty and imposing structure, 95 feet long and 74 feet wide. The basement storey, the floor of which is higher than the adjacent streets, is of massive and substantial masonry, and is in the rustic style. From this storey the walls are ornamented with pilasters, having Corinthian

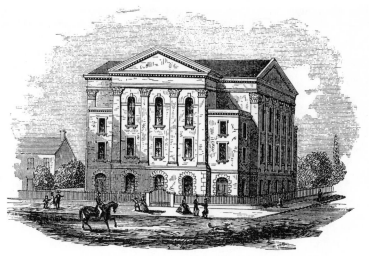

HANOVER STREET CHAPEL.

capitals, with bold and varied foliage ; the façade to the west and north being each surmounted with an elegant pediment. The lower part comprises large school-rooms, &c. The decorations are chaste and elegant. Altogether, the chapel is not only very commodious but also exceedingly handsome. PYEBANK CHAPEL, at Bridgehouses, will now accommodate nearly 700 persons. SHREWSBURY ROAD CHAPEL, Park, has been recently built and opened by this body. It is a substantial stone building, occupying an elevated and commanding situation. The interior is plain but comfortable, and will seat upwards of 500 people. MOUNT TABOR CHAPEL is situated in Wellington-street, and is a plain, substantial brick edifice. It will accommodate about 1,000 persons. SURREY STREET CHAPEL will seat about 500 people, and was erected in 1832. Plans are being prepared for the enlargement and improvement of the chapel, and for the erection of new schools and suitable rooms for the accommodation of the Young Men's Christian Institute, which now occupies rooms in Tudor-place.

DISSENTING DENOMINATIONS.

The following account of the origin of Dissent in Sheffield is abridged from an able paper read to the Congregational body by the Rev. D. Loxton :—" The Act of Uniformity, which received the royal assent of King Charles II., on the 19th of May, in the year 1662, was an Act by which all clergymen were required to give their unfeigned assent and consent to a new edition of the Book of Common Prayer. Many of them refused. Amongst them was the Rev. James Fisher, Vicar of Sheffield at the time of the passing of the Act of Uniformity.

The clergymen who were associated with him, the Rev. Matthew
Bloom, minister of Attercliffe, and the Rev. Edward Prime, both good
men, were of the same way of thinking as the Vicar.   In consequence
of their refusal to sign this declaration they were ejected from their
offices.   This was the origin of Nonconformity in the town of Sheffield.
They were the objects of very severe persecution.   Among the town
records of that period, the following entry occurs : ' Charges about
Mr. Fisher seeking and carrying to York, £1 17s. 6d.'   He survived
his ejectment and various imprisonments about four years, and died in
January, 1666.   He was succeeded as the Nonconformist pastor of the
district by the Rev. Robert Durant, who was assisted in his pastoral
work by the Rev. Richard Taylor and the Rev. Nathanial Baxter.   Mr.
Durant laboured in Sheffield about nine years.   In 1661 he was succeeded by the Rev. Timothy Jollie, a man of great zeal, wisdom, and
ability, who, for consience sake, allowed himself to be torn from the
arms of his young wife, and spent a large part of his time in jail.
During the ministry of this good man, the Upper Chapel, which is
now occupied by the Unitarians, was erected.   Previous to this the
Nonconformists met for worship in a place called New Hall, which
probably stood on the present site of Hollis's Hospital.   During this
long period—from 1662 to nearly 1700—a period of almost thirty-
eight years, the Nonconformists of Sheffield existed and held together
as churches without having any regular place of public worship.   The
Conventicle Act, which was passed in 1664, rendered a public and
open assembly impossible.   It enacted that all private meetings for
religious worship, including more than five persons, besides the members of the family, should be deemed seditious and unlawful conven-
ticles.   The offender against this Act was fined in the first instance £5,
or imprisoned three months ; for the second offence £10, or imprisoned six months ; for the third offence the penalty was £100, or
transportation for seven years.   And every offence beyond a third ex-
posed the party to a repetition of this fine, or to the consequences of its
non-payment.   Sheffield not being at that time a Corporate town, the
provisions of the Five-mile Act, which was passed in the following
year, did not apply to it.   But so far as public worship was concerned
the Conventicle Act was, in fact, a Five-mile Act.   It drove the people
out to the hills and valleys in the neighbourhood to hold their
public worship with secrecy.   The place called the Lord's Seat probably derived its name from the fact that it was one of the places
chosen by the persecuted people of God for the purpose of public worship and preaching.   On account of the non-corporate character of the
town, it was a place of refuge for ministers ejected and driven out from
other parts of the country.   Hence it is that during this period of thirty-
eight years—years in which the Nonconformist Church in the town
was a kind of under-ground Church, having no place for public open
assembly—it was yet well supplied with able and faithful ministers
from other parts of the country.   It was the sense of insecurity which

prevented the erection of a chapel till the last year of the century.   In this chapel Mr. Jollie laboured successfully till the time of his death, which took place on the 5th of April, in the year 1714.   After this the minister elected, a Mr. Wadsworth, avowed his adhesion to the principles of Arianism ; and the chapel has been occupied by the Unitarians ever since."

THE INDEPENDENTS.

NETHER CHAPEL.

This is the oldest of the existing buildings belonging to the Congregational body.   It was erected about 1715, and was rebuilt in 1826. It is a spacious building, and is under the pastorate of the Rev. T. M. Herbert, M.A.

LEE-CROFT.

This chapel was built in 1780, and enlarged about 1845.   The Rev. R. M. M'Brair, M.A., is the minister.

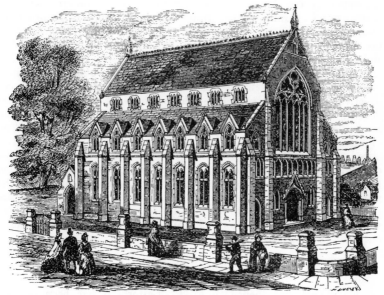

CONGREGATIONAL CHURCH, WICKER.

WICKER.

This church is situated on a triangle formed by the junction of the Barnsley and Grimesthorpe-roads, and Gower-street.   It was built in 1854, by a body of Congregationalists formerly connected with Queen-street Chapel.   The building was opened in 1855.   It cost £4,500, towards which sum £2,500 had been contributed by the time the building was completed. Handsome schools have also been erected.

The church and schools, which have been erected from plans of Mr. Hadfield, architect, are in the early English decorated style. The church is parallel with the Barnsley road, and the schools with Gower-street, whilst the triangle is completed by a spacious yard, on the side of Grimesthorpe-road. The church is 90 feet long by 60 wide, and consists of nave, side aisles, and galleries extending all round. The principal front is at the south-east end, which contains a beautiful six-light window ornamented with rich tracery. An arcade crosses the building beneath this window. In the centre is the principal door, canopied, admitting to the nave, and on each side a smaller door leading to the galleries. The side view gives a triple range of windows—first, the windows of the basement, then the gallery windows, over which is the gabled roof of the aisle ; and above these the gabled roof of the clerestory, surmounted by a high pitched roof. The interior of the building has a very pleasing and tasteful appearance. The galleries rest on a Gothic arcade. The clerestory and roof are supported by pairs of enriched metal columns, painted, and the capitals decorated in the Byzantine style. From these columns spring a second series of Gothic arches, imparting to the whole building a light and elegant appearance. The front of the gallery is of iron work of tasteful design, relieved by gilding. The pulpit is octagonal and lofty. Behind it stands a handsome organ, built by Mr. Brindley. The church is calculated to afford accommodation for about 1,000 persons.

The end next the church, fronting to the Barnsley-road, is very effective, presenting three two-light windows, of simple yet correct design, extending from the ground to the upper floor, the intervening space being tastefully filled with tracery panels ; in the lower portion of one of these windows, and harmonizing with them, a door is introduced, which opens into a porch giving access to the vestry of the church. From Gower-street the building is seen to great advantage, the length of this front being relieved by a gable broken up into the roof at the junction of the schools. The windows on this side are plain, of two-lights, except those to the house, which are ornamented with cusped heads. The end towards Ellesmere-road is plain, being only broken by one window, with tracery head.

QUEEN-STREET.

This chapel was opened in 1783. Latterly it has been deemed necessary to improve the building, which was done at a cost of £1,400, in the year 1855. The late minister, the Rev. J. H. Muir, succeeded to the pastorate in 1841. He died very suddenly in the month of February, 1862 ; and at the time we write his successor has not been appointed. The late Rev. Dr. Pye Smith was an early worshipper at this chapel.

HOWARD-STREET AND MOUNT ZION.

Howard-street Chapel was opened in 1790, and has since been enlarged. The Rev. R. C. Lumsden is the minister. Mount Zion Chapel is a handsome stone building situated in Westfield-terrace. It was opened in 1835. The Rev. D. Loxton is the pastor.

CONGREGATIONAL CHURCH, CEMETERY ROAD.

CEMETERY-ROAD, ETC.

This is a handsome edifice, which was opened in 1859. It was erected from plans of Mr. James, a London architect, and cost about £3,000. It is built in the form of a cross. There is a gallery at the south end, and another at the north end for the choir. Behind this are three handsome stained glass windows. The front of this gallery is ornamented with gilt railing. The seats are open. It will accommodate between 600 and 700 persons. The Rev. Brewin Grant, B.A., is the minister.

There is a chapel at Fulwood, under the pastorate of the Rev. H. G. Rhodes, and one at Attercliffe, of which the Rev. J. Calvert is minister. There are also chapels at Tapton-hill, Darnall, and Brightside. The foundation stone of a new chapel at Attercliffe, which is intended to be of a very handsome description, and to accommodate 900 persons, at the cost of £2,000, was laid in March, 1862.

BAPTIST CHAPEL, CEMETERY ROAD.

THE BAPTISTS.

This body has three places of worship in the borough. Townhead-street Chapel was opened in 1814; it is under the ministry of the Rev. Charles Larom. Portmahon Chapel (St. Philip's-road) was built in 1839; the Rev. J. P. Campbell is the pastor. Cemetery-road Chapel was opened in May, 1859. It cost upwards of £3,000, exclusive of the site. It will accommodate nearly 900 persons. The style of architecture is the Romanesque. The edifice was designed by Messrs. Flockton and Sons, of this town. The Rev. H. Ashbery presides over the congregation, which formerly assembled in Eyre-street Chapel (now St. Simon's Church).

CATHOLIC APOSTOLIC CHURCH.

This denomination possesses a handsome place of worship, in Victoria-street, Glossop-road. It will accommodate about 400 persons. The Rev. H. Sannick is the minister.

SOCIETY OF FRIENDS.

The Society of Friends have a plain but spacious building for worship, in Meetinghouse-lane, between the Hartshead and Bank-street.

ST. ANDREW'S CHURCH.

PRESBYTERIANS.

The Scotch Presbyterians have a place of worship in the town.   It is a handsome building in Hanover-street, Glossop-road.   It is in the geometrical English style, with a tower and spire at the end nearest Hanover-street.   The principal front is formed of the tower and nave, and contains a large five-light window.   There are north and south aisles, and a gallery at the eastern end, with another for the singers at the opposite end.   Externally, the edifice has the usual ecclesiastical form; but though there is the appearance of a chancel, there is none really, this part of the structure consisting of a school-room and sessions-room.   The building was erected at a cost of about £3,000, one-third of which was contributed by one individual, Dr. Hugh Wood.   It will

E

accommodate about 450 persons.   The foundation stone was laid by
Dr. Wood, in July, 1855, and the building was opened in the following
year.   The architects were Messrs. Flockton and Son.   The Rev. Jas.
Breakey is the pastor.

UNITARIAN.

The Unitarians have two places of worship in Sheffield.   The largest
of the two is Upper Chapel, Norfolk-street.   It was erected in 1700,
and was enlarged and partly rebuilt in 1848.   The Rev. Brooke Her-
ford is the minister.   The other chapel is at Upperthorpe.   It is a neat
stone Gothic structure, and was opened in July, 1861.   The interior
has a light and elegant appearance ; a capacious platform stands in the
place usually occupied by the pulpit ; and on either side of the platform
is a handsome window of stained and painted glass.   There is seat
accommodation for 520 persons, and the cost of erection was about
£1,500.   The Rev. J. Page Hopps is the minister.

ST. MARIE'S CHURCH.

ROMAN CATHOLICS.

ST. MARIE'S.

The principal place of worship belonging to the Roman Catholics in
Sheffield is a handsome edifice dedicated to St. Marie, in Norfolk-row.
It cost about £12,000.   It was commenced in 1846, and dedicated on

the 11th September, 1850. The total internal length from the east to the west wall within is 143 feet, the chancel being 38 feet and the nave 105 feet long. The total height to the top of the spire is 195 feet. Externally the building is a beautiful one, though the effect is marred by the confined site. In the northern aisle there is a fine view of the distant chapel of the blessed sacrament, the arched vista being closed by the beautiful window and sculptured altar. Over the northern doorway is a bunch of rich foliage, upon which stands an image of the Virgin Mother and her Divine Child. On either side in the lights of the window appear effigies of the Virgin, and also of St. Henry. This window was presented by Mr. H. T. Bulmer, in memory of his deceased mother. A little beyond is a projection from the aisle with a circular pillar in the midst, bearing upon its capital, around which is sculptured the heavenly choir of angels, two massive arches. A wooden screen of elegant design cuts off the aisle from a mortuary chapel, which has an altar consisting of a massive slab of stone, borne up by two stone shafts with sculptured capitals, whilst at the back and beneath it is a series of niches, containing sculpture of ancient date in alabastar. The subjects represented are the Annunciation, the Assumption, and Coronation of the Virgin, the Adoration of the Wise Men, the Scourging at the Pillar, and the Crucifixion. This relic was discovered in the neighbourhood of Exeter Cathedral. Above the altar, and raised upon a super-altar of stone, is a wooden dossal, containing in the centre a carving representing the Taking Down from the Cross. This work is by Herr Petts, of Munich, and was presented to the church by the Rev. D. Haigh, of Erdington, in memory of his intimate friend the late Mr. Edward Bruce. The side panels are filled with alternate rows of foliage diapers, and the first verse of the 129th Psalm. In the north transept, over the door leading to the rood loft, is a beautiful statue of the Madonna, by the same artist who produced the panel in the mortuary chapel. The blessed sacrament chapel has a floor with a rich covering of emblematic encaustic tiles. The altar is built of massive stones, and upon it stands a reredos richly decorated. The eastern window is beautifully decorated, and was the united offering of Mary Smelter, Mary Cadman, and Sarah Ellison. The side windows contain effigies respectively of St. Charles and St. Anastasia, the offering of Miss Pratt, and St. Catharine and St. Edmund ; this window being presented by the Rev. E. Scully, a former incumbent of St. Marie's. In the chancel the altar is of fair hewn stone, supporting the tabernacle, a structure of beautiful workmanship. The reredos is an admirable work. In the east window are elaborately depicted the principal events of the life of the Virgin Mary. The gift of this window was made by Mr. and Mrs. M. E. Hadfield. Upon an altar tomb, with emblazoned panels and elaborate cornice, reposes the full-length effigy of the Rev. Charles Pratt (the founder of the church), clad in the vestments of his order. Opposite to the tomb are the sedilia, or seats for the priest, deacon, and sub-deacon. A step crossing the chancel, below the sedilia, divides the sanctuary or upper choir from the choir proper. On the north side of the choir runs an elaborate iron screen with brass sconces for lights, connecting the marble column, a monolith of Derbyshire marble, with the main wall. On the south side of the chancel is an open stone screen, in front of the Norfolk chantry, and beneath these two screens and the great rood loft run the enclosed benches for the choir boys. A continuous paneling of geometric design forms the front, and four carved poppy heads crown the ends of the kneeling desk. At the entrance of the choir, in the right hand poppy-head, stands, amongst roses, Mary the Virgin, and, opposite, the angel Gabriel stands upon the lily plant. The Norfolk chantry is a revival of the ancient custom of founding chapels for the special beseeching of heaven in behalf of their builders. The ornamentation and arrangement of this portion of the edifice are not completed. The floor is, however, finished, and in alternate tiles represents the initials of the noble house of Norfolk, crowned with the ducal coronet, the initial letters of the Earl of Arundel and Surrey, and the lion of the house, with the motto, " Sola virtus invicta." In the south transept there is a fine window at the extremity, representing in diapered panels four large figures of St. Teresa, St. Anne, St. Joachim, and St. Joseph. This window is the donation of Mrs. Wright, of Revill Grange, near Sheffield. The southern aisle of the nave contains a fine window at its eastern end, which is the gift of the Rev. W. Parsons. The nave is noteworthy for the rood loft, which is very handsome. The whole of the decorative portion of the rood loft and screen is the gift of Mr. Bulmer. Passing down the nave will be seen inscribed heads terminating the labels of the beautiful arcade on either hand. These comprise the following effigies :—St. Gregory, Pope ; St. Cuthbert, bishop ; St. Edward, king ; St. Bede, monk ; St. Paul, hermit ; St. Roch, pilgrim ; and St. Francis Zavier, missionary. On the opposite side are St. Teresa, abbess ; St. Bridget, nun ; St. Elizabeth of Hungary, queen ; St. Monica, widow ; St. Catherine, martyr ; St. Mary Magdalene, penitent ; St. Walburga, pilgrim ; and St. Rose of Lima, virgin. The west window is very handsome. The Countess of Arundel and Surrey presented this splendid gift to St. Marie's Church. Leaving the nave, another window is passed, a commemoration of the late Mr. and Mrs. W. Frith, the offering of their surviving children. The baptistry is raised by an ascent of three steps above the level of the nave, and stands beneath the tower. In the centre is the font. It is of an octagonal form, borne up by a rich cluster of shafts with caps and bases, and an arrangement of angels below the bowl holding books. The eight sides of the bowl of the font are sunk in square panels, and contain sculptures of the Seven Sacraments and the Crucifixion. The belfry contains a fine peal of cast-steel bells, from the works of Messrs. Naylor, Vickers, and Co. The architects were Messrs. Weightman, Hadfield, and Goldie, of Sheffield. The present incumbent is the Rev. Canon Fisher.

ST. VINCENT'S.

This place of worship is in White-croft. It was built in 1856, at a cost of £3,100. It is a handsome structure, of combined stone and brickwork, the design of the same architects as St. Marie's. The Rev. M. Burke is the incumbent.

SISTERS OF NOTRE DAME.

The Roman Catholics have also a conventual establishment in Sheffield, consisting of the Sisters of Notre Dame, from Namur. The building hitherto used is on Sheffield-moor; but more commodious premises are being erected in Convent-walk, Glossop-road.

THE JEWS

Have a synagogue in Figtree-lane. The Rev. Mr. Herman is the rabbi.

PUBLIC BUILDINGS, MONUMENTS, CEMETERIES, &c.

THE CUTLERS' HALL.

This is a handsome structure in Church-street, opposite the Parish Church. It is elegant and commodious within; but it has become too small for the wants of the company, and arrangements are contemplated for reconstructing and enlarging it. The present building was erected in 1832-3, at a cost of £6,500. Outside are the arms of the company, which are the same as those of the London Cutlers' Company, though there is no connection between the two bodies. Underneath is the motto, "Pour parvenir a bonne foy." The sentence seems to have got corrupted, for the words mean nothing in their present shape. It has been suggested that the "a" should be changed to "ayez." In this form it might be read, as proposed, "To succeed in business, take care and keep up your credit;" or, perhaps, a better rendering would be, "If you wish to succeed, keep your word." The principal room is the dining-hall, in which the celebrated "Cutlers' Feasts" are held. It is an elegant apartment, and is also used for balls, lectures, &c. It is 80 feet long by 30 feet wide, and contains portraits of the Duke of Wellington, the Rev. Dr. Sutton (the late Vicar), and the first Lord Wharncliffe, by Briggs; *Bernard Edward, twelfth Duke of Norfolk, by Pickersgill; the late Earl Fitzwilliam, by Hugh Thompson; Mr. Hugh Parker, by Poole; and Dr. Younge. In the vestibule are portraits of Mr. Thos. Hanbey, founder of Hanbey's Charity, the Rev. J. Wilkinson, Colonel R. A. Athorpe, and Mr. George Bennet; also

* This Duke of Norfolk was born at Sheffield 1765, in "the Lord's House," which then stood on the site now occupied by the premises of Mr. Holden, jeweller, at the corner of Norfolk-row.

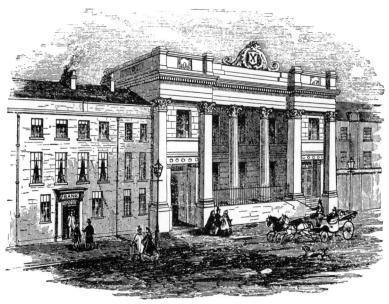

THE CUTLERS' HALL.

busts in marble, by Edwin Smith, of the first Mayor of Sheffield, Mr.
W. Jeffcock, of High Hazles; of James Montgomery, the poet; of Mr.
S. Hadfield, the founder of the Hadfield Charity; and there is one, by
Mr. Law, of the grandfather of the present Earl Fitzwilliam. There
are also casts, from sculptured busts by Chantrey, of Sir Walter Scott,
George Canning, James Watt, and Professor Lyon Playfair. In the
reception and other rooms are portraits of the Rev. Joseph Hunter, the
historian of Hallamshire, and Mr. Ebenezar Rhodes, author of "The
Peak Scenery;" and in the entrance-hall are busts of the Right Hon.
John Parker and Mr. J. S. Buckingham, the first members returned
by Sheffield to Parliament.

TOWN HALL.

This building, which is situated at the corner of Castle-street and
Waingate, was erected by the Town Trustees in 1808, and was enlarged
in 1833. It comprises a large court-room for the holding of the
quarter sessions, and a smaller room for the petty sessions, with offices
for the Chief Constable, cells for the prisoners, &c. It has, however,
grown perfectly inadequate for the wants of the town. It is now rarely
employed for large political or other town's meetings, which are commonly held in the Temperance Hall, Townhead-street. The offices
for the Chief Constable and other members of the police force, &c., are
equally inconvenient. It is in fact with the utmost difficulty that the

necessary business can be carried on in the building. The cells for prisoners are the worst of all. They are confined, partly underground, and most unhealthy. It is not unfrequent, when prisoners are confined here for any length of time, pending the preliminary inquiry before the magistrates, for them to beg to be removed to the Wakefield House of Correction, in order to escape the discomfort and unhealthiness of the local prison. At the time we write a project has been set on foot in the Town Council for building a public hall which will provide for the wants of the town.

THE COUNCIL HALL.

This building, which is in Norfolk-street, was originally erected in 1762, and was intended for Assembly Rooms. It has, however, been leased by the Town Council, and the principal room has been adapted for the general meetings of that body. At the right, on entering, over the Mayor's chair, is a portrait of Mr. William Fisher, a local worthy, lately deceased ; and at the other end of the room there is a portrait of Mr. Roebuck, M.P. Both are excellent likenesses. They are by Mr. Richard Smith. There are smaller rooms, which are used for various purposes, such as the Bankruptcy Court, bridge rate offices, &c.

MUSIC HALL.

The Music Hall is a stone building in Surrey-street, erected in 1823. It belongs to a company of proprietors, to whom Mr. Freemantle, High-street, is secretary. The large room will accommodate about 1,000 persons. It has recently been tastefully decorated, the walls being adorned with medallion portraits of eminent composers. There is also an organ. The ground floor is occupied by the Sheffield Library and the Literary and Philosophical Society.

TEMPERANCE HALLS.

There is a hall in Townhead-street belonging to the Sheffield Temperance Society. It was opened in 1856, having been built at the cost of about £2,500. The principal room is 81 feet long by 51 feet wide, and it will accommodate about 2,000 persons. There is also a commodious room underneath, in which smaller meetings are held. Considerable improvements have been made in the building since it was first constructed ; and it is now commonly used for town's meetings, popular lectures, &c. There is also a Temperance Hall on a smaller scale in Barker-pool.

FREEMASONS' HALL.

This building, which is at the corner of Surrey-street and Eyre-street, was previously used for the Sheffield and Hallamshire Savings Bank ; but on that institution being removed, in 1860, to Norfolk-street, the building under notice was purchased by the local Freemasons.

INTERIOR OF THE NORFOLK MARKET HALL

THE MARKETS.

Sheffield possesses public markets of a very spacious and convenient character. The principal one is called the Norfolk Market Hall, but is generally known as the "New Market." It owes its origin to the

THE WHOLESALE VEGETABLE MARKET AND EXTERIOR VIEW OF NORFOLK MARKET HALL.

liberality of the late Duke of Norfolk.　It was opened at Christmas, 1851.　It occupies the site of the old Tontine Hotel, which property was purchased by the Duke of Norfolk for £8,000.　The entire cost of the erection, inclusive of site, was something approaching £40,000.　It is

EAST FRONT OF SHAMBLES, WITH OFFICES OF ELECTRIC TELEGRAPH COMPANY, ETC.

built in the Tuscan style, of brick, with stone basements, quoins, and dressings. It is 296 feet long and 115 feet wide, and 45 feet high in the centre. There are six large entrance gates, two at each end and one at each side: the panels of those gates are handsomely ornamented with metal castings. The roof is of iron and glass, giving a light and pleasing appearance. In the middle of the building there is a handsome fountain of Italian design. The building is divided into stalls and shops, in which, beside fruit, vegetables, &c., a great variety of wares is sold. The engraving of the interior of the Norfolk Market Hall gives a good idea of the spaciousness of the building. A wholesale Vegetable Market is held on Tuesdays and Saturdays, on a piece of ground between the lower end of the Norfolk Market Hall and the Corn Exchange. Our artist has given a delineation no less faithful than graphic of the Market, including a view of the Norfolk Market Hall.

The Corn Exchange is a handsome building immediately below the Norfolk Market Hall already described. It was opened in 1830. The New Haymarket is immediately adjoining; and the Cattle Market is near the Victoria Railway Station. The Shambles are a very commodious structure, belonging to the Duke of Norfolk. They have been entirely reconstructed, and now furnish a most convenient mart, principally for the sale of butcher's meat, but also, on Tuesdays and Saturdays, of poultry, &c. The building ranges from the back of the Post Office to the Old Haymarket, nearly opposite the front of the New Market Hall. On each side of the interior there is a range of shops for butchers, admirably ventilated and very convenient. The rebuilding of the Shambles gave an opportunity for the reconstruction of the shops at the lower end, facing to the Old Haymarket. These now possess very handsome fronts, as are shown in the engraving of them. There are corn and other markets held at Sheffield on Tuesdays and Saturdays. There are two Fairs in the year, one at Whitsuntide and the other in November. These Fairs are of considerable importance, and there are in connection with them markets for cattle, horses, cheese, &c.

WEST FRONT VIEW OF THE SHAMBLES, WITH POST OFFICE AND ELLIOTT'S MONUMENT.

POST OFFICE, &c.

The Post-office is a neat building opposite to High-street, and with the monument to Ebenezer Elliott immediately in front. The Stamp-office is St. James's-street, and the Inland Revenue offices are in Norfolk-street.

SHEFFIELD BARRACKS.

The barracks at Sheffield are amongst the very finest in the kingdom. They are situated on about $25\frac{1}{2}$ acres of land, between the Penistone-road and the Langsett-road, the front being to the latter thoroughfare. They are quite in the outskirts of the town, on a salubrious spot, and commanding magnificent views of the surrounding scenery. They were finished in 1850. The front to Langsett-road is a handsome and imposing stone structure. There is a neat chapel at

BIRD'S EYE VIEW OF THE SHEFFIELD BARRACKS AND NEIGHBOURING SCENERY.

one end. In this magnificent erection there is complete accommodation for a regiment of cavalry and an infantry regiment, and there are ample parade and drill grounds, &c. Popularly they are known as the

"New Barracks," though the site of the old building (on the same road, nearer the town) has been sold and cut up for building purposes, and only a small part of the structure formerly in use now remains. The accompanying sketch of the Barracks also gives an excellent delineation of the surrounding country, which, as seen from the rising ground adjacent to the buildings, is very beautiful. The viaduct which is visible on the left of the background, is a very picturesque adjunct. It is on the Manchester, Sheffield, and Lincolnshire Railway, which, on the road from Sheffield to Manchester, runs through some of the most beautiful scenery in England.

THE MONTGOMERY MONUMENT.

THE MONTGOMERY MONUMENT.

The memorial to James Montgomery, the poet, is of recent erection. It is not within the town, but is placed over his grave at the General Cemetery, which is in the suburbs. The monument is near to the Cemetery-road entrance to this picturesque burial-place, and the site of it commands a beautiful view of the surrounding scenery. It was opened in July, 1861. This interesting memorial was in a large measure the work of the Sunday school teachers and scholars of Sheffield, who thus testified in the most practical way to the actively religious disposition of the departed bard as well as to his poetic fame. At the opening of the statue there was a public procession in which the Town Council and all the local public bodies took part. The cost of the statue was £1,000. It was designed by John Bell, the eminent sculptor, and cast in bronze by the Coalbrook Dale Iron Company. It is a satisfactory work of art, and not unsuccessful as a likeness. The figure is in a standing posture, with one arm encircling a book. The following inscriptions are on the pedestal:—

[FRONT.]

JAMES MONTGOMERY,

BORN

AT IRVINE, SCOTLAND,

November 4th, 1771;

DIED

AT THE MOUNT, SHEFFIELD,

(After a Residence in the Town of 62 Years),

April 30th, 1854,

IN THE 83RD YEAR OF HIS AGE.

THE TEACHERS, SCHOLARS, AND FRIENDS OF SUNDAY SCHOOLS

IN SHEFFIELD,

Assisted by Public Subscription,

HAVE ERECTED THIS MONUMENT

IN MEMORY OF

THEIR REVERED TOWNSMAN,

MDCCCLX.

[BACK.]

HERE LIES INTERRED,

Beloved by all who knew him,

THE CHRISTIAN POET,

PATRIOT,

AND PHILANTHROPIST.

WHEREVER POETRY IS READ, OR CHRISTIAN HYMNS

ARE SUNG,

IN THE ENGLISH LANGUAGE,

" HE, BEING DEAD, YET SPEAKETH,"

BY THE

GENIUS, PIETY, AND TASTE EMBODIED IN HIS

WRITINGS.

On the two sides are inscribed extracts from Montgomery's beautiful poems "The Grave" and "Prayer."

THE MONUMENT TO EBENEZER ELLIOTT.

The monument to Ebenezer Elliott, "the Corn Law Rhymer," is in the Market-place, fronting the Post-office. It cost about £600, the amount being raised by public subscription. It was erected in August, 1854. The artist was Mr. Burnard, of London. The figure is of bronze and the pedestal of granite. It bears no inscription but the word Elliott. The poet is supposed to be seated on a rustic bank in one of those spots he has so charmingly described in his works. Some account of the events in Elliott's life connecting him with Sheffield, and a similar sketch in respect to the poet Montgomery, will be found in another place.

THE CRIMEAN MONUMENT AND VIEW OF MOOR HEAD, ETC.

MONUMENT TO THE CRIMEAN HEROES.

A monument is in course of erection to the memory of the Sheffield soldiers and sailors who died in the service of their country in the Russian war in the Crimea. The foundation stone was laid by his Royal

Highness the Duke of Cambridge. Though the work is not completed at the time we write, we are enabled, through the courtesy of Mr. G. Goldie, of London, the architect who has designed the monument, to furnish an engraving and description of it. The monument will be composed of Darley Dale stone and Aberdeen granite. The granite shaft will be 18 feet long, the total height of the monument being about 58 feet. The statue of Victoria, as "Honour," will be nearly 10 feet high. Mr. Henry Lane, of Birmingham, is the sculptor. The site of the monument is at the junction of Sheffield-moor and Union-street. From £1,300 to £1,400 has been collected for the construction of the memorial. The engraving of the monument also gives a view of Sheffield-moor, one of the broadest and best thoroughfares in the town, and affords an idea of the picturesque glimpses of houses, manufactories, and hillsides, one above another, which are to be seen in almost every direction, looking towards the outside of the town.

THE CHOLERA MONUMENT.

THE CHOLERA MONUMENT.

A neat and appropriate monument has been erected in Norfolk-road, opposite the Shrewsbury Hospitals, in memory of those who died in Sheffield from the ravages of the cholera in 1832, and who were buried on this spot. The disease raged from the beginning of July till the end of October. The numbers attacked were 1,347, of whom 402 died. Amongst the victims was Mr. John Blake, the Master Cutler. The cross which commemorates the visit of the terrible malady was erected in 1834-5, the corner stone having been laid by Montgomery the poet in December of the former year.

DRINKING FOUNTAINS.

A number of gentlemen have munificently come forward to erect drinking fountains for the use of the town. There is one in the Wicker, at the entrance to the Midland Railway Station, which is very handsome, and which was built by Mr. J. H. Sales, coal merchant, at a cost of about £200. The Town Trustees have erected one in front of the Town Hall in Castle-street. There is one within the Free Library building, given by Mr. Alderman Fisher. There is one at the head of Sheffield-moor, erected by Mr. John Brown, of the Atlas Iron and Steel works. There is one at the junction of Shalesmoor and Gibraltar-street, erected by Mr. Nadin, herbalist, Shalesmoor; and this fountain may be taken by the stranger as a guide to the business premises last occupied by Ebenezer Elliott, being nearly opposite to them. The teachers and friends of the Redhill Sunday Schools have erected a fountain in that locality; and there is also one given by Mr. Henry Levy, outside the Parish Churchyard, at the top of High-street.

CEMETERIES.

The burial grounds adjoining the churches having been most of them closed by the action of the Legislature, it has been necessary to construct cemeteries outside the town. There was, however, one in existence previously to the closing of the old grave-yards, namely, the General Cemetery, opened in 1836, by a company of shareholders, who had at that time expended on it about £13,000. It then comprised about six acres, but in 1848 about eight acres more were added. It is situated at Sharrow, in the suburbs of the town, on a very beautiful spot, and the Cemetery itself is most picturesque and tasteful in appearance. There are two entrances, one in Ecclesall-road and the other in Cemetery-road. There is a handsome church in the decorated style, with tower and spire, and also a chapel in the Doric order. Immediately under the west end of the church, in a circular space set apart for the purpose, is the grave of James Montgomery the poet, with the monument to his memory. The Rev. G. Sandford, M.A., is chaplain for the consecrated portion, and the Rev. W. T. Kidd for the unconsecrated.

On closing St. Philip's Church in 1857, a new parochial burial ground was projected by the Incumbent at the further extremity of the parish, on the dry and picturesque acclivity which overlooks Birley Meadows and the vale of the Don. The area of this cemetery exceeds five acres. It has a neat mortuary chapel, and a lodge for the sexton

F

and vestry office. It is approached by the old road leading from Neepsend by the Club Mill, and from Owlerton by a new road and bridge recently erected over the River Don. This burial ground was consecrated in 1859 by the late Archbishop of York.

The cemetery of the Brightside Bierlow district was constructed in 1859-60, on about 27 acres of land, verging upon Burngreave-road, Pitsmoor, and the Occupation-road. The cemetery was formed by the ratepayers, a Burial Board having been constituted for the purpose. The land cost about £5,400, and about £4,000 more has been spent in laying out the ground, building the necessary edifices, &c. The chaplains are the Rev. J. Aldous for the consecrated and the Rev. J. Jefferson for the unconsecrated portions.

A Burial Board was also formed for the construction of the Attercliffe cemetery, which is pleasantly situated and joins Christ Church, Attercliffe. It was consecrated August, 1859. It contains about four acres, and cost £1,332. The Board have spent a further sum of £968 in laying out the ground and building a neat chapel on the unconsecrated portion.

At Darnall a Burial Board has been formed and a cemetery opened. Its extent is six acres, and there are a church and chapel attached. The cost of land, buildings, &c., has been about £1,600. The Rev. C. T. Wilkinson is chairman of the Attercliffe, and the Rev. W. L. Gibson of the Darnall, Board.

COMMERCIAL, LITERARY, AND OTHER PUBLIC INSTITUTIONS.

CHAMBER OF COMMERCE.

The Chamber of Commerce is a valuable institution, of which many of the principal manufacturers and merchants are members. It takes part in the discussion and direction of all questions affecting the trade of the town, Mr. J. Jobson Smith is president, and Mr. W. Smith, jun., solicitor, of Campo-lane, is acting secretary.

THE ATHENÆUM.

The Athenæum, which was established in 1847, is one of the most prominent institutions of the town, and combines within itself all the conveniences and attractions of a well-conducted club. The present building, which was purchased, and in a great measure rebuilt, three years ago, at a cost of about £4,000, is admirably adapted for all the purposes for which it was designed, containing commodious and well-furnished coffee, dining, smoke, and chess rooms, a capacious, light, and well-ventilated news-room, an extensive and well-assorted library,

and a suite of rooms elegantly fitted up for the sole and especial use of
ladies. In addition to these advantages, arrangements have recently
been made for the regular supply of all the latest information by
electric telegraph, thereby adding to the institution all the facilitiesand
requirements of a Commercial Exchange. The site, which is in George-
street, adjoining the Sheffield Fire Office, is perhaps the most eligible
that could have been selected, being not only central, quiet, and respectable, but readily accessible from the leading thoroughfares, High-
street and Norfolk-street. Another important feature in connection
with the Athenæum is the series of first-class concerts provided every
year, exclusively for the members. In fact, of late this institution has
been the chief means of introducing to Sheffield most of the great
musical celebrities of the day. The annual subscription for £5 proprietors is £1; members, £1 10s.; and lady members, 15s. each. The
present number of members (including £20 proprietors) is about 600,
no extraordinary number when we consider the size and importance of
the district, and the varied inducements held out by the Athenæum for
the social and intellectual gratification of its supporters. According to
the rules of the institution strangers residing ten or more miles from
the town can have the privilege of attending the news-room for a
certain time without any payment whatever, providing they are introduced by a member, and their names are duly enrolled in the strangers'
admission book. M. M. de Bartolomé, M.D., is the president, and Mr.
J. H. Greaves the honorary secretary.

THE ATHENÆUM.

THE SHEFFIELD CLUB.

THE CLUB.

The Sheffield Club is an institution for social purposes, similar to the clubs of London. It is supported by the *élite* of the town, and is carried on with great spirit. The club was first opened in premises at the lower end of Norfolk-street; but a new and handsome building (of which we give a sketch) has been erected at the corner of Mulberry-street and Norfolk-street, and will be opened in a few days after the publication of this work.

MEDICAL INSTITUTION.

The building belonging to this institution, for the instruction of students in practical surgery, is situated at the end of Surrey-street, near Arundel-street. It was erected in 1829. It bears in front the motto, " Ars longa vita brevis."

LITERARY AND PHILOSOPHICAL SOCIETY.

This association, the nature of which is indicated by its name, was established in 1822. The society is now carried on with great vigour.

Monthly meetings are held, lectures of a high class are frequently delivered, and a conversazione of a very attractive character is annually given. The rooms of the society are at the Music Hall, in Surrey-street, where they have a museum of scientific objects. Mr. John Holland is the curator.

SHEFFIELD LIBRARY.

This valuable institution belongs to a body of shareholders, and the library contains about 30,000 books. The rooms are at the Music Hall, in Surrey-street.

PUBLIC FREE LIBRARY.

This institution, which is maintained by the Corporation out of the public rates, is located in Surrey-street, in premises rented from the Mechanics' Institute. The rooms have been recently reconstructed, and are now exceedingly commodious. Besides the library, there is a spacious and comfortable reading-room, where all the leading magazines and reviews are kept. The library contains about 19,000 books, which are free for the use of all the burgesses in the borough. Mr. Walter Parsonson, F.R.A.S., is the librarian.

THE VOLUNTEER FORCES.

Sheffield has not been backward in respect to the Volunteer movement which has become so popular throughout the country. There is a local squadron forming part of the 1st West York Yeomanry Cavalry —a body which has remained in existence ever since the great French Revolution at the end of the last century. Directly in connection with the recent movement, however, there are three corps, one of Rifles, another of Artillery, and the third of Engineers. The oldest is the body of Rifles, which was originated in May, 1859. They are called the Hallamshire Rifles. The total number belonging to the corps is about 480. Lieut.-Colonel Lord Wharncliffe is the commanding officer. The depôt is in Eyre-street. The Engineers were established in connection with the School of Art. They number about 160. Captain Young Mitchell is the commander. The depôt is in Convent-walk, Glossop-road. The Artillery Volunteers number about 200. Captain Nathaniel Creswick commands. The depôt is in Tudor-street. The corps has received four guns from Government, and ground has been provided at Wadsley-common for a battery, magazine, and other appliances necessary for exercise. The above numbers comprise only the actual members of the corps, each of them having in addition a numerous and excellent band. Including the members of the bands, the number of the Volunteer forces in Sheffield approaches 1,000. The different corps vie with each other in attaining a high state of discipline and efficiency, and they are not to be surpassed by any similar bodies in the kingdom.

EDUCATIONAL INSTITUTIONS.

COLLEGIATE SCHOOL.

This institution is situated at Collegiate-crescent, Broomhall Park. It belongs to a company of proprietors, having been established to provide a thoroughly sound education for the youth of the upper classes, preparatory to the University course or to commercial pursuits. It cost nearly £10,000, the school house, which is a handsome building in the Tudor style, having been erected in 1835. There are 3½ acres of pleasure grounds, tastefully laid out, and a commodious residence for the principal and for the reception of boarders. The building is situated in the best and most picturesque part of the suburbs, and is quite outside the smoke and bustle of the town. In connection with this institution is being organized a School of Practical Science, for the training of young men, so as to fit them for manufacturing pursuits. The principal is the Rev. G. B. Atkinson, M.A.

COLLEGIATE SCHOOL.

GRAMMAR SCHOOL.

This institution was founded in 1603 by Thomas Smith, an attorney at Crowland, in Lincolnshire, but no doubt a native of Sheffield, who bequeathed £30 a year to the town "as long as the world shall endure," for the maintenance of "two sufficient learned men to teach and bring up the young children there with godliness and learning." In the following year the bequest seems to have come into force; and King James, on the petition of the inhabitants, granted a charter incorporating the Vicar and twelve of the principal inhabitants governors to carry out the undertaking. The estates belonging to the school have increased in value, and now produce about £200 a year. The present building is a stone structure in St. George's-square. It was erected by subscription in 1824, and replaced a building in Townhead-street, which was constructed in 1648, partly from the ruins of Sheffield Castle. In the original charter it is styled " The Free Grammar School of King James ;" but it has been found that the endowment is not large enough to admit of gratuitous instruction. The benefit which the inhabitants receive from the school is that the masters are required to teach from thirty-five to forty boys at half the ordinary charge. These boys are nominated by the governors. The Rev. P. Bowen, M.A., is head master. The school is free to all religious denominations.

WESLEY COLLEGE.

This is a handsome building devoted to educational uses, and belonging to the Wesleyan body. It is situated in the Glossop-road. It is the property of a company of shareholders, and is a most prosperous undertaking. It was opened in 1838, and cost about £14,500, including the land, the grounds surrounding the building being very spacious. There is accommodation for about 250 boarders. The Rev. Dr. Waddy is governor and chaplain.

SCHOOL OF ART.

This is an institution which has grown rapidly, yet with sound prosperity. The history of the Sheffield School of Art is peculiarly interesting. The idea of establishing a " School of Design" (as these institutions were then entitled) was first mooted in Sheffield in 1841. A public meeting was called, but it was attended only by three individuals. Of this meeting, humble as it was, a record remains not to be surpassed for interest in the history of modern art in this country. Everybody remembers poor Haydon the historical painter; his disgust at the success of Barnum's Tom Thumb, while his own historical paintings next door were almost unvisited; his growing despair; and his ultimate suicide. It happened that when the meeting was called in 1841, Haydon was in Sheffield, and, having a deep desire for the spread of his beloved art, he was one of the three persons who attended for the purpose of establishing the school. The other two were Dr. Harwood and Mr. H. P. Parker. During the progress of the " meeting" Haydon amused himself by drawing a pen-and-ink sketch of the persons present. This drawing has been framed, and may be seen at the institution. Underneath the sketch are the following words in Haydon's writing, showing a latent humour in the painter's mind the existence

THE SCHOOL OF ART.

of which would hardly have been suspected:—"Public meeting at Sheffield, to establish a School of Design, October 13, 1841. Symptoms of great enthusiasm. Sketched by B. R. Haydon." Accompanying the sketch, also in Haydon's handwriting, is a transcript of the resolutions passed. An extract from these we give, on account of its proving so remarkably prophetic of the future of the institution :— " That notwithstanding the neglect of the leading men of the town in not meeting, it is the duty of those who are assembled, amounting to *three*, to persevere till the great object be accomplished, aware from history that much greater revolutions have been accomplished and begun by much more incompetent means."

Miserable as this first attempt was, subsequent efforts were successful; and a school was opened in 1843, in Victoria-street, Glossop-road. It grew and prospered, and larger premises were taken in Arundel-street. Still these were inconvenient and unsightly, and an effort was set on foot to raise a structure which would be a credit to the town. The foundation stone of the present building was laid by Dr. Branson on the 24th October, 1855, and it was opened in January, 1857. It is in Arundel-street, opposite the end of Surrey-street, is one of the most handsome and commodious educational structures in the town, and is scarcely equalled by any other School of Art in the kingdom. The architects were Messrs. Manning and Mew, of London, and the total cost was about £7,000. The building covers about 900 yards of land. It was erected in a most enterprizing spirit, being adapted not merely to supply the existing wants of the town, but to afford room for every possible expansion during many years to come. Going in at the front door in Arundel-street, the visitor finds himself in a spacious entrance hall, leading into the lobby, on the right of which is the geometrical-room (26 feet by 19), for the study of architecture, engineering, &c.; and on the left is the Council-room (13 feet by 19). Further on he comes to the lecture-room; and, occupying the entire range at the back, he finds the elementary class room (70 feet by 39 feet, and 21 feet high). In the middle of the lobby there is a handsome staircase, leading to a passage, at one end of which is a room (45 feet by 25) running along the whole front of the building, and used for the ladies' classes. At the other end are the painting-room (35 feet by 27) and the sculpture gallery (69 feet by 39). The latter room contains an excellent collection of casts from celebrated works. Besides the above, which are the principal apartments, there are a number of other rooms, such as the head master's, the modelling-room, studios, &c. The exterior appearance is striking and handsome. It is a mixture of the Byzantine and Romanesque styles. There are alternate layers of red and black brick, with columns, &c., of stone.

The condition of the school as an educational institution fully corresponds with the structure. The general position of the institution is in the very first rank of the schools of art throughout the kingdom. The head master under whom it has been brought to this state of excellence is Mr. Young Mitchell.

THE PEOPLE'S COLLEGE.

This institution is one of the most interesting educational establishments in the town, or, indeed in the kingdom, because it is genuinely and entirely what its name purports—a " People's College." It is for the use of the working classes, and it is fully self-supporting, the members neither asking nor accepting pecuniary aid. The following account of the origin and early progress of the college is abridged from an article in the " Working Men's College Magazine," written by Mr. Rowbotham, president of the Sheffield College:—" The People's College at Sheffield originated seventeen years ago with the Rev. R. S. Bayley, an Independent minister then residing in the town. He considered that Mechanics' Institutions generally had fallen far short in their efforts at popular education, and that the time was come when studies of a higher range, and more likely to be really useful, ought to be placed within the reach of the youth of the middle and working classes. To carry out his views he proposed to establish classes embracing Latin, Greek, French, and German, mathematics, English literature in its various branches, logic, elocution, and drawing, in addition to the more elementary subjects that commonly formed the curriculum of night schools. The classes were opened August 11th, 1842; the times of meeting were *before* and *after* the hours of labour. The morning classes met from half-past six to half-past seven; the evening from half-past seven to half-past nine. The greatest novelty was the admission of *women* to the classes. The result was good, an increased degree of decorum and self-respect being exhibited by both sexes. The principal portion of the work in the classes fell upon Mr. Bayley. The class-room, for the first year and a half, was a ghastly, whitewashed, unplastered garret, in George-street. The morning classes in winter were especially uninviting, and it required considerable devotion to study to travel through snow at half-past six in the morning, before breakfast, to find a room probably without fire, or one but newly lighted. But there was no trial that the principal himself did not willingly endure, and no morning, however rough and uncomfortable, but found him in attendance. In December, 1843, the college removed to better rooms in Orchard-street. Here the same labours were renewed, and attended for several years with success ; but from a succession of untoward circumstances, the members began gradually to fall off, till at length, in September, 1848, on Mr. Bayley leaving Sheffield for London, the college was all but extinct. A few young men—sixteen in number, many of them under age—felt that with them rested the question of the continuance of the institution. A public meeting was held in the rooms of the institution, Mr. Wilson Overend in the chair, when a full statement of the objects of the future People's College, and the plans whereby they were to be secured, was read on behalf of the committee by the president, Mr. Thomas Rowbotham, and resolutions of approval were passed : and thus the institution was fairly launched upon its future career. It was stated at the meeting that the committee did not possess a single book and had not a single farthing to invest in furniture. Indeed to outside observers things looked so hopeless that Mr. Overend and his brother earnestly asked the committee to estimate the probable expenses of the first year, that they might subscribe a portion, and beg the rest. Although the generosity of this offer was perfectly appreciated, it was nevertheless respectfully declined. A principle had been laid down, and it was abided by. On the day following the public meeting the classes were opened. Before the end of the month there were nearly two hundred students in the classes. Such faith had the committee in the success of the scheme, that in less than six months they had incurred liabilities of upwards £200. Extensive alterations were made, and the whole of the rooms were properly fitted up with new furniture. At the end of the first forty-seven weeks it was found that there had been 530 students on the books : 426 of these were young men ; and the rest, 104, women ; the average attendance had been 135, and the amount received for fees had been £203 1s. 3d."

Since that time the institution has gone on in an unpretending but very successful manner. It still occupies the building in Orchard-street ; but more commodious rooms are needed. It is greatly to the credit of those who have the management of the college that they have not only paid their way, but have a small sum in hand as a nucleus for a building fund.

MECHANICS' INSTITUTE.

This institution has a handsome stone building at the junction of Surrey-street and Tudor-street; but it is to a large extent devoted to other uses. The institution was established in 1832, and was for many years in a flourishing condition. In 1847-8 the building referred to was constructed, at a cost of about £7,000. From this time the institution languished, partly because the building was too ambitious and costly, and partly because, the lower rooms being devoted to the use of a club, the upper rooms which are set apart for the students were found to be inconvenient. The building consists of three storeys. The lowest is rented by the Corporation, and is used for the Free Library. On the second storey there is a handsome lecture hall. The rooms at the top are still used for the students of the Mechanics' Institute, and many useful classes are held. Mr. T. Dunn is president, Mr. J. Brown (the Mayor), vice-president, and Mr. Edwin Round honorary secretary.

CHURCH OF ENGLAND EDUCATIONAL INSTITUTE.

This institution is entitled to emphatic mention, ranking as it does amongst the first of the kind in the country. Conscious of the want of an instrument of instruction for the working population after business hours, to be conducted upon Church principles, a number of gentlemen set on foot, in the year 1840, "The Church of England Instruction Society," for the use of which a suite of rooms were opened in Carver-street. Chiefly by the voluntary aid of unpaid teachers, the good work was carried on, but with comparatively little success, till 1856,

CHURCH OF ENGLAND EDUCATIONAL INSTITUTE.

when the institution took quite a new start under the auspices of the Rev. James Moorhouse and others of the clergy and laity, who willingly came forward to render assistance to the old staff of teachers who had borne the burden for many years. The constitution of the society was modified, and its operations largely extended; and the modest "instruction society" expanded into the more ambitious "educational institute"—a title amply justified by the results which have been realized. One immediate effect of this new impetus was a want of greater space, to meet which supplementary accommodation was procured at St. Peter's and St. James's national schools, New Queen-street. A public subscription was set on foot for a new and more commodious building, and proceeded with alacrity, the popularity of the institution being proved by the facility with which the requisite funds were subscribed. The result was the erection of the handsome and very commodious edifice in St. James's-street, from designs by Messrs. Flockton and Son. The building was opened—free from debt—in the year 1860. A considerable sum was required for furnishing, and this was obtained by the proceeds of a bazaar.

Unlike most undertakings of the same nature, it may without exaggeration be said of this institution that it fully answers the expectation of its promoters. Its success is unequivocal. The subjects taught comprehend the Hebrew, Latin, German and French languages; natural theology and religions of the world, and other Biblical and sacred subjects; English literature; reading with the poets, and critical papers by the students; Shaksperian readings; Euclid; book-keeping; singing, geography, English grammar, dictation and composition; shorthand writing; reading, writing, arithmetic, &c. There are nearly a hundred teachers on the list at the present time, all of them, with the exception of the modern language master, giving their services gratuitously. Amongst the teachers are to be found seventeen clergymen, men of science, and members of liberal professions. An educational institution, indeed, which includes amongst its voluntary instructors a senior wrangler of the University of Cambridge may well be considered a great boon to young persons who are striving to emancipate themselves from the thraldom of ignorance. Here, as at the People's College, the practice of combining young persons of both sexes in the same classes has been found to work satisfactorily. Shortly after the opening of the new structure the admission book exhibited a total of 512 students, and the class rooms being now quite full it became necessary to announce publicly that no more could be admitted. The recent and still prevailing commercial depression, with its attendant poverty, combined with a change in the mode of payment of the class fees (causing a larger amount to be paid at one time than heretofore), has resulted in a diminution of the numbers, but there is every reason to believe that when trade revives there will again be as many students as the building can hold. The Rev. Canon Sale, D.D., is president. The Rev. T. Smith and Mr. Henry Pawson are the honorary secretaries.

YOUNG MEN'S CHRISTIAN ASSOCIATION.

The rooms of this society are in Norfolk-row. The object of it, as its name indicates, is to bring young men together for the purpose of imparting to them education of a religious tone. In this direction it has done considerable good. The society has assisted materially in advancing the Early Closing Movement. There are classes and a reading room attached to the association; but its chief feature is a series of lectures every winter in the Music Hall, which are always numerously attended. Mr. Ald. Fawcett is president. Mr. Adam Wood and Mr. Wm. G. Snowden are the honorary secretaries.

NATIONAL SCHOOLS, &c.

There is a good supply of National Schools in the town, conveniently distributed so that no quarter is unsupplied, and the working man, in whatever part he lives, has a choice of schools within an easy distance to which he may send his children. The oldest of these schools are those which are situated in Carver-street, and were built in 1812, and opened the year following, soon after the formation of the National Society.   In most of them large numbers of children are receiving a sound education adapted to their position in life, under the surveillance of the Education Committee of Privy Council, whose reports generally give a favourable account of the state and progress of the schools in the town.   Indeed we believe that the Sheffield National Schools, as compared with those in Yorkshire generally, stand well in the list both for the excellence of their arrangements and the education given in them.   In a late report presented to the Privy Council Committee by her Majesty's Inspector for Yorkshire, in which he has arranged all the large towns in four classes of merit, we find that out of the 23 schools of which the first-class consists, seven are in Sheffield.   Leeds claims six.   Thus, according to the judgment of her Majesty's Inspector, Sheffield stands at the head of all the large towns in Yorkshire for its number of first-class National Schools.   There are also in the town Lancasterian and other schools conducted with vigour on the voluntary principle.

Sheffield possesses a large number of Sunday schools.   There are belonging to the Church of England Sunday School Union 21 school,s 485 teachers, and 5,500 children, besides several schools which have not joined the union.   In the Wesleyan body there are 34 schools, having 1,096 teachers and 5,694 children.   The Sheffield Sunday School Union (comprising the Dissenting bodies) has 41 schools, with 1,708 teachers and 12,776 scholars.

BOYS' AND GIRLS' CHARITY SCHOOLS.

The Boys' and Girls' Charity Schools are kindred institutions, situated in the opposite sides of the Parish Church, the first being at the bottom of East-parade and the latter of St. James's-row.   The school for boys was erected in 1710 and rebuilt in 1825-6.   It affords support and education to 100 destitute boys, the cost being defrayed out of endowments and subscriptions.   The other school, which was built in 1786, supports in a similar manner sixty girls.

GIRLS' INDUSTRIAL SCHOOL.

This is an unpretending institution, but little known.   It is, however, quietly producing valuable results.   It has been established mainly through the instrumentality of the Rev. W. Wilkinson.   Premises are rented at Broadfield, Heeley.   The institution is in the nature of a charity as well as a school, the girls being entirely maintained for 2s. 6d. a week over twelve years of age.   They are also taken under that age occasionally, but at 3s. 6d. a week.   Nothing which can be of use to them, either as domestic servants, or in their own homes should they become wives, is neglected.   They are taught washing, cooking, baking, sewing, house-cleaning—in fact, everything that can be required.   Besides the matron, a schoolmistress, two laundresses, and a washerwoman, are employed to instruct the girls. A number of ladies also assist in the instruction of the inmates. Each girl is brought up in habits of saving, by having small sums of money allowed her for marks for good conduct. It may be added by way of explanation, in the words of the committee, that "this school is not to be looked upon in the light of a reformatory, as its object is not to reclaim the vicious, but to qualify virtuous, well-conducted girls for respectable situations."

ROMAN CATHOLIC REFORMATORY.

The Girls' Reformatory School for the North of England is situated at Howard Hill, Steel-bank, and was opened in August, 1861. It is under the management of the Sisters of Charity of St. Vincent of Paul. At the time of the report being printed there were eight inmates. As its name indicates, the institution is intended for the reclamation of children who have fallen into crime, and who belong to Roman Catholic parents.

RAGGED SCHOOLS.

These schools are in Peacroft, where there is a commodious structure, built in 1856, at a cost of £1,000. They were originally established in 1848. They are in a prosperous condition. The last annual report states that there are nearly 600 scholars in daily attendance. The average attendance at the evening classes is about 120; their ages varying from 10 to 20. These scholars do not attend any day school, but are most of them engaged in some sort of employment. A teacher from the School of Art attends (gratuitously) one evening in the week, to give instruction in elementary drawing. Bread is distributed, and clothing is supplied at a cheap rate.

CHARITABLE INSTITUTIONS.

GENERAL INFIRMARY.

This handsome building and most valuable institution is situated at the end of Shalesmoor, near St. Philip's Church. It was erected by public subscription, and was opened in 1795. In 1841 extensive additions were made, at a cost of about £6,000. It is now a most efficient charity, accommodating about 150 patients, who are wholly provided for within the house, and giving medical aid constantly to an average of about 650 out-patients. Outside the entrance door to the Infirmary there are two figures, representing Hope and Charity, which are interesting because they are believed to be the very first effort, literally of the "'prentice hand," of the great sculptor Chantrey. Within the building there is an excellent bust, by Chantrey, of Dr. Browne, who was mainly instrumental in the original establishment of the institution.　There are also a copy of the bust, by Chantrey, of the Rev. J. Wilkinson, the original of which is in the Parish Church, and a marble bust, by Mr. Edwin Law, of the late Mr. Thos. Rawson, of Wardsend, with other portraits and busts of individuals of local celebrity.

SHEFFIELD GENERAL INFIRMARY.

PUBLIC HOSPITAL AND DISPENSARY.

This institution is situated in West-street, and the front of the building has a most elegant and tasteful appearance. It is of red and white brick. The institution was originally established as a Dispensary only, in 1832. Subsequently, as the town grew, the want of another infirmary became felt, and in 1857 a project was started for establishing a hospital at the Dispensary, not in competition with the existing Infirmary, but to provide for wants which that institution could not wholly supply. Mainly through the efforts of Dr. J. C. Hall, sufficient money was obtained during 1857 and the two following years to carry out the undertaking. Accordingly the building was reconstructed so as to provide accommodation for about fifty beds. The dispensary and hospital are now carried on simultaneously at the institution, which has proved to be of great utility in cases of serious accident occurring on that side of the town.

HOLLIS' HOSPITAL.

This institution was founded in 1703 by Mr. Thomas Hollis, a merchant residing in London, but a native of Sheffield. He was an earnest Nonconformist. He purchased the first Dissenting meeting-house in Sheffield, called New Hall, together with the adjoining house, which he converted into dwellings for sixteen poor widows. Though the chapel has disappeared, the almshouses remain, in what is still called Newhall-street. The trust property is yearly increasing in value. Besides 7s. per week each paid to sixteen women, stipends are also provided for various Dissenting ministers and schoolmasters in the locality.

G

DEAKIN INSTITUTION.

This is a very valuable charity, the benefits of which are extending considerably. It was established by Mr. Thomas Deakin, merchant, who, at his death in 1849, bequeathed £3,000 to found an institution for the benefit of unmarried women who need pecuniary help and who believe the doctrine of the Holy Trinity as taught by the Church of England. It was left on condition that another £3,000 should be raised and added to it for the same object. This was accomplished in 1851, and the fund is still increasing year by year. The annuitants now receive £20 per annum each, and they are selected from all parts of England ; but they must not be less than forty years of age. The annuitants are elected by those who subscribe to the fund. The funds of this excellent charity now amounts to about £10,700. At present twenty persons are receiving annuities, and two more are to be elected at the annual meeting in October, 1862. The Archbishop of York is president, and Mr. A. Thomas, of Bank-street, solicitor, is honorary secretary.

SHREWSBURY HOSPITAL.

This charity was founded in 1616, by Gilbert Earl of Shrewsbury. The building formerly stood adjoining the Lady's bridge, and subsequently occupied the site of the existing Corn Exchange and Haymarket ; but this structure was pulled down in 1827, and the present buildings in the Norfolk-road (opposite the Cholera Monument) were erected. They comprise (with the spacious grounds adjoining) a series of almshouses not to be surpassed in the kingdom, for convenience, comfort, healthfulness, and handsome appearance. The property belonging to the charity has greatly increased in value, and the recipients of it are very liberally treated. The patronage is vested in the Duke of Norfolk. There are dwellings for twenty men and twenty women. Each of the men receives 10s. a week, and each of the women 8s. a week, besides which there is a periodical allowance of coal and clothing. There are also twenty out-pensioners who receive 5s. a week. There is a chapel and a commodious house for the governor and chaplain, the Rev. J. Stacye, M.A. In the original bequest it was directed that the charity should be for such as had " seen better days, but had been reduced by misfortune."

HANBEY'S AND HADFIELD'S CHARITIES.

The first of these charities arises from property bequeathed by Mr. Thomas Hanbey in 1796. Besides a sum devoted to the maintenance of six boys in the Charity School, there is an income of about £150 a year, which is employed for the annual distribution of clothing and money to poor aged housekeepers, who must be respectable members of the Church of England. This charity is under the management of the Cutlers' Company. Emulating the example set by Mr. Hanbey, Mr. Samuel Hadfield, as a Nonconformist, entertained the idea of pro-

SHREWSBURY HOSPITAL.—FOUNDED BY GILBERT EARL OF SHREWSBURY.

viding the same benefit for his poor Dissenting brethren that his pre-
decessor had for members of the Church.   Mr. Hadfield expressed this
determination to his brother, Mr. George Hadfield (one of the present
members for the borough).   When he died the bulk of his property
was left to Mr. George Hadfield; but there was no provision for the
fulfilment of his charitable desires.   Mr. George Hadfield, however,
scrupulously carried out what he knew to be his brother's intentions,
and set apart £3,000, the interest of which is annually distributed, after
the manner of Hanbey's Charity, to "all classes and denominations
excluded from the benefits of Hanbey's Charity by reason of their not
being members of the Church of England."   The charity is under the
control of the Cutlers' Company and the Mayor and aldermen for the
time being.   There are some other minor bequests distributed among
the poor of the town, besides which there are

THE WITHERS' PENSIONS,

A charity which has just been established by the late Miss Withers,
who in her will bequeathed £10,000 to the founding of a charity in
commemoration of her late brother, Benjamin Withers.   It is provided
that the trustees of the fund are to keep in good repair the monuments
in St. Paul's Church of the Withers family, and to divide the annual
income in pensions of £10 each among widows or single women in reduced and needy circumstances, members of the Church of England,
and of the age of 50 years or upwards.   The trustees are to meet
annually on the 26th October, the anniversary of the birthday of the
late Mr. Withers, in order to elect the pensioners for the ensuing year,
those of the past year being eligible for re-appointment.

INSTITUTION FOR THE BLIND.

An institution for the support of blind persons has been originated by
Miss Harrison, a lady noted throughout this neighbourhood for her
Christian munificence.   It is situated in West-street.   It is entitled
the North of England Institution for the Blind, and is partly self-
supporting and partly maintained by subscription.   The persons assisted are taught such trades as they can carry on without the use of
the eyesight, such as basket and mat-making, &c.   The produce of
their fingers is purchased from them at a certain rate, and is disposed
of at the shop in West-street at fair market prices.   About twenty
blind persons are maintained in this way.

LICENSED VICTUALLERS' ASYLUM.

This institution, which is in connection with the Sheffield and
Rotherham Licensed Victuallers' Protection Society, is intended for the
residence and support of members of the society, or their widows, who
need such help.   It is a neat building situated within view of the Midland Railway, on the way from Masbro' to Sheffield.   It is near Grimesthorpe, about three miles from the town.   It was commenced in 1848,

LICENSED VICTUALLERS' ASYLUM

and was erected at a cost (with land) of £2,487. There are residences occupied by two widowers and five widows; and to each dwelling is attached a plot of garden ground, the whole area comprising 4½ acres. Each unmarried person receives £15 a year for life, and each married couple (when there are such inmates) £22 a year. It is intended to establish, in connection with this building, a school for the orphan children of licensed victuallers.

BANKS, NEWSPAPERS, PUBLIC COMPANIES, &c.

BANKS.

There are the following banks in Sheffield:—SHEFFIELD BANKING COMPANY, George-street (draw on Smith, Payne, and Smiths), J. H. Barber, manager; SHEFFIELD AND ROTHERHAM BANKING COMPANY, Church-street (draw on London and Westminster Bank, and on Barclay, Bevan, Tritton, and Co.), W. Wild, manager; SHEFFIELD AND HALLAMSHIRE BANKING COMPANY, Church-street (draw on Glyn, Halifax, Mills, and Co.), W. Waterfall, manager; SHEFFIELD UNION BANKING COMPANY, Bank-street (draw on Prescott, Grote, and Co.), E. Liddell, manager.

THE HALLAMSHIRE SAVINGS BANK.

SAVINGS BANKS.

The Sheffield and Hallamshire Savings Bank was established in 1819, and has prospered greatly, the managers having been enabled to build out of the surplus fund, at a cost of between £6,000 and £7,000, the present very handsome and commodious stone structure in Norfolk-street.   In 1836 the total amount deposited was £147,136, and in 1861 it was £331,958, though this was a year of great commercial depression.   Mr. Frank Wever is the actuary.   The bank is open for the reception of deposits every day except Thursday.   The Sheffield Penny Savings Bank was opened in 1857 under the auspices of Mr. Ald. Mycock and others.   When the bank had been in existence twelve months the number of depositors amounted to 900, and there had been paid into the bank the sum of £231 16s. 3d. in deposits of one penny and upwards.   From that period the business gradually increased till in 1862 the number of depositors had reached 10,000, and there had been paid in no less a sum than £7,600, and paid out in withdrawals, wholly and partially, the sum of £6,320, thus leaving in the treasurer's hands a balance of £1,280.   There have been 123,530 deposits made during the existence of the bank, and 10,830 withdrawals, making a total of 124,360 individual transactions.   The average number of weekly deposits is from 800 to 1,000, and the amount from £50 to £60.   The business is transacted at the Council Hall. Mr. A. F. Charles, of High-street, is the general manager.   The Ecclesall Penny Savings Bank is the offspring of the penny bank at the Council Hall, and was opened in 1860. It numbers 800 deposi-tors, and £250 has been received in sums of one penny and upwards. There is a balance in hand of £100. Mr. A. F. Charles is the manager. The business is transacted at the Vestry Hall, Cemetery-road, on Mon-day evenings.

NEWSPAPERS.

There are three weekly and the same number of daily newspapers now published in Sheffield. The oldest of these, *the Independent*, was commenced in 1819, and under the editorial management of Mr. R. Leader has attained a position of great prosperity. Since the repeal of the paper duty in October, 1861, the proprietors (Messrs. Leader and Sons) have issued a penny *Daily Independent*, but the old form of weekly issue has also been kept up, and by a great reduction in price the circulation has largely increased. The *Sheffield Times*, a weekly (Saturday) newspaper, was first published in 1846, and has since had incorporated with it the *Iris* and *Mercury*, the former being the paper with which the poet Montgomery was so long connected, and the latter a well-conducted paper, long the organ of the Conservatives ; Mr. S. Harrison is now the proprietor of the *Times*. The *Daily Telegraph*, which is published by Mr. Joseph Pearce, jun., was the first daily newspaper issued in Sheffield, being one of several provincial daily papers which the repeal of the newspaper stamp duty, in 1855, brought into existence. It was carried on for years with heavy loss, but has now become a well established property. The proprietor has latterly commenced the publication of a *Weekly Telegraph*, on Saturday, at 2d. The remaining daily paper is the *Daily News*, published by Mr. S. Harrison, every afternoon, at a halfpenny.

GAS AND WATER WORKS.

There is only one Gas Company in Sheffield, two others which have been started at different times having been amalgamated with it. The offices are in Shude-hill. Mr. Edwin Unwin is managing director, and Mr. T. Roberts is secretary.

The Waterworks Company have very extensive reservoirs for the supply of the town. Two of the principal of them are at Redmires, about six miles outside. From these the water is conveyed to the town in culverts. The offices are in Division-street. Mr. G. B. Greening is secretary.

FIRE OFFICES.

There are two fire insurance establishments in the town. The Sheffield Company has its offices and engines in George-street. The Liverpool and London Company has a branch office in the Old Haymarket, and its engines in Norfolk-street. There is a fire escape kept under the care of the police at the Town Hall.

TELEGRAPH COMPANIES.

There are two companies for the conveyance of messages by telegraph. The Electric Telegraph Company has an office in the Old Haymarket, at the corner of the Fruit-market. The other, the British and Irish Magnetic Company, has its office on the opposite side of the Haymarket.

RAILWAY COMPANIES.

The Midland Railway Company connects Sheffield with the north and south of England. At present, however, owing to a blunder in the original selection of the route, it does not come nearer than six miles of Sheffield, and passengers to the town have to change carriages at Masbro' Station, in order to get on a branch line which has been constructed to Sheffield. In order to remedy this inconvenience, the directors have proposed to change the direction of the trunk line, so as to carry it directly through Sheffield. Surveys have been made for the purpose, and it is believed that the Directors will next session apply for parliamentary power. They have also determined to build a new station, the present structure in the Wicker having become quite inadequate in size. The route taken by the Manchester, Sheffield, and Lincolnshire Railway is sufficiently indicated by its title. By alliance of this with the Great Northern, the town of Sheffield is now brought on the direct route of traffic between Liverpool and London. The Company have provided the Victoria Station, a handsome structure near the Cattle Market. The South Yorkshire Railway also runs into Sheffield, and the Company have the use of the Midland station in the Wicker.

HOTELS.

Since the destruction of the old Tontine Hotel, a place of accommodation upon a similarly large scale has been greatly needed in Sheffield. This has been supplied by a number of shareholders, who have erected, at a cost of about £15,000, the Victoria Hotel, a spacious building adjoining the station of the Manchester, Sheffield, and Lincolnshire Railway, of which we give an engraving. The hotel is one of the finest and most complete in the kingdom. It is five stories high and along with the ordinary range of lofty public rooms on the ground floor has billiard and smoke rooms, suites of private rooms, and upwards of fifty bed rooms. It is leased to Mr. George Meyer, of Manchester, who has expended near £10,000 in fittings and furnishing, and will be opened in July. There are other excellent inns in the town. Such, for instance, are the Royal Hotel, at the corner of Waingate and Castle-folds; the Angel, in Angel-street; the King's Head, in Change-alley; the Commercial, Old Haymarket; the Black Swan, in Snig-hill; The George, Market-place; and others. A great convenience to persons residing in the suburbs and strangers

VIEW OF VICTORIA RAILWAY STATION AND HOTEL.

visiting the town are the Commercial Dining-rooms, the best of which are Mr. Eaton's, in High-street; Mr. Bland's, in the Haymarket; and Mr. Steer's, at the top of Dixon-lane.

OMNIBUS ROUTES.

As the town has grown in size, a number of omnibuses have been provided to run to and from various parts in the suburbs. These all start from the vicinity of the Market Hall. They run to Attercliffe, Owlerton, Hillsbro', Broomhill, Botanical Gardens, Heeley, Ranmoor, Cherry-tree, Upperthorpe, Pitsmoor, Wadsley-bridge, Grenoside, &c.

FREEHOLD LAND SOCIETIES.

We have on page 28 referred to the existence of numerous Freehold Land Societies, which mark the growing intelligence and providence of the working classes. The following table (which has been prepared by Mr. H. Bates), shows the name of each society, the amount expended, the extent of the allotments, &c. :—

NAME OF SOCIETY.	No. of Lots	Quantity of Land.			Amount of Purchase.			Expended on Roads.			Total Cost.			Length of Roads.
		A.	R.	P.	£	s.	D.	£	s.	D.	£	s.	D.	Yards.
Abbeydale View	48	10	1	0	1,537	10	0	100	0	0	1,637	10	0	680
Artisan View	25	3	3	28	720	0	0	200	0	0	920	0	0	266
Bellfield	11	0	3	26	732	15	0	50	0	0	782	15	0	119
Birkendale.............	32	8	3	0	2,187	0	0	300	0	0	2,487	0	0	814
Botanical Gardens	23	5	0	29	3,108	0	0	424	0	0	3,532	0	0	377
*Brightside (First)	12	1	2	15	200	0	0	0	0	0	200	0	0	70
Brightside (Second)	82	11	1	1	2,251	1	0	9 00	0	0	3,151	1	0	858
Barrow Lee	79	9	3	24	3,200	0	0	1,417	0	0	4,617	0	0	1,055
Carbrook (First)	189	55	3	16	8,529	0	0	4,161	4	7	12,690	4	7	3,045
*Carbrook (Second)......	66	13	1	1	1,995	0	0	193	0	0	2,188	0	0	780
Cobden View...........	35	4	1	25	700	0	0	220	0	0	920	0	0	217
*Elliottville	21	2	2	30	525	0	0	85	0	0	610	0	0	120
Fir View................	100	27	2	24	4,995	0	0	1,300	0	0	6,295	0	0	1,300
Freedom Hill	151	21	3	20	3,937	10	0	1,500	0	0	5,437	10	0	1,540
*Fruits of Toil	24	3	3	10	381	5	0	77	0	0	458	5	0	422
†Grimesthorpe														
*Hall Carr Lane	16	4	0	0	575	0	0	75	0	0	650	0	0	190
Hadfield	70	8	1	30	3,900	0	0	490	0	0	4,390	0	0	686
Hampden View..........	133	20	1	34	4,565	5	5	1,640	7	3	6,205	12	3	1,500
Heeley	70	8	3	0	5,650	0	0	1,308	5	9	6,958	5	9	835
Heeley Bank...........	134	24	2	14	7,950	0	0	2,500	0	0	10,450	0	0	2,370
Hillsbrough	19 2	25	2	27	5,326	0	0	2,760	0	0	8,006	0	0	2,103
*Ivy House	17	11	2	35	1,640	12	6	0	0	0	1,640	12	6	725
Mount View	121	27	3	30	3,061	17	0	1,500	0	0	4,561	17	0	1,600
Municipal (First)	121	17	3	10	3,212	10	0	1,298	0	0	4,510	10	0	1,836
Municipal (Second)	82	12	3	22½	3,178	0	0	831	1	4	4,009	1	4	967
Nether Edge	250	38	3	5	6,980	12	6	2,200	0	0	9,180	12	6	2,500
Parkwood Springs	95	27	0	0	4,860	0	0	2,018	0	0	6,878	0	0	2,018
Rivelin View	220	32	3	25	5,429	10	7	2,000	0	0	7,429	10	7	2,200
Sheaf View	78	12	0	23	2,750	0	0	722	0	0	3,472	0	0	712
Shirebrook...............	171	30	2	30	4,100	0	0	2,100	0	0	6,200	0	0	2,200
Spring Vale	66	10	1	15	5,689	0	0	770	0	0	6,459	0	0	558
Steel Bank.............	79	21	2	9	5,160	0	0	831	13	4	5,991	13	4	1,500
Upperthorpe Vale........	40	5	2	0	2,750	0	0	650	0	0	3,400	0	0	382
Whitehouse Lane (First)..	137	18	0	36	7,397	10	0	1,800	0	0	9,197	10	0	1,970
Whitehouse Lane (Second)	97	15	0	16	6,040	0	0	2,800	0	0	8,840	0	0	1,330
*Woodland View (First)..	37	5	0	0	600	0	0	100	0	0	700	0	0	200
*Woodland View (Second)	30	4	0	0	480	0	0	130	0	0	610	0	0	200
Totals	3154	564	3	10½	126,294	18	7	39,451	12	3	165,746	10	10	‡40,245

* Roads not completed.
+ 14a. 0r. 22p. land purchased. Cost £6,371 17s. Not yet set out in Allotments, April 1862.
‡ Upwards of twenty miles.

PLACES OF RECREATION.

THE BOTANICAL GARDENS.

These gardens are amongst the most beautiful in the country. They are moreover situated in one of the most charming spots in the immediate vicinity of the town. They occupy about 18 acres of land between Clarkhouse-road and Ecclesall-road. They slope down towards the valley of the Porter, and from them may be seen, on the opposite hill-side, the picturesque grounds and the graceful church of the General Cemetery. The gardens were established by a company in 1836, at a total cost of about £18,000. They were at first a failure, and the original proprietors sold their interest in them to a new company for £9,000. Since that time the undertaking has, amidst many difficulties, gone on very prosperously. Though the property belongs to a company, it is not at all carried on with a view to profit, but solely that the use of the gardens may be enjoyed by the town. They are admirably managed. There are large and handsome conservatories, spacious gardens tastefully laid out, with beautiful lawns, walks, grottoes, and arbours. During the summer "promenades" are periodically held. Upon these occasions music is provided, and the gardens are numerously attended by the leading inhabitants. Nor are the general public uncared for. Several galas are held in the course of every summer, when the price of admission is fixed at a low rate. Sometimes twenty or thirty thousand people crowd the place on these occasions. Constant access to the gardens is of course only permitted to shareholders and subscribers ; but visitors from other towns can always obtain admission through a shareholder. The gardens are open the whole of every day except Sunday, when they are closed during the morning. Mr. Marshall, solicitor, Chapel-walk, Fargate, is secretary ; and Mr. John Ewing, who resides at the gardens, is the curator.

NORFOLK PARK.

These are spacious pleasure grounds constantly open to the public, situated on the estates of the Duke of Norfolk, and which the town owes to the munificence of the grandfather of the present inheritor of the title. The park comprises altogether more than 60 acres. It has been laid out in ornamental walks, carriage drives, &c., and is well planted with shrubs and trees. In the centre there is a large open space covered with grass, which is used for cricket matches, &c. Here also has been held for some years past a poultry show on a large scale. Very beautiful views of the surrounding scenery are to be obtained from various spots in Norfolk Park.

THEATRE ROYAL.

This building is situated at the corner of Arundel-street and Tudor-street. It belongs to a company of proprietors. It is a spacious edifice and very commodious.   It was erected in 1773.   In 1855 it was re-opened, after having been entirely rebuilt except the outer walls, at a cost of about £3,000.   The re-construction of the general edifice was carried out by Messrs. Flockton and Sons, of Sheffield, and that of the stage by Mr. Straughan, of London.   When these alterations were adopted, many modern improvements were introduced.   Since that time other changes have been made, the result of which is a commodious and elegant building.   It is at present under the lesseeship of Mr. Charles Pitt.

CRICKET GROUNDS, &c.

There are two public cricket grounds.   One is in Bramall-lane, and was opened in 1855.   It cost (without land) nearly £3,000.   It is commodious and well kept : the entire extent is more than eight acres.   The other cricket ground is at Hyde-park.   Norfolk-park is also used as a cricket ground.   There are three bowling greens kept up by annual subscription, one in Broomgrove-road, another at the Bramall-lane cricket ground, and the third at Pitsmoor.   There are three Football Clubs, the Sheffield, the Pitsmoor, and the Hallam.   In connection with these there are annual sports and athletic games, which, especially those of the Sheffield Club, are attended by the *élite* of the town.   There is also a Racket Club in Tudor-street.

SHEFFIELD CELEBRITIES.

JAMES MONTGOMERY THE POET.

The name of James Montgomery is directly associated with Sheffield from an early period of his life down to his decease.   Pre-eminently known as "the Christian poet," the mention of him calls up in the mind of the general reader ideas of serene and peaceful purity, from which the tumult of passion, the fierce contest of political rivalry, and the bitter strife of competition, are equally absent.   Yet there have been few men in later times who have undergone greater hardships, fought a sterner battle with the world, or struggled more fervently in the cause of political freedom, than did James Montgomery.   It was in the moments of leisure which he snatched from the pursuit of his business, and during the tranquil after-years earned by a long life of energy, that he penned those sweet and placid strains from which the popular idea of the poet is formed, and which will live as long as the English language remains.   Montgomery was born on November 4th, 1771, at Irvine, in Ayrshire.   He was the son of a minister in the Moravian body, and was educated at Fulneck school, in all the peculiar strictness of that denomination.   He was intended for the same profession as his father, but this idea was abandoned, and he was placed in a retail shop at Mirfield, near Wakefield. However, he remained long enough at school to acquire a good education, which materially assisted him in after-life. His poetic tendency showed itself when he was only ten years of age, and from that period he spent a great deal of time in writing verses which his friends at that time considered might have been more profitably employed.

Montgomery's career on his own account did not begin in that grave and staid manner which persons who know the poet only from his writings would be apt to picture to themselves. On the 19th of July, 1789, when he had been at Mirfield about a year and a half, and when he was about eighteen years of age, he fairly began life for himself by running away, with just three and sixpence in his pocket. He found the world harsher and harder than he had imagined, and in five days he was forced to take a situation similar to that he had left, at Wath, a village near Rotherham. He remained at this place till August, 1790, when he had saved money enough to realize the great object of his ambition—a trial of his fortunes in the great world of London. He obtained some employment in the metropolis, but was unsuccessful in his efforts to get any of his works published. At the end of eight months the young poet quitted London in disgust, and returned to Wath, where he was cordially welcomed back by his former employer. One day he saw an advertisement in the *Sheffield Register*, for a literary assistant. He answered it, and obtained the appointment. Thus, in 1792, began Montgomery's connection with the town of Sheffield, which only ended at his death.

Stirring and troublous times now came upon the young poet. Much was feared throughout the country from the spirit of disaffection created by the French Revolution, and the Government acted with a severity which, in these peaceful days, it is difficult to realize. The *Register* was a newspaper on the suspected list, as one of the organs of the revolutionary party ; and in those times to be suspected was to be crushed, if the means could be found. In 1794, Mr. Gales, the proprietor of the paper, who had engaged Montgomery, considered it prudent, for political reasons, to leave the country ; and the poet undertook to stay and manage the business for Mr. Gales' two sisters, a gentleman of the town joining in the proprietorship. As a precautionary measure, the name "*Register*" was changed to "*Iris.*" But this was not likely to deceive the Government, any more than the protestations of loyalty and neutrality which the first number of the newly-named paper contained were to propitiate them. The change took place in July, 1794, and next month poor Montgomery was in the meshes of the law. It was a cruel piece of injustice. He printed a few copies of a ballad which he found ready set-up in type in the office, and sold them to a travelling ballad-vendor. The song was declared to be seditious, although it was written in 1792, and referred to the then pending invasion of France by the Prussians and Austrians. The ballad really had to be tortured into a seditious meaning to give

colour to a prosecution. But the chance was too good to be missed.
Montgomery was indicted for sedition, and, being proved to be the
printer of the song, was convicted. He was sentenced to pay a fine of
£20, and suffer three months imprisonment. It became known afterwards that this was a State prosecution, carried on for political purposes.

Far from crushing Montgomery, the persecution he underwent only
seems to have stimulated his energies. In 1795, he became the sole
proprietor of the *Iris*, and managed it alone. He was so careful in
his political writings, that he gave no chance of a prosecution on that
ground. Still he was unfortunate enough again to be a victim to law
proceedings. In August of the same year, a riot took place in the
town. The Volunteers were called out, and Colonel Athorpe, the commanding officer, ordered them to fire on the crowd. Two men were
killed, and others were wounded. Montgomery, in the *Iris*, thus described what followed :—" A person, who shall be nameless, plunged
with his horse among the unarmed, defenceless people, and wounded
with his sword men, women, and children promiscuously." It was
well known that the "nameless person" was Colonel Athorpe, and he
suffered great odium from the affair, increased no doubt from Montgomery's account of it. Colonel Athorpe prosecuted Montgomery for
libel, and he was again convicted. There can be little doubt, from all
the reports, and even from the proceedings at the trial itself, that Montgomery's version of the affair was in the main correct ; but verdicts
cannot always be accounted for, and there was doubtless a prejudice
against Montgomery, from his having been previously convicted. He
was fined £30, sentenced to six months' imprisonment, and ordered to
find sureties for his good conduct for two years.

Montgomery was still uncrushed. During his imprisonment, the
Iris was conducted by John Pye Smith, a name well-known in
literature and religion, and an honoured representative of which
still remains in Sheffield. Upon his return to his business in the
summer of 1796, Montgomery re-introduced himself to his friends in
an address which, in its simple and Christian, yet manly tone, is very
touching. From this time the poet went on in an untroubled career
of prosperity, his paper gradually increasing in mercantile value, until
he obtained a handsome competence. He had leisure, too, to pursue
his more genial poetic pursuits, and he was able to risk the publication
of his poetry on his own account. "The Wanderer of Switzerland"
was the first lengthy poem he put forth. It was printed in his own
office at his leisure, and was published in 1806. It was at once successful. It went rapidly through two editions, and was benefited rather
than injured in its sale by one of those fierce and unscrupulous attacks
which were at that time made by the *Edinburgh Review*. "The West
Indies" followed in the next year. His other principal works were
"Greenland," "The World before the Flood," and "The Pelican Island."

Montgomery's poems were a source of profit to him, and, combined
with his newspaper income, enabled him to retire from business.

During the later years of his life, Montgomery was amply compensated for his early persecution. Indeed it is rarely that " poetic justice" is is so fully done in this world. From the Government he received a pension of £200 a year. His fellow-townsmen honoured him by public testimonials, and in every way in which it was possible to recognise his talents and his virtues. Though out of business, Montgomery was far from inactive. He was ever busy for the promotion of benevolent and Christian undertakings. He never left the Moravian body ; but his religion was of a singularly unsectarian character, and he aided every evangelical denomination in its primary object—that of spreading the Gospel. Montgomery never married. Miss Gales, the survivor of the two sisters already mentioned, continued to reside with him to the last, and was with him at his death, which took place on the 30th April, 1854. He was in the 83rd year of his age. He suffered little, his death being like a falling to sleep ; and he was at his usual avocations on the previous day. His remains were interred in the General Cemetery, and there was a public demonstration on the occasion, such as probably was never before seen in Sheffield. All the public bodies took part in the funeral procession, every building on the route was crowded, and it is not too much to say that the whole town took part in the manifestation.

It would be out of place to enter upon any critical estimate of the poetical works of Montgomery. He published many well-known pieces besides the principal ones enumerated ; and they still retain a hold on the public, as is proved by the issue of new editions. Many of his hymns, which were collected and published by himself in a volume the year before his death, have found their way into the collections of all evangelical Christians.

It now remains to point out, what will be very interesting to the stranger, the localities hallowed by an association with Montgomery. There are only two to which a direct interest attaches in this way. One is the house which was his residence after he retired from business, and where he died It is in one of the most beautiful parts of the suburbs, in a row of handsome residences, called the Mount, near to the Glossop road, and opposite Wesley College. The house occupied by the poet is now tenanted by Mr. George Wilson, and is the second residence at the east end of the Mount. The monument to Montgomery in the Cemetery, a bronze statue on a granite pedestal with inscriptions on its four sides, may be seen from its upper windows. The other locality, which is even more interesting, is in one of the very dirtiest and most unsavoury neighbourhoods in the whole. town. It is on a spot called the Hartshead. In the engraving which we give, the view taken is from the narrow passage leading out of the top of Angel-street. The house in which Montgomery published his newspaper and wrote the greater part of his poems is the prominent one, with a still handsome old doorway. The space in front has been widened in the drawing, to give

MONTGOMERY'S SHOP AND OFFICE, HARTSHEAD, FROM A SKETCH BY MR. C. THOMSON.

a better view of the house. It is now a beerhouse known as the "Montgomery Tavern."* The rooms in which Montgomery toiled and rested still remain, just as they were, except that they are filled with the inelegant appurtenances of a public house of not the very highest class. The room in which Montgomery wrote is at the back, and furnishes an outlook over one of the most anti-poetic scenes imaginable. We may add that Miss Gales, the old and tried friend of the poet, has died since his decease, and is buried at Eckington, near Sheffield. Montgomery's newspaper, the *Iris*, no longer exists as a separate undertaking, but is incorporated with the *Sheffield Times*.

* Howitt in his "Homes and Haunts of the English Poets" remarks upon the coincidence that many of the haunts which had been occupied by poetical authors ultimately came to be used as drinking places. Montgomery, in commenting upon this to his friend Mr. Holland, said, " I was amused with his (Howitt's) statement to the effect that the house in which Moore was born is now a whisky shop; that Burns's native cottage is a public-house; Shelley's house at Great Marlow a beer-shop: the spot where Scott was born occupied with a building used for a similar purpose; and even Coleridge's residence at Nether Stowey, the very house in which the poet composed that sweet ' Ode to the Nightingale,' is now an ordinary beer-house. Had his visit to Sheffield been only a few weeks later, my own forty years' residence would doubtless have been added to this list; for as Miss Gales and I walked up the Hartshead the other day, talking of '*auld langsyne*,' and not forgetful of the very complimentary character which Mr. Howitt had given of that locality, what was our consternation to perceive that our old house was actually converted into a Tom-and-Jerry shop !"

EBENEZER ELLIOTT.

Like Montgomery, Ebenezer Elliott, " the Corn Law Rhymer," was not born in Sheffield, but was brought by circumstances to spend the greater part of his life in the town, and the whole of the poetry by which he became celebrated was written here. Elliott was born at Masbro', the station on the Midland line at which travellers stop to change carriages for Sheffield. His birth took place on the 17th March, 1781. Elliott's father was employed at the Masbro' Iron works. In a brief autobiography which Elliott wrote he gives very graphic descriptions of his parents. " From my mother," he says, " I have derived my nervous irritation, my bashful awkwardness, my miserable proneness to anticipate evil, that makes existence all catastrophe." In another place he tells us, " My poor mother, who was a first-rate dreamer, and a true believer in dreams, related to me one of her visions. ' I had placed under my pillow,' she said, ' a shank-bone of mutton to dream upon, and I dreamed that I saw a little, broad-set, dark, ill-favoured man, with black hair, black eyes, thick stub-nose, and tup-shins : it was thy father.' " Elliott describes this parent as a man possessing immense energy, and very decided political opinions, from which the Corn-Law Rhymer obtained that bias which is strongly manifested in so much of what he wrote. Elliott's early life was very far from congenial, being spent among the rough workmen at the iron foundry. He soon felt the impulses of that poetic genius which eventually made him celebrated. His first effort was an humble imitation of Thomson's " Seasons." His early education was very meagre, and, like many men of brilliant genius, he was a dull boy. The love of rhyming, however, which he discovered in himself, seems to have stimulated his dormant faculties, and to have caused him to study hard, having moreover the additional good effect of weaning him from debasing pursuits.

The outward circumstances of Elliott's life are very simple, from the outset to the close. Up to manhood he remained a workman with his father. " From my sixteenth to my twenty-third year," he says, " I worked for my father at Masbro' as laboriously as any servant he had, and without wages, except an occasional shilling or two for pocket money ; weighing every morning all the unfinished castings as they were made, and afterwards in a finished state, besides opening and closing the shop in Rotherham when my brother happened to be ill or absent." Subsequently Elliott entered into trade on his own account at Rotherham ; but it was a complete failure. Then he came to Sheffield, where he started in the steel business with £100 ; and that was borrowed. He had many difficulties to encounter. Speaking to a friend of his literary compositions written at this period, Elliott said, " I had to rock the cradle and stir the melted butter while I wrote my poetry. The poetry was spoilt, and the melted butter was burnt." Elliott continued to struggle hard, and eventually he made his way to independence. The story, however, which Mr. William Howitt tells of

H

him, as " making £20 a day," is not strictly correct in the way that writer relates it. What Elliott meant to tell Mr. Howitt was that he *occasionally* made £20 a day. Be that as it may, Elliott succeeded to a reasonable extent ; and he stated himself that he retired with £6,000. Towards the close of his life he purchased a residence at Great Houghton, near Barnsley, where he died on the 1st December, 1849. He was interred in Darfield churchyard.

Elliott's poetic fame was made by his " Corn-Law Rhymes," which show immense energy and force, and became celebrated because they expressed the popular sentiments in opposition to the Bread Tax. But these rhymes are far from affording a full and adequate conception of Elliott's poetic powers, which in the " Dying Boy to the Sloe Blossom," " The Excursion," &c., show a depth of tenderness and a power of fancy which are hardly to be surpassed. The reminiscences of those who knew Elliott personally are very interesting. His love of the beautiful and his quick poetic instincts were strangely mingled with a brusque manner and expression, sometimes amounting to coarseness. This can only be accounted for by his early association with the workmen at Masbro', which no doubt gave an unfavourable tone to his mind. He had that nervous irritability and bashful desire for seclusion which he himself describes ; but his strong sense of duty forced him to take a prominent part in political and other meetings. The Corn-Law question was a sort of mania with him. Elliott lived a happy and married life, and had several children. They inherit his shrinking sensitiveness of disposition, which in them is manifested even to a larger extent. One of his sons, Mr. John G. Elliott, keeps a druggist's shop in Gibraltar-street, not far from his father's old place of business. Another, Mr. Henry Elliott, lives on the same premises, independent. A third son, Mr. Benjamin G. Elliott, also independent, resides at Shire-green, near Sheffield. There are three other brothers at a distance, two being clergymen in the West Indies. The poet also left two daughters, who are still living.

The place in which Elliott commenced business in Sheffield was at the upper corner of Barker's-pool and Burgess-street, now occupied as a boot maker's. This served him both as a shop and a residence, and here he wrote the greater part of his poetry. He subsequently removed to larger premises, at the end of Gibraltar-street, which are still called the " Elliott Steel Works." When he occupied these premises he was able to rent a country residence, and he lived in the house at Upperthorpe in which Mr. Francis Milns now resides.

SIR FRANCIS CHANTREY, R.A.

Sir Francis Chantrey, the greatest sculptor whom England has ever produced, is essentially a Sheffield celebrity, for though he was not born here, his early genius was developed in Sheffield, and the town possesses his very earliest works, in the Parish Church and at the

Infirmary. The illustrious sculptor was born at Norton, a village about four miles from Sheffield, on the 7th April, 1781.

Chantrey has been commonly designated a "milk-boy," and not entirely without truth, for he did during his boyhood ocasionally drive an ass laden with milk barrels between Norton and Sheffield. This period of the sculptor's life is thus referred to by Ebenezer Elliott :—

> " Calmly seated on his pannier'd ass,
> Where travellers hear the steel hiss as they pass,
> A milk boy, sheltering from the transient storm,
> Chalked on the grinder's walls an infant's form.
> Young Chantrey smiled ; no critic praised or blamed ;
> And golden promise smiled, and thus exclaimed—
> ' Go, child of genius, rich be thine increase—
> Go, be the Phidias of the second Greece.' "

Escaping a lengthened stay in the grocery business, to which he was put, but which proved very distasteful to him, young Chantrey was permitted to enter a more congenial occupation. He was apprenticed to Mr. Robert Ramsay, a carver and gilder, then carrying on business in High street, Sheffield. Chantrey did not finish the term of his apprenticeship, but got his friends to advance £50, to pay to Ramsay for cancelling the indentures some two or three years before his period of servitude had expired. He was mainly induced to take this course by his ardent desire for higher artistic labours. Shortly afterwards, in 1802, we find Chantrey started in Sheffield in business on his own account as a portrait painter, and advertising in the *Sheffield Iris*, (the poet Montgomery's paper,) as follows :—

" F. Chantrey, with all due deference, begs permission to inform the ladies and gentlemen of Sheffield that, during his stay here, he wishes to employ his time in taking portraits in crayons and miniatures, at the pleasure of the person who shall do him the honour to sit. F. C., though a young artist, has had the opportunity of acquiring improvement from a strict attention to the works and productions of Messrs. Smith, Arnold, &c., gentlemen of eminence. He trusts in being happy to produce good and satisfactory likenesses; and no exertion shall be wanting on his part, to render his humble efforts deserving some small share of public patronage. Terms—from two to three guineas. 24, Paradise-square."

This announcement, prosaic enough in itself, becomes in its excessive modesty quite romantic, as associated with the name of England's most celebrated sculptor. Young Chantrey for a while alternated his Sheffield portrait painting with visits to London for study: but he soon found that his real vocation was not painting but sculpture ; for in October, 1804, we find the following advertisement in the *Iris* :—

" SCULPTURE AND PORTRAIT PAINTING.

" F. Chantrey respectfully solicits the patronage of the ladies and gentlemen of Sheffield and its environs in the above art during the recess of the Royal Academy, which he hopes to merit from the specimens he has to offer to their attention at his apartments, No. 14, Norfolk-street. As models from life are not generally attempted in the country, F. C. hopes te meet the liberal sentiments of an impartial public."

Chantrey's first work in marble was executed in the autumn of 1806. It consisted of a bust of the Rev. James Wilkinson, the late Vicar of Sheffield. This was the great turning point of the sculptor's career. The work was universally admired, and it fixed the young artist's determination to persevere in the development of his hitherto comparatively untried powers.

From this time Chantrey gradually made his way in London. In 1808 he found himself in a position to leave Sheffield, and establish himself altogether in the metropolis. The current of fortune turned in his favour, and his own industry never allowed the stream to be diverted. In 1818 his merit was recognized by the Royal Academy, and he was elected a member. Besides the magnificent statues from the chisel of the great sculptor, which adorn the Cathedrals of Worcestor, Lichfield, &c., Chantrey executed a multitude of minor works ; and he had the peculiar honour of modelling from life four English sovereigns, the last being that of our own Queen, which he executed in 1840. Chantrey was knighted by William IV. He died in London, on the 25th November, 1841, aged 60. He retained a deep affection for his birthplace, and, by his own direction, his body was interred in a vault in Norton Church yard. Chantrey left directions in his will, that so long as his tomb was preserved (after the decease of his widow), £50 should be paid annually out of his estate for the instruction of ten poor boys at Norton, and £10 a year each to ten poor old people, five of each sex. Lady Chantrey, we may add, is still living.

The existing memorials of Chantrey, at his birth-place and burial-place at Norton, are described in our account of that village. The following is a list of the most interesting of the works of art by Chantrey, in this neighbourhood :—Two stone figures, being his first essay with the chisel, at the Infirmary ; his first work in marble, and another more matured piece of sculpture, in the Parish Church ; a monument in St. Paul's Church ; four casts of busts at the Cutlers' Hall ; and a bust of Dr. Browne at the Infirmary. These are referred to in detail in our descriptions of the buildings mentioned. We may a ld that there are three other works by the great sculptor within reach of the visitor to this district. One of these is a monument to the late Sir Richard Arkwright, in Cromford Church ; the second a monument to the memory of Mrs. Cooke, in Owston Church, near Doncaster. The third and most interesting is a monumental group in Ilam Church, Dovedale, to the memory of one of the Watts-Russell family. In this fine work of art the venerable David Pike Watts is represented on his bed of death, from whence he has half raised himself by a final effort of expiring nature to perform the last solemn act of a long and virtuous life ; his only daughter and her children surround his couch as they receive from his lips the blessings and benedictions of a dying parent, when the last half-uttered farewell falters upon them.

OTHER NOTABILITIES.

Amongst the persons of note who have been connected with Sheffield, were two eminent medical men. Dr. James, the inventor of the well-known "James's Fever Powder," practised here as a surgeon in the early part of his life. The other was Dr. Buchan, author of the still popular "Domestic Medicine." Wm. Buchan, M.D., was born at

Ancrum, Roxburghshire, 1729. He practised in Yorkshire, and was physician at the Ackworth Foundling Hospital. When Parliament had withdrawn the grant from the hospital, he settled in Sheffield, which he left for Edinburgh in 1766. In all probability he wrote his " Domestic Medicine" in Sheffield. He resided in the Hartshead, in the house afterwards occupied by Montgomery He died in 1805.

Two eminent divines are associated with Sheffield, though in the case of the first the connection is but slight. Archbishop Secker (born in 1693, died 1768) was educated under the Rev. Timothy Jollie, minister of the Upper Chapel, Sheffield, at the Dissenting Academy at Atter-cliffe, a suburb of Sheffield. Bishop Butler persuaded Secker to conform to the Church of England. He became Bishop of Bristol, Bishop of Oxford, and eventually Archbishop of Canterbury. The other was John Pye Smith, D.D., LL.D., F.R.S., an eminent Nonconformist preacher and writer. Dr. Pye Smith was born at Sheffield in 1774. He was the son of a bookseller, remembered by several persons still living, and was intended to follow his father's business ; but his talents and his great piety of disposition led to his entering the ministry. He became a student at Rotherham College in 1796. At the early age of twenty-five he was appointed theological tutor and principal of Homerton College. He was minister of Gravel Pit Chapel for about 47 years. He was a man of immense erudition and unsullied piety. His " Scripture and Geology," which took its place as the standard work reconciling geology and revelation, obtained for him the fellowship of the Royal Society. The learning and power of his other great work, " Scripture Testimony to the Messiah," may be judged from the fact that, though the production of a Dissenter, it is used as a text-book in the Universities. Dr. Pye Smith died at Guildford in 1851.

Mrs. Hofland, once one of the most popular writers of the day, was directly connected with Sheffield. She was daughter of Mr. Thomas Wreaks, a manufacturer, and was born in 1770. She first married Mr. Hoole, of Sheffield, who dying in two years, she afterwards married Thomas Christopher Hofland, an artist, who was born at Worksop in 1777. This latter marriage, against the wishes of her friends, was not a very happy one. She was for a time mistress of a school at Harrogate. She survived her husband two years, and died in 1844. Mr. Richard Bailey, of Castle Dyke, Sheffield, possesses a view of Sheffield from Crookes-moor, by Mr. Hofland. It is engraved in Knight's " Land we Live in." Mrs. Hofland wrote a large number of tales, some of which still keep a hold upon the public. The book entitled " Son of a Genius" is most likely to live the longest. It gives in all probability some of her own experience. Amongst the other literary persons who have been distinguished here, the Rev. Joseph Hunter, author of " The History of Hallamshire," demands a passing notice. Mr. Hunter was born in Sheffield in 1783, and died in London in 1861. He was originally a minister in the Unitarian

body; but he became one of the vice-keepers of the National Records—
an office for which he was, by his antiquarian researches and his great
learning, admirably fitted. His "History of Hallamshire," from its
immense research, its copiousness of detail, and its trustworthiness,
must form the basis of every account of Sheffield and the neighbourhood. Mr. Hunter published several other works of a similar character,
especially a History of the "Deanery of Doncaster," 2 vols. folio.
The late Mr. Ebenezer Rhodes was celebrated as the author of "Peak
Scenery," a magnificent work illustrated with engravings from drawings by Chantrey, and containing descriptions scarcely less attractive of
the beautiful scenery of the most pictorial parts of Derbyshire. Mr.
Rhodes was a merchant and manufacturer carrying on business in
Sheffield. The late Mr. Samuel Roberts, who built the Queen's
Tower referred to in our sketch of the Manor, was a man of cultivated
tastes, who published several works, was an intimate personal friend
of the poet Montgomery, and co-operated with him in many of his
benevolent projects. Another friend of the poet's, Mr. John Holland,
is still vigorously engaged in literary and scientific pursuits. Mr.
Holland has published an elaborate life of Montgomery, in seven
volumes. He has also published a life of Chantrey and many other
works both in prose and verse. Mr. Samuel Bailey has an almost
European reputation as a philosophic writer. Ebenezer Elliott styles
him "The Bentham of Hallamshire." Some of his principal works
are "Essays on the Formation and Publication of Opinions," "Truth,
Knowledge, Evidence, and Expectation," "The Nature, Measure, and
Causes of Value," &c. Mr. Bailey is still busy with his pen, and he
occasionally takes part in the public business of the town. He resides
at Norbury, Pitsmoor.

Sheffield is worthily represented in music and painting by Professor
Bennett and Mr. Creswick, R.A. Wm. Sterndale Bennett, Mus. Doc.,
was born in Sheffield, April 13, 1816. His father was organist at the
Parish Church. He died when Mr. Bennett was three years old, and
the infant musician was taken care of by his grandfather, who lived at
Cambridge. In 1824 he entered the choir of King's College there.
He was pupil at the Royal Academy. Mr. Lucas and Dr. Crotch in-
structed him in composition, and Mr. Holmes in the piano. In 1849
he founded the Bath Society. In 1856 he was elected Professor of
Music at Cambridge, and Mus. Doc. soon after. In 1856 he also became
permanent conductor of the Philharmonic Concerts. Mr. Bennett's reputation as a composer is steadily increasing. At the opening of the
International Exhibition, his beautiful cantata to the ode composed by
the poet laureate for the occasion, was universally considered as a
worthy setting for a poetic gem of the highest kind. Thomas Creswick,
R.A., the eminent landscape painter, was born at Sheffield in 1811. He
exhibited at the Royal Academy first in 1828, was elected Associate
in 1842, and Academician in 1851. Mr. Creswick's works are highly
valued for their truthfulness of detail and their poetic feeling.

MANUFACTURES OF SHEFFIELD.

We now come to the manufacturing processes of the town, which are, after all, the most interesting objects in a busy hive of industry like Sheffield. The number of trades carried on in Sheffield has increased very greatly during the present century. They now include the general manufacture of iron and steel, railway and carriage springs, buffers, tyres, &c., heavy ordnance, steel bells, crinoline, steel wire, files, saws, edge tools, scythes, sickles, all kinds of table and pocket knives, scissors, shears, razors, skates, spades and shovels, axes, hatchets, surgical instruments, machine fittings, steel collars for shirts, paper collars, silver, silver-plated, and Britannia metal wares, brass chandeliers, stove grates and fenders, optical instruments, combs, powder flasks, railway carriage and wagon building, &c., &c.

STEEL AND IRON TRADES.

BAR AND SHEAR STEEL.

The use of steel dates back to a very remote period, having been common amongst the ancients. The reason of its manufacture is obvious from the peculiar uses to which it is put and for which iron could not be employed. Steel is in fact simply a compound of iron and carbon, or charcoal, or as at present believed by some chemists, a compound of iron, carbon, and nitrogen intimately combined by means of heat. The best iron for steel purposes is produced from the mines of Danemara in Sweden. Swedish iron generally, with Russian, has been for many years in high repute for the best steel. Iron from India has also been making its way into use during the last few years ; and some of our native ores are capable of being changed into very useful steel.

The process of converting iron into steel, as pursued in Sheffield, may be thus described :—The converting furnace is composed of two troughs (about 12 feet long, 3 feet wide, and 3 feet deep), one at each side, the place for the fire being between and under them, and the whole being arched over, so that the heat may be kept in and equalized. Bar iron is cut into lengths and placed in layers, with charcoal strewed between each layer, in the two troughs. When these are full they are covered with sand or loam, which cakes together with the heat of the furnace, and excludes the air from the iron and charcoal beneath. All the apertures in the furnace are closed with loose bricks and plastered over with fire-clay. The troughs usually contain from 8 to 20 tons of iron. A large fire is made in the space left for that purpose between and under the two troughs. It takes from sixty to seventy hours to heat thoroughly the metal in the troughs. The process of conversion takes place from this point. The pores of the iron being opened by the excessive heat, the carbon becomes gradually absorbed in it, and the iron is transformed into steel; the process taking several days to accomplish after the mass is heated through. When the metal is sufficiently carbonized it is taken out, and the bars are called "blister steel," from the small raised portions which are left on the surface. This steel, after rolling, tilting, or shearing, is employed for many purposes when a very high degree of polish is not required.

When the bars of steel are put together heated and welded under the tilt or forge hammer as hereafter described, they are called "shear steel." The origin of the name is not very clear; but it was formerly, from its superior qualities, employed for the better class of goods. Shear steel is called "double," "single," or "half" from the number of bars which have been welded together.

CAST STEEL.

The manufacture of cast steel, which was discovered in 1740 by Mr. Benjamin Huntsman, of Handsworth, near Sheffield, has come into general use, and has to a large extent displaced the use of shear steel. The casting of steel is a simple process, but very interesting. The bar steel is broken into small pieces, and, with manganese, &c., put into a crucible of very peculiar make, composed principally of fireclay. The quality of the steel depends a great deal upon the suitable selection of the blistered bars, and also upon the skill of the melter in the management of his furnace, the production of cast steel properly melted requiring great care and long experience. There are a number of furnaces, which are in reality merely holes in the floor of the casting-room, each hole being about three feet deep. The furnaces having been raised to an intense heat with coke fuel, the crucibles of steel are lowered into them. In about three hours the steel is in a liquid state; and the crucible is then lifted out and the steel poured into cast-iron moulds of various shapes and sizes, in which it cools in the form of ingots. The most interesting part of the process is the taking out of the crucible and pouring of the metal into the mould. The lid of the furnace is removed, and the dazzled eye falls with a wavering glance on the glowing mass within, from which pours out a stream of intense heat. A workman—his legs protected with wet sacking—proceeds to the hole. He looks down with an unshrinking gaze. Guided by quick and experienced hands, his huge iron pincers firmly grasp the crucible, and the liquid metal is carried to the moulds, which stand at a short distance. The crucible is turned on one side, and the molten steel runs out in a thin white stream, from which shoot out a number of brilliant coruscations. This process is very beautiful when performed at night. The excessive heat makes the crucibles worthless after two or three castings. When the steel is cooled into ingots it is tilted or rolled, in the same way as bar steel. The difference is that cast steel is for many purposes of a superior quality, and is used for articles in which the highest kind of finish is

STEEL CASTING SHOP—MESSRS. C CAMMELL AND CO., CYCLOPS WORKS.

required. In the accompanying illustration of steel casting the work-men on the left are standing over the furnaces in the floor, while in the centre a crucible of molten steel is being poured into the ingot mould. On the right corner is a heap of the moulds, and on the shelves on the left are rows of crucibles, looking not unlike skittle-pins.

BESSEMER STEEL.

The Bessemer process has been in use in Sheffield for the last two or three years. It is the invention of Mr. Henry Bessemer, who has a manufactory here for making steel upon his own method. The plan is exceedingly simple, but very remarkable in its results. The time required for making bar steel, reckoning from the period when it is put into the furnace till it is cool enough to take out, is from fifteen to twenty days ; and then three hours and a half more are required to change the bars into cast steel. Looking at these facts, it seems hardly credible that by the Bessemer process crude iron can be changed into steel within thirty minutes. Yet such is the fact. The vessel in which the steel conversion takes place upon Mr. Bessemer's plan is made of strong boiler plate, the interior being preserved with a lining of powdered stone called " ganister," found in the neighbourhood of the town. The vessel is oval, with an aperture at the top for pouring the metal in and out. At the bottom there are inserted seven tuyeres of fireclay, each having seven holes in it ; and through these a blast from the engine enters. Though the converting vessel is made large enough to hold several tons of metal, it is constructed so that it will readily swing about in any direction required. In the commencement of the process the vessel is thoroughly heated with coke. A sufficient quantity of pig iron having been melted in an adjoining furnace, the converting vessel is turned on one side, and the iron is poured in at the hole in the top already described. The vessel is then put back into its ordinary position, the blast having been turned on into the interior through the holes mentioned in the bottom. This causes a most powerful combustion to take place. As the fire increases in intensity, it causes a series of miniature explosions of spark and flame, which are interesting to watch ; while the place is illuminated with a beautiful white light. The most pleasing part of the process, however, to the visitor, is when the vessel is swung down again, at the close of the operation. He has to stand on one side, where he is perfectly secure while the molten metal sends forth a torrent of large and brilliant sparks, which dart straight ahead with great force. When the practised eye of the workman sees that the metal is ripe for his purpose, the vessel is tilted forward, and he puts in a quantity of charcoal pig iron containing a certain proportion of carbon. The carbon combines with the mass of molten iron, and thus it becomes steel. The vessel is then placed in a position in which the metal will run out, and it is poured into a large ladle, and thence into the ingot moulds. The process of conversion occupies about 28 minutes.

STEEL ROLLING AND TILTING.

After leaving the converting furnace, or the mould of the caster, steel, before being manufactured into cutlery, tools, or the various other forms in which it reaches the general public, has to undergo the process of rolling or tilting, by which its quality is very much

STEEL ROLLING MILLS.—MESSRS. C. CAMMELL AND Co., CYCLOPS WORKS.

improved. Both these are interesting to witness. The engraving which is appended gives an accurate idea of the process of rolling. On the left the workmen are pulling out of the fire, with iron pincers, the red-hot bars of steel. In the centre are the rollers,

which are kept revolving by steam power. A workman stands on
each side, in order to turn the bar after it has passed between the
rollers. The object of the rolling is to close the pores and give the
steel a more perfect grain. It is rolled in flat sheets for saws, shovels,
and other articles which have a broad surface, and circular rods for wire,
needles, &c. The tilting or hammering process is even more picturesque and interesting. The object is the same as in the case of rolling ;
but hammering is considered to adapt the steel better for a certain class
of articles, such as razors, knives, &c. The hammers with which the
steel is worked are very curious and peculiar objects. When the
visitor enters one of the large rooms in which the process is carried on,
as represented on the opposite page, it seems at first sight as though
a number of heads belonging to some antediluvian monsters were at
work nodding up and down, some with frantic rapidity, some with de-
liberation, and some apparently just on the point of coming to a pause.
Upon examining them more closely he finds that they are really hammers fastened to huge lengths of timber, which, impelled by steam,
are coming down with greater or less force and rapidity on the hot and
yielding steel. The process, like that of rolling, is carried on amidst
a most bewildering noise. The voice is inaudible except by shouting,
while the building strains and trembles from the great vibration caused
by the hammers. There are fires for the heating of the steel, as
in the rolling department ; and in both the men drag about the red-hot
bars in a manner which creates an uncomfortable feeling in the stranger's
mind ; but the workmen are very dexterous, and accidents rarely occur.
The hammers referred to are called " tilt" and " forge" Both the
forge and tilt hammers are precisely the same, except that the forge are
made larger and heavier. The hammer is merely a piece of iron,
bound round the end of the timber, and with a portion of hard composite
metal fastened on the under part of the iron where it strikes the steel.
Water is kept pouring on the framework to keep it cool. The workman sits in front on a seat which moves to and fro, to accommodate
the varying action of his body. In this posture he skilfully guides the
iron under the hammer, moving it carefully so that the blows shall be
distributed evenly over the whole surface. In this way the steel is
made of the desired size and consistency, a number of bars, when it is
necessary, being welded together under the action of the hammer until
they form one united mass. The tilt and forge hammers vary in weight
from about $2\frac{1}{2}$ cwt. to 5 cwt. each. A tilt hammer can deliver about
300 strokes per minute and a forge hammer about half as many. The
sketch of the tilt and forge hammering process which we publish is from
the works of Messrs. Sanderson Brothers and Co., at Attercliffe, the most
extensive tilting mills in the trade. In the building depicted there are
twelve of these ponderous hammers under one roof, and in other parts
of the works eleven others. The large fires which are used to heat
the steel are kept in a red glow by a beautiful piece of machinery acting
the part of bellows on a large scale. Huge wheels moved by steam-power

STEEL TILTING.—MESSRS SANDERSON BROTHERS AND CO, ATTERCLIFFE.

STEEL TILTING.—MESSRS SANDERSON BROTHERS, ATTERCLIFFE.

revolve on the fan principle, and create a draught which maintains the
fires in a glow. On the same principle as the tilt and forge hammer
as regards the effect on the metal, though quite different in the mode of

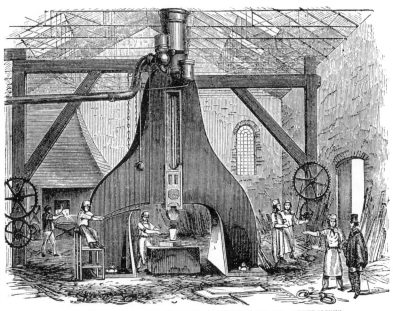

STEAM HAMMER.—MESSRS. SANDERSON BROTHERS AND CO., ATTERCLIFFE.

working, are the large hammers similar to the one invented by Nasmyth. These are used for masses of steel too large for the tilts or forges to deal with. The one of which an illustration is annexed is at Messrs. Sanderson Brothers', and weighs two tons. This hammer, which moves up and down in a fixed frame of iron, works with wonderful precision, and the blow of it can be so regulated as to bring the two-ton hammer down upon the heated steel with the greatest force, or so gently as to crack a nut.

EXTENSION OF THE STEEL TRADE.

It is in the steel department that the enormous increase in the trade of Sheffield, to which we have previously adverted (page 27), has principally taken place. The introduction of railways and the growth of labour-saving machinery, are probably the main causes of calling steel into more general use; and hence the impulse given to the steel trade in Sheffield. The manufacture of steel elsewhere is of so trifling extent that it may be said with truth that Sheffield furnishes the whole of the United Kingdom with steel, and, in large part, the entire world. It is true that recently Germany, France, and the United States have entered the lists as rival manufacturers; but Sheffield steel, especially the best cast steel, has still an unequalled reputation for quality throughout the world. It is only one foreign manufacturer (Krupp, of Essen, in Prussia), who may be said to have taken a position formidable to Sheffield, and that only in one special and peculiar branch—the manufacture of large masses of steel. Our manufacturers have not, however, been wanting in activity and enterprise ; and if we may judge from the progress made in Sheffield during the short time it has been known what strides Krupp was taking, we can confidently assert that it will not be long before, in that branch also, Sheffield is without a rival.

The Sheffield steel trade may very properly be divided into the following two classes :—1st, that devoted to the old staple trade of steel for tools, cutlery, springs, &c., which is followed by all the leading firms. 2ndly, that used in the production of steel in large masses and forgings adapted to special purposes, for which formerly steel was not employed. This branch of the steel trade is as yet in its infancy. Owing to its newness, it is followed up by a few manufacturers only. The extensive application of steel which is now beginning to take place has only begun to dawn upon the world ; but it is evident, from the rapid impetus which has already been given, that it is not easy to fix limits to its future use. The great benefit which is obtainable by the use of steel in place of iron, is its great durability and strength, to a large extent outweighing the additional cost incurred. Nevertheless, the expense is a serious item in the question ; and should the Bessemer process be found to produce metal of sufficiently good quality, there can be no doubt that it will have a material effect in spreading the use of steel. The necessity of cheapness is strikingly shown in the use of steel for rails for railways. The vast superiority of steel, on account of its great durability, cannot be disputed. For instance, at the Pimlico station, on some parts of the London and North Western, and on the Caledonian Railway, steel rails have been put down, and have been found at the end of a year to be nearly as good as new, whereas the old iron rails required to be renewed about once in three months. Notwithstanding these remarkable facts, steel has not hitherto come into general use for rails because of its costliness. One expedient adopted has been to have merely the surface of the rail composed of steel ; but this does not wear like a solid mass of steel. Steel rails are now gradually coming into use for places like busy stations, where there is a very large amount of traffic; and probably they will eventually be used throughout the railways. Solid steel tyres, &c., are also made for the wheels of railway carriages ; and as regards these, there is, in addition to the great durability, the advantage given by the increased safety to travellers by railway from the wheels being less liable to accident in breakage. Besides the above, there are a multiplicity of new uses to which steel is being adapted. Cast steel bells are growing into general favour; and amongst other new manufactures may be mentioned the following:—Cast steel locomotive double crank axles, and tender and carriage axles; single crank and other marine shafts; cannon blocks, jackets, tubes, and hoops for ordnance and hydraulics, forged out of solid ingots of cast steel ; solid castings in steel, not forged or rolled, for railway wheels (with tyres in one solid piece), railway crossings,

BRIGHTSIDE STEEL WORKS.—MESSRS. W. JESSOP AND SONS.

hornblocks or cheek plates, and a variety of other castings and forgings
in steel for railway rolling stock, permanent way, machinery, ordnance,
&c., &c.   Quite a different class of manufacture is that of crinoline,

PARK STEEL WORKS.—MESSRS. W. JESSOP AND SONS.

SOHO STEEL ROLLING MILLS.—MESSRS. W. JESSOP AND SONS.

which has grown so largely during the last few years.   For some time
Sheffield produced all the crinoline steel that was used.   It is now made

I

in limited quantities in France, Germany, and America ; but still an enormous and increasing amount is yearly manufactured in Sheffield. It is exported in various shapes, from raw steel to the made-up skirts, all over the Continent, to Australia, America, and every portion of the civilized world. It is computed that Sheffield manufactures something like 10,000 tons of steel for crinoline during the year—rather a heavy load for the ladies who have to carry it. All the raw material for the steel pens manufactured so largely at Birmingham is made at Sheffield ; and it is reckoned that about six hundred tons a year are supplied for this purpose. It was estimated that in the year 1856 the steel manfactured in Sheffield amounted in value to £1,854,500, Since that time the quantity made has so largely increased that it probably approaches in value £3,000,000 yearly.

MANUFACTURERS OF STEEL.

Messrs. Naylor, Vickers, and Co., who have works at Millsands and Wadsley-bridge, are the oldest steel manufacturers in Sheffield, and amongst the largest and most enterprising. They produce almost all the different kinds of materials already enumerated, and were the first to introduce into the town some of the most important of them. A very interesting process to the stranger is one which Messrs. Naylor, Vickers, and Co., carry on without competitors in Sheffield— the making of cast-steel bells. We give an engraving of the scene at the casting of a bell. This process is similar to what is witnessed at the pouring of the molten metal into the ingot mould in the operation of making cast steel. It is, however, upon a larger scale, and is more picturesque. The steel being ready melted, the crucibles are taken up by relays of workmen, who carry them to the bell- moulds, and pour them in in quick succession. The process is a most delicate one, for any access of cold to the poured-out steel or any delay in the addition of the remainder of the metal, would make the bell worthless. As crucible after crucible is emptied, the bright colours and countless myriads of sparks shooting out from the masses of molten metal are seen to great advantage. In making the large bell which is being shown by the firm in the International Exhibition, and which weighs nearly five tons, no less than 176 crucibles of steel had to be poured out in this way without a moment's cessation. In fact, the process only occupied eleven minutes. The manufacture of steel bells was commenced by Messrs. Naylor, Vickers, and Co., in 1855, since which time they have made more than 3,000 bells of all sizes, including some 90 inches in diameter. From this it is evident that the prejudices against steel bells are giving way. Their qualities are highly spoken of by connoisseurs. Amongst the most successful peals which have been made by the firm are the following :—St. Marie's, Sheffield : a peal of eight ; tenor 54 inches, note E flat ; total weight of peal, 8,500 lbs. St. Clement's, Hastings : a peal of eight ; tenor 52 inches, note E ; total weight of peal, 7,880 lbs. Ingleton, Lanca-

STEEL BELL CASTING.—MESSRS. NAYLOR, VICKERS, AND CO., DON WORKS.

shire: a peal of six; tenor 48 inches, note E; total weight of peal, 5,700 lbs. A singular fact has been noted in connection with these cast steel bells. Although they are made one-third lighter than the old bronze bells, they are not by any means so liable to break from the concussion caused by ringing them during severe frosts. In fact, these steel bells have been rung without injury in Russia and Canada, when the thermometer was so low that bronze bells could not be rung without being cracked. The cast steel bells are produced much cheaper than bronze. Messrs. Naylor, Vickers, and Co., also manufacture field-pieces made from a solid block of cast steel. The firm are still greatly extending their operations, and are about erecting new works on land adjoining the Midland Railway, which will cover 20 acres. These are to be devoted entirely to the production of steel in large masses, while the present works are to be continued for the old productions of steel manufacture for which they have become famous.

Messrs. Sanderson Brothers and Co., are amongst the largest as they are of the oldest manufacturers of steel, for which, with the various descriptions of files, saws, edge tools, cutlery, &c., of which they are general merchants, they have a deservedly high repute throughout the Continent, the United States, and Russia. They have works in West-street, Sheffield, at Attercliffe, and at Darnall, where the processes of converting, melting, rolling, tilting, and forging are carried on. The illustrations of steel tilting at page 117, and of the steam forge hammer at page 118, are taken from the works of this firm at Attercliffe.

The engravings at pages 120 and 121 show the three separate steel works of Messrs. W. Jessop and Sons—Park, Soho, and Brightside. This house, long the most extensive engaged exclusively in the steel trade, has branch establishments or depôts in Manchester, Paris, Canada, and at no less than six of the principal cities of America. Park Works, at which the converting and melting processes are carried on, were many years ago, from the quantity of steel manufactured there, entitled to the first rank in the trade. The subsequent expansion of the steel trade induced the firm to establish the larger works at Brightside along both sides of the River Don, a bridge over which connects them together. To these were subsequently added Soho Works, where the various descriptions of sheet steel are rolled, particularly the sheets from which steel pens are made, and of which this house manufactures the greater part for Birmingham and the foreign trade. Mr. T. Jessop, the senior partner in the firm, is one of the Jurors of the Exhibition.

The largest development of manufacturing industry in the steel trade is on the line of the Midland Railway, from outside the Wicker Station towards Brightside. The first of the large manufactories erected in this neighbourhood was by Mr. Charles Cammell, now the head of the firm of Messrs. Charles Cammell and Co., of Cyclops Steel and Iron Works; and, the building being once opened, the advantages of the contiguity to the railway became so obvious that many other large business premises were shortly afterwards erected there. Mr. Cammell was followed by Messrs. Spear and Jackson; by Messrs. J. Beet and Son (now Peace, Ward, and Co.), Agenoria Works; Messrs. John

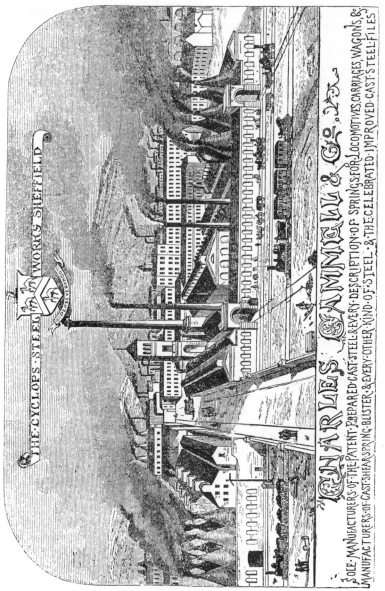

CYCLOPS STEEL IRON, AND SPRING WORKS.—MESSRS. C. CAMMELL AND CO.

Brown and Co., Atlas Iron, Steel, and Spring Works ; Messrs. Thomas Firth and Sons, Norfolk Works, who carry on a large steel trade, manufacture heavy ordnance, and also send out files, edge tools, &c.;

Messrs. Moses Eadon and Sons, President Works ; Mr. Bessemer, who
carries on the manufacture of steel by his own process ; Messrs.
Wilson Hawksworth, Ellison, and Co. Carlisle Works ; Messrs.
Sybray, Searls, and Co. ; and others.   Indeed, the advantages of
the locality are so apparent, that all the new steel manufactories are
being built in this direction.   The large extensions already referred
to as contemplated by Messrs. Naylor, Vickers, and Co., are on land
further outside the town, near Brightside, and on the estates of Earl
Fitzwilliam.   The other manufactories mentioned are on land belonging to the Duke of Norfolk.   Some idea of the extent of the works
in this locality, may be formed from the fact that, on the estates of
the Duke of Norfolk alone, about 50 acres have been taken for manufactories, and about 70 acres more for dwellings for the workpeople,
while upwards of ten miles of roads have been made.   These figures
refer only to this one particular locality, there being other extensions
within the same township of Brightside.

The large increase of works referred to has all taken place since 1845,
when Mr. Charles Cammell removed to this spot.   The business premises of the large firm of which that gentleman is the founder, are called
the Cyclops Works, where Messrs. Cammell and Co., carry on the manufacture of steel, heavy forgings of all kinds both in steel and iron,
railway springs and buffers, and files, upon a very extensive scale.   To
their other branches of trade, Messrs. Cammell and Co. have recently
superadded that of iron manufacture, previously unknown in this town.
They convert pig iron into malleable wrought iron for the best qualities
of work.   The extensions of the business premises are a good test of
the progress of the firm.   In 1845 the works of Messrs. Cammell and
Co. occupied four acres, and the covering of this extent of land with a
huge manufactory appeared so bold a venture that many were startled,
and prognosticated that so rapid a progress could not be sustained.
The new works, however, were no sooner erected than Mr. Cammell's
enterprize and energy brought in orders more than could be executed.
In a short time another piece was taken.   Since then the works have
been further enlarged, and they now cover about nine acres of land.
A good notion of the extensiveness of the works may be gathered from
the fact that from 5,000 to 6,000 tons of coal and coke are consumed
during the month.

The engraving at page 113 showing the process of steel refining and
casting, and that at page 115 of the interior of a steel rolling mill,
are both taken from the works of Messrs. Cammell and Co.   The
railway spring department, at the Cyclops Works, is very interesting to visit.   The forging shop, of which we give an illustration,
is close to the mills where the steel is rolled into bars for making up
into springs.   The bars are put under machinery which cuts them up
as easily as paper is snipped with scissors, and with the utmost nicety
in regard to length.   The pieces of steel have then many processes to
go through.   Holes are punched in them, and they are " slitted " and

FORGE SHOP.—MESSRS. C. CAMMELL AND CO., CYCLOPS WORKS.

"studded"—that is, apertures are made of various shapes for the purpose of fastening the pieces of steel together, so that they shall make up into the complete spring. After the plates have gone through these and other operations, they are bent by hammering into the shape in which they are seen, and are also hardened and tempered. We give an engraving of the shop in which these processes are performed. They are then fitted together and fastened with very strong rivets. Being thus complete, nothing remains but to test them. This, however, is a very important process, as is evident from the serious consequences which would follow if they were to give way in actual use. They are tested by a very beautiful hydraulic machine, which works with great rapidity, precision, and certainty. The spring is put in the arched part upwards, on a flat iron table, and a weight is brought down on it, which quickly flattens it till it is perfectly level with the table. It is marvellous to see, when the weight is withdrawn, how these thick pieces of steel rebound with all the elasticity of a watch-spring, till they resume their proper position, without any perceptible variation. Nothing can be more perfect than the test. In many instances, in fact, they are bent beyond the straight line. The engine springs are frequently made to carry as much as 25 tons weight each. We have only described one kind of springs, but there are all kinds made here.

Another very interesting piece of machinery in regular use at the Cyclops Works is one shown by the firm in the Exhibition, and rendered indispensable by the necessity for testing the iron and steel to the utmost possible extent. By this machine the metal is tested in every imaginable way—by tension, torsion, crushing, and breaking. The steel and iron produced at Messrs. Cammell and Co.'s are constantly tested in these ways, and a register of the results is kept. It is possible to put a power equal to 388,000 lbs. weight, or about 175 tons, upon a section of half a square inch. The machine is very simple, only two levers being used in its construction, and when not moved by steam power two men can work it.

The rolling of armour plates at the manufactory of Messrs. Brown and Co. is not to be surpassed in interest. The process is commenced by taking about 132 slabs of iron, measuring about 30 inches by 12, and an inch and a half thick. Four of these pieces, after being heated in a furnace, are rolled into a solid plate about four feet square. In this way the whole of the slabs are by degrees welded together until they form four plates, each 10 feet long by 4 feet 4 inches wide, and $2\frac{1}{2}$ inches thick. These four have to be rolled together to make the armour plate which is used for the protection of the ship. As may well be imagined, it requires peculiar machinery and gigantic appliances to deal with such masses of metal. The four plates are placed in an enormous furnace, where they are left until they are red hot all through. And now comes the final and exciting operation. The huge rollers are at a distance of about 20 yards in front of the furnace; and along this space the mass of metal has to be drawn. Seventy men are employed in the work. The door of the furnace opens, and an iron carriage is pushed up to its mouth for the conveyance of the red-hot

SPRING SHOP.—MESSRS. C. CAMMELL AND CO., CYCLOPS WORKS.

plates. They are drawn out partly by means of a chain passed round the rolls and partly with huge pincers, each pair of which is so heavy that the strength of three men is necessary to lift it. These two forces are put into action, and the vast mass of metal shoots out and rests itself on the carriage. The chain is rapidly detached, and the men run the carriage up to the rollers, the huge bulk of red hot iron sending out a stream of heat which is felt far and near. It passes between the rollers, and the pliable bulk of the mass is reduced by the pressure from ten to eight inches. By a mechanical contrivance the action of the rollers is now reversed, so that the iron passes through backwards; but this time it only loses half an inch in thickness. Altogether it passes through the rollers eight times. Upon each occasion of the plate coming from between the rollers the surface is swept with brooms dipped in water. At intervals buckets of water are also thrown upon the mass of metal, to remove the impurities on the surface. The water goes hissing and bubbling over the iron, but it is powerless to make any perceptible diminution in the heat. There is another operation which has to be occasionally performed with great care. Whenever there is the appearance of a blister, or raised lump of metal, on the surface, it has to be removed. This is effected by placing a sharp punch, at the end of a long shaft, on the blistered spot. The punch is struck into the blister with a heavy hammer; and this restores the iron to a level. The rolling of the plate being now completed, it is conveyed by means of a crane to the place for straightening it. This is performed by placing it on flat iron plates, where two rollers, each weighing nine tons, pass over it to make it perfectly straight. After about twelve hours, the plate is sufficiently cool to be conveyed to the planing tables, where the edges are cut square and grooved, so as to adapt it for being fastened to the sides of the ship for which it is intended. The plates vary in size; but the general average is about 20 feet long, 4 feet 4 inches broad, $4\frac{1}{2}$ inches thick, and about six tons in weight. The largest Messrs. Brown have hitherto made are shown in the Exhibition. One of these is 5 inches thick, 24 feet long, and 3 feet 8 broad. The largest is $6\frac{1}{2}$ inches thick, 21 feet long, 4 feet 3 wide, and weighs 11 tons.

The accompanying engraving represents very accurately the scene at the commencement of the process of rolling armour plates at Messrs. Brown's. The plate, it will be seen, is in progress of removal, in the red-hot state, from the furnace to the rollers.

The process of making these armour plates is one of vast and increasing importance, considering the changes which are taking place in naval warfare. Messrs. Brown and Co. are devoting great attention to the subject, with a view to manufacture plates with the greatest possible resisting power; and they have made many improvements in those which they have produced. They believe that the rolled plates are superior to the hammered, because the latter are more brittle and liable to be shattered by the effects of the shot. The rolling process preserves the fibre of the metal. Iron of different kinds of fibre is used, and these are rolled so that the fibres cross each other. In this way an additional amount of resisting power is obtained.

ROLLING OF ARMOUR PLATES FOR SHIPS OF WAR.—MESSRS. JOHN BROWN AND CO., ATLAS WORKS.

ROLLING OF ARMOUR PLATES FOR SHIPS OF WAR.—MESSRS. JOHN BROWN AND CO.

The Atlas Iron, Steel, and Spring Works of Messrs. John Brown and Co., at which the manufacture of armour plates just referred to is carried on, is one of those immense ranges of buildings which

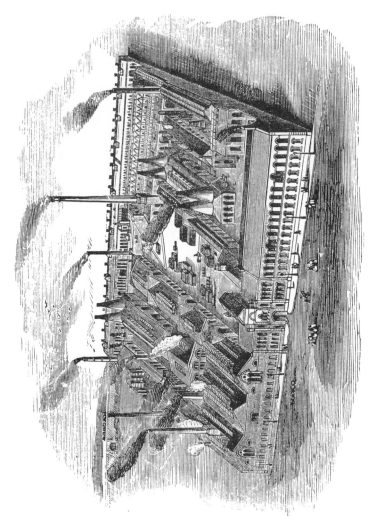

ATLAS STEEL, IRON, AND SPRING WORKS.—MESSRS. JOHN BROWN AND CO.

we have referred to as having been constructed on the line of the Midland railway. The above engraving, having been executed before the
recent large extension of the works, does not show near their full extent. It is, in fact, the largest of these extensive manufactories, the
ground on which the works stand comprising altogether between 14
and 15 acres. Messrs. J. Brown and Co., besides the general steel trade,
carry on the manufacture of files and railway springs and buffers. They
introduced a patent buffer some years since, which came into general

REGENT WORKS.—MESSRS. BURYS AND CO., MANUFACTURERS OF STEEL, FILES, SAWS, EDGE TOOLS, ETC.

use and greatly promoted the prosperity of the firm. With that enterprise which has always characterized Messrs. Brown and Co., they have
adopted the Bessemer process, which is carried out at their works upon

a more extensive scale than is any where else to be seen.   They have two converting vessels each capable of holding four tons of iron.   These are worked simultaneously, and, their contents being poured into the same mould, they produce an ingot of steel weighing seven tons.   The Bessemer process, as seen in operation at Messrs. Brown's upon a scale like this, is exceedingly interesting.   Another process which Messrs. Brown and Co. are carrying out is that (already described) of iron armour plates for war ships, for the manufacture of which the firm has become celebrated throughout the country, having made some of the best plates that have been produced.   Indeed, their position in the opinion of the Admiralty may be judged from the fact that they have been entrusted with the contract for the armour plates for the cupola ship which is about to be constructed on Captain Coles' principle.   So extensive has become this branch of their manufacture, that Messrs. Brown and Co. are about to construct a mill specially for it, and capable of turning out from 300 to 400 tons of finished plates weekly—twelve inches thick if necessary.

With the exception of Messrs. W. Jessop and Sons, there are few large firms engaged *exclusively* in the manufacture of steel, but great numbers who combine that with other manufactures, some of whom will be found specially referred to in subsequent portions of this work. Amongst the principal houses may be named the Turtons, Butchers, Burys, Shortridge, Howell, Ibbotsons, Spencers, Unwins, Machens, Doncaster, Wardlows, Cockers, Hall, the Nicholsons, the Peaces, Eadons, Fisher, Brittain, Beardshaws, Burgin, Smiths, Becketts, Makin, Osborne, Moss, Hunter, Turner, Horn, Rossell, Jowitt, Brooksbank, Parkin, Sybray, Searls, &c., &c.

CUTLERY MANUFACTURES.

The early reputation of Sheffield was for its cutlery wares ; and this reputation it still maintains.   In spite of all that has been done to damage the character of the town, it is well known to those who are conversant with the facts, that Sheffield produces the best cutlery that is made.   A Sheffield knife or razor, with the mark of a good firm upon it, will hold its ground against the world.   The superiority of the goods sent out by the leading manufacturers must indeed be decided, to enable them to maintain the supremacy which they unquestionably hold ; for both on the Continent and in America a most dishonest system of piracy has been pursued, in such a way as not only to obtain the benefit of the marks of Sheffield firms but to injure their reputation.   A Prussian manufacturer, for instance, makes some very bad cutlery or edge tools, and also some as good as he can send out.   On the good articles he stamps his own name, and thus obtains a reputation as the maker of respectable goods.   But upon the worthless trash he affixes the well-known name and mark of some eminent Sheffield firm, and thus effects the double object of selling his rubbish and bringing the name of the English house into bad odour. These piracies are carried out in a most systematic manner. In some instances firms in Prussia send out circulars offering to imitate the labels and packages of any particular house required. The law of that country gives no redress to the English manufacturer in such cases; but a strenuous effort is being made to induce the English Government to obtain international protection for trade marks. In France the state of things was at one time almost as bad as in Prussia; but the Government of the Emperor has, with great liberality, given to English firms the same protection that is open for French houses; and the legal process is found to be thoroughly effective. The system which is enforced by the Sheffield Cutlers' Company for the protection of trade marks is very satisfactory. Within the district of Hallamshire the piracy of marks is almost unknown, because the Cutlers' Company have special powers by which summary proceedings can be taken before the magistrates; while they have a registry of all the marks granted, so that there can be no infringement without its being discovered. Until some plan like this is adopted, not only in this country, but, by mutual arrangement, internationally with other countries, the dishonest trader will get advantages at the cost of the purchaser and of the fair-dealing, honest manufacturer. Under the protection afforded by the Cutlers' Company's system, many Sheffield firms have built up a reputation for their marks which it would be difficult to measure by a money value. Recently an attempt has been made to decry Sheffield cutlery as inferior to that manufactured in London. To those who are aware of the facts, this is nothing better than a joke; for it is well known that most of the first-class cutlery passed off by the Metropolitan shopkeepers as "London-made" is produced in Sheffield.* The purchaser never can get wrong so long as he obtains articles bearing the name or mark of one of the many eminent firms in Sheffield which have earned a reputation for their goods.

We now proceed to give a description of the various processes of cutlery manufacture. Having shown how steel is made, we shall trace the progress of the metal until it comes from the hands of the workman a finished article suitable for pocket or table use.

SPRING KNIVES.

We commence with spring cutlery, or knives that shut with a spring, to go in the pocket. The ingot of steel, rolled to the required size, is first placed in the hands of the "forger" or "blademaker." It may be here remarked, incidentally, that the principle of sub-division of labour is very fully carried out in the cutlery trades. Not only is each department, as forging, grinding, &c., carried out by separate workmen, but the

---

* The London *City Press*, in an interesting article on the Cutlers' Company, says:—" The Londoner, when traversing the streets of the metropolis of the world, may, perhaps, remark to himself the limited number of cutlers. In London there are about 200 cutlers, who employ about 1,000 hands." This is not so large a number of workmen as is employed by three of the foremost firms in Sheffield. Taking into account, too, the fact that a very large part of the hands in London must be employed in the repairing of goods, not many are left for the manufacture of cutlery.

man who grinds or forges one particular class of blades, such as for pen knives, does not work at table knife blades ; and so on throughout all the different branches. The forger works in a small room containing a fire-place or hearth, a trough to hold water, and another for the small and specially-prepared coke for the fire, an anvil weighing from two to four hundredweight, and other tools. The forger buries the end of the bar of steel in his fire, to the extent required ; then, working his bellows, he soon raises the steel to the proper heat. This has to be done very carefully, for if over-heated the steel becomes what is called "burnt"—that is, it is changed from steel, which is a carburet, into a sulphuret of iron, which is useless for cutlery purposes. Again, if not adequately heated it is not sufficiently soft to take the shape which the forger intends. Duly heated, the end of the bar is brought to the anvil, and is there fashioned with very few strokes by an expert hand into a blade of the required shape, and is cut off the bar, which is again heated for the renewal of the process.

The end of the blade where it is attached to the handle is called the "tang," and the next stage in the knife's history is the grinding of this part. The building in which the grinder works is commonly called a "wheel," and each separate shop in it is denominated a "hull." The annexed engraving gives a very faithful description of

A SHEFFIELD GRINDERS' "HULL."

a grinders' "hull." The grinding wheels are amongst the most curious and characteristic of the manufacturing sights of Sheffield. The stranger looks in through the open door or window, and, after he has grown accustomed to the confused hubbub caused by the whirling and rattling of the machinery, the hiss of the steam-engine, and the noise of the grinding, he examines with lively interest the " wheel" and its occupants. The whole place is tinged with a peculiar brownish yellow hue, caused by the particles thrown off from the stones on which the blades are ground. These stones are revolving rapidly, and at each of them sits a workman, his hand grasping the steel, which, held dexterously to the surface of the stone, sends forth a continuous shower of sparks. In this way the tangs before described are ground, together with one side of the blade, preparatory to its being marked. This process is technically termed " laying on."

The next process the blades undergo is that of " marking." The marker's shop is the counterpart of the forger's. On a coke fire a narrow iron tray is laid, on which the blades to be marked are arranged. The fire is intensified by the application of the bellows until the blades assume a dull red heat, called " worm red." Then, the blades being sufficiently soft, the marker takes up six or eight of them with his tongs, lays them upon the anvil, and, lifting his mark and hammer, cuts the manufacturer's name and corporate or distinguishing mark into the tang, and in many instances on the side of the blade as well. The mark resembles a broad punch, and is made of the very best and hardest steel. In the bottom (or what would be the point of a punch), is carved the name or design of the firm, and this is transferred sufficiently deep into the tang or blade by a single blow.

The blades thus marked are returned to the forger for the purpose of being hardened and tempered. The hardening is done by laying them again upon a small iron tray and heating them to a dull red colour, when they are plunged into cold water. The sudden abstraction of the heat renders the blade very hard and brittle. To overcome this brittleness, what is called the tempering process must be carried out. The blades are first rubbed with some finely-powdered sand, to remove any scaling or unevenness of surface produced by the hardening; they are then placed on an oblong tray made of steel, which is put on the fire, where it remains until the blades assume a straw colour or bright blue tint, when they are removed and allowed to cool. All that the blades now require is giving an edge to them. For this purpose they are again taken to the grinder's " hull," before described, and are there ground. The blades pass thence to the " cutler," accompanied by the other portions necessary to make up the complete knife. First there is the " spring." This constitutes the back of a pocket knife, and is made of steel. The springs used in a knife vary according to the number of blades. There are also the outer and inner " scales." The outer scale is in reality the covering of the knife, and consists of pearl, ivory, horn, shell, wood, or other suitable material. The inner scale is composed of iron, brass, or German silver, and forms the small chambers into which the various blades fit within the outer covering. These materials, with bolsters, rivets, &c., for fastening the whole together, are carried to the cutler's shop, where, besides the

K

tools required for this purpose, there are what are called "buffs" and "glazers" These are necessary for polishing portions of the knife. The process of fitting the materials together and properly securing them is a delicate one, and requires careful and experienced manipulation. The knives, being so far finished, are protected by paper wrapping and returned once more to the grinder for the purpose of being polished. They are brought back to the warehouse, where they are whetted or sharpened, by the edge of each blade being skilfully and rapidly passed over a very hard and peculiar stone, the surface of which is lubricated with olive oil. The knife may now be considered absolutely finished, and only requires to be cleaned before it is ready to be sent away.

In spring knives and every other description of cutlery, the name and mark of Messrs. Joseph Rodgers and Sons are universally known as indicative of goods of the very highest quality and finish. Their showrooms, in Norfolk-street, have for many years been a great attraction to strangers visiting Sheffield who desire to see some of the most elegant productions of the town, or to make purchases of cutlery, plate, articles for presentation, &c., &c., which are here displayed in great profusion and variety. The rooms also contain various pieces of cutlery, curious in workmanship or design, including the celebrated knife made for the International Exhibition, and also one containing as many blades as the date of the year. The success of the firm, and the great and extensive reputation which its productions have acquired, have caused it to be amongst the principal sufferers from the piracies to which we have already referred. In order to prevent these practices as much as possible, Messrs. Rodgers and Sons stamp their goods with their own well-known name, and also their corporate mark ✶ ✠ granted by the Cutlers' Company, and the piracy of which is attended with such heavy penalties that it is seldom attempted. This therefore affords a great protection to the purchasers of their manufactures.

Those who have not recently visited the establisment of Messrs. Rodgers and Sons will be gratified at the great improvement which has been made in the erection of new show-rooms, offices, &c. The former are very tastefully designed, spacious, and most elegantly fitted up. The accompanying engraving gives a good idea of the spacious pile of buildings now occupied by Messrs. Rodgers and Sons, which are amongst the most handsome business structures in the kingdom. The principal front, in Norfolk-street, is about 150 feet in length, and three storeys high in addition to the basement. The room appropriated to the display of cutlery is 45 feet long by 21 feet 6 inches wide, and, communicating with this room at the upper end by an archway, is the department, 54 feet by 20 feet, for silver and plated articles. These rooms are very elegantly fitted up and furnished. It is impossible for the visitor to get a better idea of what is accomplished in the finish and elaboration of cutlery and other Sheffield manufactures, than

FRONT VIEW OF MESSRS. JOSEPH RODGERS AND SONS' WORKS, NORFOLK STREET.

by an inspection of these show-rooms; and nothing can furnish a more striking example of the industry and skill of man, acting upon the raw products of nature.

FRONT VIEW OF WASHINGTON WORKS.—MESSRS. G. WOSTENHOLM AND SON, CUTLERY MANUFACTURERS.

FRONT VIEW OF WASHINGTON WORKS.—MESSRS. G. WOSTENHOLM AND SON.

The largest establishment for the manufacture of spring knives is that of Messrs. George Wostenholm and Son, whose I.XL cutlery takes the highest rank in the United States of America. The two ac-

BACK VIEW OF WASHINGTON WORKS.—MESSRS. G. WOSTENHOLM AND SON, CUTLERY MANUFACTURERS.

BACK VIEW OF WASHINGTON WORKS.—MESSRS. G. WOSTENHOLM AND SON.

companying engravings will convey to the reader an idea of the extent of the premises, which, from the business of the firm being almost exclusively American, are appropriately named Washington Works.

Besides spring knives, however, an immense number of "bowie" knives are made here, together with razors, particularly the razor known as the "Doubly Carbonized I.XL," which is hardened and tempered by a peculiar and secret process. The manufactory stands upon a piece of ground considerably more than an acre in extent, the front being towards Wellington-street. Although the firm is styled "George Wostenholm and Son," it consists only of Mr. George Wostenholm, his father having died nearly thirty years ago. At that period large cutlery works in the town were almost unknown. Indeed, when the Washington Works were erected, the speculation was considered gigantic, and its projector failed in consequence of the place being so large as to be greatly in advance of the requirements of the trade. At that period Mr. Wostenholm, the present proprietor, became the purchaser, and with considerable hesitation removed from his comparatively limited establishment in Rockingham-street. Yet such have been the results of his enterprize that addition after addition has had to be made to the buildings till they have become nearly four times their original size, and no fewer than 800 workpeople find employment on the premises in times of ordinary trade. At the International Exhibition of 1851, Messrs. Wostenholm and Son obtained a prize medal, and at the Paris Exhibition in 1855 they had awarded to them the large gold medal, the only one presented for English cutlery.

TABLE KNIVES AND FORKS.

The ample description we have given of the process of making spring knives will serve to furnish a general idea of the way in which table knives are made, as the operation only varies in detail. In forging the blade of a table knife, two persons are necessary—the maker and the "striker." The cutting part of the blade is first shaped from the end of a bar of steel. It is then welded to a piece of iron which forms the "bolster"—that is, the part which rises round the edge of the handle of the knife ; the "tang," which fastens into the handle, is also shaped. After it has been again heated, the blade is re-hammered on the anvil, and it next goes through the processes of grinding, hardening, tempering, &c. It is then passed to the cutler, and after being hafted again finds its way to the grinder's room to be "buffed" or finished. The hardening and tempering not only of knives but of all cutlery are, it is obvious, processes upon the effectual performance of which the value of the articles, as to their practical use, must very greatly depend ; and it is by the peculiar skill of the workmen in these difficult departments that the reputation of Sheffield cutlery has been in a large measure created and kept up. Besides the trade in table knives with steel blades, there is a large demand for dessert cutlery, which is made of a more elaborate and ornamental character, the handles being commonly of pearl, silver plated, &c., and the blades of silver, or steel or German silver plated with silver. Much taste is shown in the ornamentation of the handles and blades.

GLOBE WORKS.—MESSRS. J. WALTERS AND CO., CUTLERY MANUFACTURERS AND MERCHANTS.

GLOBE WORKS.—MESSRS. J. WALTERS AND CO., CUTLERY MANUFACTURERS.

Forks are forged from a rod of steel about three-eighths of an inch square. The tang, shoulder, and shank are first shaped, and then cut off, leaving at one end about an inch of the square part of the steel.

This is drawn out flat to the length and thickness required for the prongs.   This flat piece is heated till it becomes soft.   It is then placed under a die, which descends upon it and cuts out pieces of the steel in such a way as to leave only the narrow portions that form the prongs of the fork.   The prongs, however, are by this process only roughly shaped, and they have to be carefully filed smooth.   The fork is then ground,* &c., and fixed in the haft, the same as the knife.

Amongst the largest manufacturers of table knives are Messrs. John Walters and Co., of the Globe Works, who send out goods not merely to the United Kingdom but to America, the Continent, &c.   They have obtained a wide reputation for their balance-handled table knives, which possess a peculiar merit.   The preponderance of weight which the handle ought to possess over the blade is ordinarily attained by loading the inside of the haft with lead ; but in the case of ivory-handled knives this expedient is open to the serious objection of discoloration, the lead being visible through the ivory.   "Walters's Patent" obviates this defect by a peculiarity in the "bolster" at the junction of the handle with the blade, which imparts the requisite excess of weight to the handle without presenting any unsightly appearance.   The engraving on the preceding page gives a very accurate delineation of Messrs. J. Walters and Co.'s extensive works.

RAZORS AND SCISSORS.

It is notorious that nothing varies in quality more than razors, and in no kind of cutlery is finish of workmanship so perceptibly valuable. Razors of the highest excellence are forged from the very best qualities of cast steel, and are made with the utmost finish and care in every stage of their progress through the manufactory.   The bars from which they are formed are about half-an-inch in breadth and no thicker than suffices for the back of the razor.   The blade having been forged, the concave surface which is seen on the sides of the razor is made by dexterously working it on the rounded edge of the anvil.   It is then cut off, and the tang is formed either by drawing out the steel or welding on a piece of iron.   The blade after this undergoes the processes of hardening, tempering, &c.

* The "grinder's disease" is peculiar to this occupation, and creates much suffering. It is caused by the particles of stone and metal which are thrown off, lodging in the lungs of the grinders and producing asthma, consumption, and other diseases.   The evil is worst among the fork, razor, and other departments in which *dry* grinding is used.   It is called *wet* grinding when the stone revolves through water.   This of course has a tendency to prevent the particles from flying off.   But in *dry* grinding, which is necessary in some cases, no water is used, and the atoms of stone and steel fly about much more freely, to the great injury of the workmen.   The pain and mortality caused are very great.   A few years ago it was calculated that the average age of all the workmen in the fork-grinding trade was 29, and in the razor-grinding 31.   No doubt the mortality is on the decrease, though but slowly.   In the first place, wet grinding is as far as practicable being substituted for dry; and, secondly, an apparatus has been discovered by which the lungs of the grinders in all the departments are protected from the dust flying from the stones. It consists of a fan on the principle of a winnowing machine, and with a flue to take away the dust from each of the different stones in the room.   When this is properly carried out it in a great measure prevents the dangerous effects of the grinding.   But it is with much difficulty that the grinders can be induced to use the apparatus, though the cost is only about 30s.   Dr. Holland and Dr. J. C. Hall, of Sheffield, have paid great attention to this question.

There are great varieties of scissors, and they vary very much in quality. We may mention, amongst the different kinds, button-hole, cutting-out, tailors', drapers', flower, garden, grape, hair, lace, nail, pocket scissors, &c., &c. In making scissors a single blade is forged, with enough steel at the end for the shank and bow. To shape the bow a hole is punched through, and in this aperture the projecting point of a small anvil is placed, the bow being worked upon it with the hammer. After being softened in the fire, the shank is shaped and the bow is more perfectly rounded with the file. The joint is also squared, and the hole is bored and fitted for the rivet. The blades are next ground and the bows and ornamental work are smooth-filed, &c. The separate blades are then screwed together so as to form the complete scissors. When it is seen that they work properly they are unfastened and hardened and tempered, after which the whetting, polishing, and other finishing processes are performed.

Scissors are frequently manufactured in a most costly and elaborate manner. Those of which we give illustrations have been made by Messrs. Thomas Wilkinson and Son, of New Church-street, who are noted for the manufacture of all kinds of scissors. The first pair of scissors which is shown in the annexed engravings embodies very tastefully the arms of the Duke of Norfolk. The second contains the arms of the Duke of Devonshire, and is a very beautiful piece of workmanship. But the third pair is the gem of the whole. For beauty and finish of detail probably no scissors were ever produced to equal them. They are called the "Victoria Scissors," because they were presented to her Majesty, who expressed her

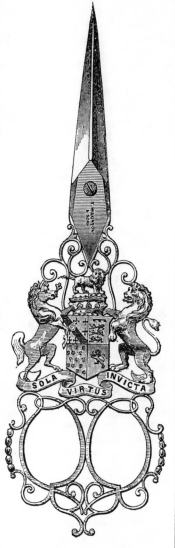

THE NORFOLK SCISSORS.
THOMAS WILKINSON AND SON.

admiration of them. They are from a design furnished by Mr. George Wilkinson (the present Master Cutler.) The scroll-work was executed with small files, of which seventy-two were used, and six weeks

THE DEVONSHIRE SCISSORS.
THOMAS WILKINSON AND SON.

THE VICTORIA SCISSORS.
THOS. WILKINSON & SON.

were spent in the task. The firm has been most enterprizing, not only in introducing new patterns and new styles of ornamentation, but in assisting to maintain the position of Sheffield in the great Exhibitions which have been held. Messrs. Wilkinson and Son were the only Sheffield house which sent goods to the first of these Exhibitions which took place, and which was held at Manchester in 1846. They obtained a medal at the Exhibition of 1851, and were the only manufacturers of scissors who obtained a first-class medal at the Paris Exhibition; and Mr. George Wilkinson was mainly instrumental in establishing the Sheffield Court in the Crystal Palace at Sydenham. Messrs. Wilkinson and Son have paid great attention to the manufacture of tailors' scissors and shears, for which they have a great reputation, and have constructed scissors with springs and other improvements so as to give the greatest possible facility for their use. Quoting from an article on Messrs. Wilkinson and Son's contribution of scissors to the Exhibition of 1851, we may conclude by saying that they "vary in size from one-sixteenth of an inch to 24 inches; in weight, from the twenty-fourth part of a grain to 8 lbs.; and in value, from 2½d. to 20 guineas."

It is impossible in a work of this description to give anything like a complete list even of the principal manufacturers of cutlery, but the following are a selection; those marked * having obtained prize medals at the Exhibition of 1851:—CUTLERY: *Joseph Rodgers and Sons, *G. Wostenholm and Son, *W. and S. Butcher, *T. Turner and Co., M. Hunter and Son, *J. Walters and Co., *Unwin and Rodgers, *J. Nowill and Sons, Mappin Brothers, *J. Wilson and Son; Corsan, Denton, Burdekin, and Co.; F. Newton and Sons, Messrs. Fenton; Wingfield,

Rowbotham, and Co.; Cutler, Chambers, and Co.; W. and S. Horrabin, Harrison Brothers and Howson, Joseph Haywood and Co., Brookes and Crookes, B. Matthewman and Son, Parkin and Marshall, Newbould Brothers, W. Shirley, *S. Hague, *W. Matthews, *J. and G. Morton. RAZORS.—*F. Fenny (now C. Bingham and Co.), *S. Martin, J. and W. Ragg. *Hawcroft and Sons, J. Heiffor, and Gilbert Brothers. SCISSORS.—*W. Wilkinson and Son, *E. Hunter, *Steer and Webster, J. Cousins and Son, *G. W. Higginbotham, J. Gibbons and Sons, W. Badger, Isaac Read and Sons, and G. Wilkin.

FILES, EDGE TOOLS, AND SAWS, ENGINEERS' TOOLS, &c.,

Although Sheffield is popularly known principally as the world's great cutlery mart, an enormous trade is done in files, saws, and edge tools. These goods, unlike cutlery, are in most cases produced by firms which also make steel.

The manufacture of files is very interesting, from the peculiar skill which is manifested in one department of the process. Files vary greatly in shape and size, according to the purposes for which they are wanted. For good files, the best steel has obviously to be used, or the file itself would be worn away instead of the metal operated upon. The bar of steel for the file is first forged in the usual way, and the tang having been shaped, &c., the smooth file, if it may be so called, is taken to the cutters' shop to be roughened in that way which gives

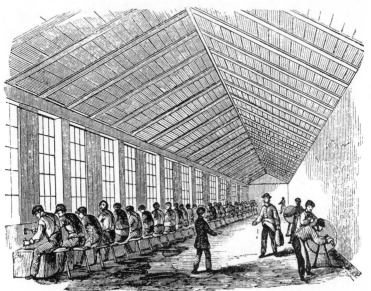

FILE CUTTERS' SHOP.—W. HALL AND SON, ALMA WORKS.

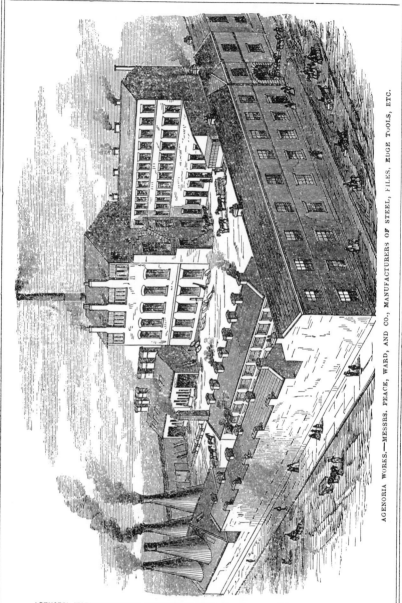

AGENORIA WORKS.—MESSRS. PEACE, WARD, AND CO., MANUFACTURERS OF STEEL, FILES, EDGE TOOLS, ETC.

AGENORIA WORKS.—MESSRS. PEACE, WARD, AND CO., MANUFACTURERS OF STEEL, ETC.

the characteristic property to the tool. File cutting is all done by hand, and the process furnishes one of the most remarkable instances of manual dexterity which is to be seen in the whole round of human

MESSRS. BEARDSHAW AND SONS, MANUFACTURERS OF STEEL, FILES, SAWS, ETC.

industry. The engraving at page 147 gives a representation of a row of file-cutters at work. Under the windows there are a number of low stone benches, and close to them the seats for the workmen. The hammer which the cutter uses weighs from one to six pounds, according to the size of the file to be operated upon ; and it is constructed so as to allow the metal which composes its head to be pulled towards the workman while he is making the blows on the file. The chisel is formed of very strong, tough steel, and, like the hammer, varies with the size of the file it is used upon. When the workman proceeds to cut, the chisel is held in the left hand, somewhat in the same way as a pen, and so that the hollow of the hand is turned towards the workman. But this is only a general description, and the mode of working varies with the different kinds of files. The file is held in its place by means of a leather strap passing over each end, and going round the feet of the workman, like stirrups. At each blow of the chisel a tooth is cut, and the blows are repeated in rapid succession until the whole surface of the file is covered, the file being moved as required by loosening the tread on the straps. When one side of the file is finished, the workman deals with the other in the same manner ; but as the finished part would be liable to injury if unprotected while the second side is cut, a flat piece of metal, being a mixture of lead and tin, is placed under it during the process. It is quite impossible to obtain an adequate notion of the skill of the workmen in cutting the various kinds of files, without an inspection of their labours. Some idea, however, of the dexterity required, may be gathered from the fact that in fine round files as many as from ten to twenty rows of cuts are required to cover the surface with teeth ; and there are sometimes more than a hundred teeth within the space of an inch.

The question of file-cutting machines is one of great interest in the trade. Many attempts have been made to carry out the process by machinery, but hitherto without success. Simple as the operation appears, there are certain qualities of manipulation which it seems almost impossible to impart by means of machinery. For instance, the clever workman not only adapts the strength of his blow to the kind of steel he is operating on, but, even in the same file, if he finds one part softer than another, he regulates the fall of his chisel so that the size of the teeth shall be the same in every part. The most recent of the machines for file-cutting is one which is now in use in Manchester, and the practical merits of which remain to be tested.*

Messrs. Turton and Sons are large manufacturers of files, saws, edge tools, and also of steel and railway springs. Their place of business, called the Sheaf Works, is close beneath the ticket platform at the Victoria Station of the Manchester, Sheffield, and Lincolnshire Railway, approached from the south or east. The platform is situated right over the chief thoroughfare of Sheaf Works, intersecting it about the centre. The scene, looking down from the railway platform into the works, is very striking, especially at night. The railway viaduct is here very high, and composed of open-arched masonry. One of the arches completely spans the road, the crown of which is at an elevation of about 30 feet from the base. The next arch on each side is used for a spring maker's shop. The works are very large. The

---

* The file-cutters of Sheffield show a very natural antipathy towards the machines which have been invented, and entertain great contempt for their mechanical rivals. The present undertaking at Manchester has called forth from one of their number an effusion which is far more vigorous and poetic ; but a few verses of it will give in a characteristic shape the views of the workmen :—

> " It's the wonder of wonders, is this mighty steam hammer,
> What folks say it will do, it would make any one stammer;
> They say it will cut files as fast as three men and a lad,
> But two out of three, it's a fact, they are bad.
>
> " They say it will strike 300 strokes in a minute,
> If this is a fact, there will be something serious in it ;
> The tooth that is on them looks fine to the eye,
> But they're not worth a rush when fairly they're tried.
>
> " These Manchester cotton lords seem mighty keen
> To take trade from old Sheffield with this cutting machine :
> They've a secret to learn—they know it's a truth—
> The machine's naught like flesh and blood to raise up the tooth.
>
> " So unite well together, by good moral means,
> Don't be intimidated by these infernal machines ;
> Let them boast as they will—and though the press clamour,
> After all, lads, there's nothing like wrist, chisel, and hammer."

SHEAF WORKS.—MESSRS. T. TURTON AND SONS, MANUFACTURERS OF STEEL, FILES, ETC.

canal which runs from Hull intersects them; and this is a great convenience, as the Swedish iron which they use in large quantities is
carried from that port direct to the works and landed there.   Messrs.

Turton and Sons are amongst the oldest firms in the town, and possess a high reputation for all their various manufactures. They make steel of all kinds, and for every purpose. They are especially noted for files and edge tools. In edge tools they succeeded the eminent house of Messrs. William Greaves and Sons, of the same works ; and they have greatly increased the former reputation of this firm. Their " Boracic" edge tools are made by a peculiar process, and are of such repute that they command a higher price than any other goods of the same kind. Messrs. Turton and Sons may be considered to be at the head of the file trade.

The quality of Messrs. Turton & Sons' files is amusingly illustrated by the following extract from *The Times* of July 26th, 1851 :—" Sheffield *v* France.—At a public dinner given last week at the Cutlers' Hall, Sheffield, to the Great Exhibition Local Commissioners for that town, one of these gentlemen (Mr. Overend) related the following interesting anecdote :—' There was a French gentleman among the jurors, who very properly showed great zeal in protecting the interests of his countrymen. He had admitted that Sheffield made very good files, but he maintained that there was a house in France that could make better. He challenged Sheffield to the trial, and selected the house with which he would make the trial. It happened to be that of which my worthy friend, the Mayor (Mr. Turton) is the head. He sent to France to have files made for that purpose. He brought over a French engineer to use them, and he challenged Messrs. Turton and Sons to the contest. Two pieces of steel were selected upon which to try the files, and they were fixed in two vices. Messrs. Turton accepted the challenge, but they did not send to Sheffield to have any files made specially for the occasion. They merely went to a London customer whom they supplied with files, and took files indiscriminately from his stock. They chose a man from among the Sappers and Miners in the Exhibition to use their file against the French engineer and the French files made for the trial. The two pieces of steel being fixed in the vices, the men began to work upon them simultaneously. The Englishman, with Messrs. Turton's file, had filed the steel down to the vice before the French engineer had got one-third through. When the files were examined, Messrs. Turton's file was found to be as good as ever, while the French file was nearly worn out. The French juror then said, no doubt he was beaten in that trial, but Messrs. Turton's file must have been made to cut steel alone, whereas the French file was better adapted for iron. A new trial then took place upon iron, and the result was still more in favour of the English file.' "

The jury on cutlery and edge tools in connection with the 1851 Exhibition stated :—" In the United Kingdom, London, Sheffield, Birmingham, Warrington and Stourbridge, Edinburgh and Glasgow, Cork, Clonmel, and Limerick sent contributions to this class. But for extent, variety, and excellence of collection, none could compare with Sheffield. In the collection from this town were articles of the

most refined as well as the most ordinary character with various degrees of merit, but with a large proportion of the highest.   Had
singular excellence of workmanship and quality been a sufficient title
to a Council medal, the jury would have felt called upon to award it
to Messrs. Turton and Sons, of Sheffield, who displayed a complete
assortment of files of various sizes for ordinary manufacturing purposes, which for large dimensions, combined with the utmost strength
and efficiency of material, far surpassed others of the same class.   The
jury deemed them worthy of the highest assignable reward in respect
of these points of merit." At the Paris Exhibition, in 1855, Messrs.
Turton and Sons obtained the gold medal.

Edge tools, which are made very largely in Sheffield, comprise chisels,
gouges, plane irons, axes, adzes, &c.   The processes of manufacture vary
much in detail, but none of them exhibits any principle which requires
illustration, beyond what has already been described.   Formerly the
whole of the edge tools used were made in Sheffield ; but there are
some now manufactured at Birmingham.   Sheffield, however, need not
fear the competition of the makers of that town.   There are also edge
tools produced to some extent in America and Germany ; but the
quality of the goods made in Sheffield is evidenced by the fact that
very large consignments are regularly ordered for use in Germany.
Akin to the trade in edge tools is that of joiners' tools, which are made
here upon an extensive scale.

The manufacture of saws is one of the oldest of the staple trades,
and is almost exclusively confined to Sheffield.   Steel of the best
quality for saws being cast into ingots of proper weight, and reduced by rolling into sheets, is then cut into the shape required
by a paring machine worked by steam power, which will cut metal,
at a stroke, 3 feet 6 inches long and three-eighths of an inch
thick, with the greatest rapidity and accuracy.   It is then taken to
the toother, who places the sawplate on a bed.   A punch is forced
down by steam power and cuts out a piece of steel, leaving the edge
standing of the exact size and form required for the tooth.   The
saw is then moved a space, and a similar process is performed until
the whole saw is toothed.   It is then marked and filed, after which
it is submitted to the hardening process, which is peculiar. The saw
is placed in a furnace heated to a high and uniform temperature,
after which it is taken out and immersed in oil, resin, &c., which
have the property of hardening the saw to the proper degree.   This
process requires great care and experience ; for, heated too highly, the
saw becomes brittle, and if the heat does not reach a certain temperature it will be too soft.   It is then carefully tempered, after which it is
submitted to the action of hammering on an anvil.   This process requires the exercise of great skill and judgment on the part of the workman, to reduce the uneven face produced by hardening into a perfectly level and solid surface.   It is now prepared for the grinder,
under whose hands it undergoes very elaborate manipulations.   The

L

stones at which saws are ground are much larger than those previously described. The grinder, after shaping the back, places the saw on a "scorching" board, and brings it then across the grindstone. Unlike the grinder of cutlery or edge tools, he does not sit at his work, but, placing his knees on one edge of the scorching board and his hands at the other, works the saw across the stone from the tooth edge to the back, moving it transversely from heel to point. Having thus ground it on both sides crossway, which is called "scorching," he then grinds it lengthway, which is called "drawing," the grinder bringing the whole weight of his body to bear upon the saw as it moves along the surface of the rapidly-revolving stone. Straight saws are usually ground thinner towards the back. The circular saw in the process of grinding is secured to a vertical circular-faced plate, opposite to which is a "lap," which reduces the surface to a smooth face, sliding backwards and forwards slightly reducing it from the circumference to the centre; the emery, sand, or grit for grinding is fed into the lap-box in a wet state by the attendant, and the saw revolves in its plate against the reducing lap. The next process is hammering, which corrects any irregularity that has arisen from the friction caused by grinding. Long saws are then stiffened or tempered by being placed over a coke fire until they assume a straw colour. The saw is next polished, and then rubbed by a machine, which obviates the laborious and unhealthy process of rubbing by hand. If a short saw, it goes to the setter and sharper, who sets or bends the teeth alternately with a hammer, so as to enable it in actual work to cut with little friction. After setting, the teeth are made sharp by filing, and the saw is ready for the handle.

At the Ætna Works of Messrs. Spear and Jackson the process of saw-making in all its branches may be seen carried out upon a very large scale. These extensive premises are situated in Saville-street East, adjoining the Midland Railway. Besides their other branches of industry, Messrs. Spear and Jackson are large manufacturers of steel. In the saw department the most interesting process is that of making the large circular saws. It is curious to see the ease and accuracy with which the immense pieces of steel (some of them weighing nearly 8 cwt., and being three-eighths of an inch thick) are passed through the various processes of manufacture; machinery being used to facilitate much of the work. Files and edge tools of all kinds are also made here. Some new branches of manufacture have been during the last few years introduced by this firm—namely, spades and shovels for agricultural and horticultural purposes, and also hay, manure, and digging forks. These are superior from being made of the best hand-hammered cast steel, and tempered by a peculiar process. Each of the tools is forged out of a solid piece of steel, so that there is no chance of any flaw from welding. The consequence of their being made, by improved processes, entirely of the best qualities of steel instead of partly iron, is that they are lighter, more elastic, will stand a considerable strain without fear of breaking, and are

ÆTNA WORKS.—MESSRS. SPEAR AND JACKSON, MANUFACTURERS OF SAWS, FILES, EDGE TOOLS, ETC.

ÆTNA WORKS.—MESSRS. SPEAR AND JACKSON, MANUFACTURERS OF SAWS, ETC.

much more durable; so that, while the persons using them can get through a considerably increased amount of labour, they wear about four times as long as the old-fashioned spades and forks.   Their superiority is so manifest that they bid fair in a short time entirely to supersede the former kind of forks. The firm has obtained a great reputation for these goods, of which a vast number are used not only in this country, but also on the Continent, in Australia, &c. Messrs. Spear and Jackson have received first-class distinctions at the Exhibitions of 1851 and 1855, at the former taking the only Council medal, and at the latter the only gold medal and decoration, for their class of goods. As one of the members has been selected as juror for the present Exhibition of 1862, they have altogether refrained from sending anything to it, leaving the field open for other manfacturers. Mr. Samuel Jackson received from the Emperor of the French, at the Exhibition of 1855, the cross of the Legion of Honour.

President Works, of which we give an engraving on the opposite page, are the business premises of another extensive house in the saw trade—Messrs. Moses Eadon and Sons. The business was originally founded by the late Mr. Moses Eadon, and by the excellence of his manufactures, aided by the enterprize and energy of his sons, who now carry it on, the house has rapidly risen to that of one of the first in the trade. Saw making has wonderfully improved of late. Up to the beginning of the present century saws worked by machinery were unknown. Since that period there have been brought into use the circular saw; the balk or timber frame saw, cutting six deals at one time; the segment saw, 20 feet in diameter, cutting Honduras mahogany 5 feet wide and 16 veneers to the inch; the endless-band saw with its perpetual cut, doing its work with marvellous truth and celerity. These and other changes have called for improved methods in manufacture, which have been carried out by no firm more fully than by Messrs Eadon and Sons. The solid endless band or belt saw is patented by Messrs. Eadon. It is of the greatest use in cutting large timber, and may be seen, with Messrs. Eadon's other saws, at work in the Government dockyards. A circular saw shown by Messrs. Eadon in the Exhibition is believed to be the largest ever made. It is 7 feet $2\frac{1}{2}$ inches in diameter. In this description of saws, contrasted with those which preceded it, the progress is very remarkable. Fifty years ago a pit-saw was used in the saw-pit, and with it two men painfully toiled along, getting through a tree probably in the course of a day. The circular saws have come into use, and have progressed till we have the enormous one alluded to, with which a man might cut his way through the thickest timber as fast as he could walk. The President Works are situated in Saville-street East, on the Midland Railway; and there Messrs. Eadon and Sons manufacture not only saws but also steel, files, tools, machine knives, &c. They roll steel for crinoline, and also make steel for the royal small-arms factory at Enfield. Messrs. Eadon and Sons have an extensive demand for their goods in this country, and also in Russia and Canada. It is in saws that the great reputation of the firm consists. The solid saw tillars or buckles which are

PRESIDENT WORKS.—MESSRS. MOSES EADON AND SONS, MANUFACTURERS OF SAWS, ETC.

now so generally adopted by the trade were first made by Messrs,
Eadon. Solid cylinder saws are made here of the largest size, and
also the finest saws used in the most delicate surgical operations.

Mr. William Hall, of the Alma Works, Barker-pool, is a large manufacturer of steel, files, edge-tools, saws, &c. The firm has been extensively known in the trade for seventy or eighty years. It has acquired a high reputation for the manufacture of these articles. The premises of the firm were originally in Porter-street, whence they were removed, from the necessity of extension, to the present works in Barker-pool. The accompanying sketch gives an idea of their extent. The illustrations of grinding and file-cutting, which accompany the description of these processes, are taken from the manufactory at the Alma-Works. In erecting the present buildings, great attention has been paid to sanitary requirements, which in the construction of such works were formerly altogether overlooked. The forging shops, instead of being each a small separate building, as used to be the case, are open to each other for the purpose of ventilation through the whole length of the building, without anything to break the free current of air. There is every convenience for carrying on the various trades; and furnaces for the conversion and casting of the best kinds of steel have been erected since the original construction of the works.

The pre-eminence of Sheffield for its manufacture of files, edge-tools, joiners' tools, saws, &c., was demonstrated by the large proportion of prize medals awarded in these departments to Sheffield houses. Without attempting to give anything like a complete list of the trade, we may, for the guidance of strangers, name the following as amongst the principal houses:—FILES: *Turton and Sons, *C. Cammell and Co., J. Kenyon and Co., Spencer and Sons, *Jowitt and Son, *T. Turner and Co., *Joseph Peace and Co., Peace, Ward, and Co., Peace Brothers, W. K. Peace and Co., Marriott and Atkinson, Shortridge, Howill, & Co.; Machen, Miller, & Co.; Hobson, Hill & Son , Tyzack and Sons, Henry Rossell and Co., Earl, Smith, and Co.; M. and J. Wing, J. Wing and Co., S. Wing and Co., Beardshaw and Stevenson, &c. EDGE TOOLS, JOINERS' TOOLS, &c.—*R. Sorby and Sons, *Ward and Payne, Lockwood Brothers, *Ibbotson Brothers, *J. Ibbotson, *Brookes and Sons, *Marsden Brothers, *Mathewman & Son, *W. Makin and Son, *J. Howarth, *Blake and Parkin (now J. Parkin and Co.,) F. G. Pearson and Co., &c. SAWS, &c.—*Spear and Jackson, Slack, Sellars, and Co.; S. S. Brittain and Co., J. Beardshaw and Son, Eadon and Sons, Groves and Sons, A. Beckett, Wheatman and Smith, C. Gray and Son, Taylor Brothers, &c. Those marked * obtained prize medals at the Exhibition of 1851.

CRINOLINE.

The making up of crinoline from the raw steel into the finished skirts is a most interesting process. Probably Messrs. R. and G. Gray and Co. make a greater quantity of crinoline than any one else in the world. The firm has two places where the manufacture is carried on, one in Pond-hill and the other at the Castle-mills. The steel arrives at the works in lengths, rolled sufficiently thin for use, and about three

ALMA WORKS.—MR. WILLIAM HALL, MANUFACTURER OF STEEL, FILES, SAWS, ETC.

inches in width.   The first operation is to cut the metal into narrow
strips, which is done by a machine that performs the operation with
wonderful celerity and precision.   The width of the steel, as it is thus

CRINOLINE ROOM.—MESSRS R. AND G. GRAY AND CO.

cut up for use, varies from about an inch to one-sixteenth of an inch.
The best class of skirts are made of the narrowest kinds of steel, a
greater number of which are put in, and the skirt is thus made more
light and elastic.   The steel is next hardened and tempered, after
which it is wound round large bobbins and carried into the room where
the cotton is bound round it.   Probably there is not a more curious
manufacturing sight to be seen than is contained in this room.   Upon
first entering the scene is quite bewildering, and the effect is increased
by the noise, which is deafeningly loud.   It seems at a glance as though
hundreds and hundreds of large reels of cotton had become animated,
and were frantically whirling about in a dance-like motion.   When the
details of the room are examined, the interest of the spectacle is increased rather than diminished.   The saltatory motion is in reality the
action of myriads upon myriads of yards of cotton in the process of
being twisted round the steel.   This is done by means of a mass of
intricate machinery, worked by steam power.   The bobbin of steel is
placed below, and a number of smaller bobbins of cotton are fixed over
it.   The steel unwinds itself slowly, and the threads of cotton are
rapidly unwound, braided round the steel, and firmly fixed there so as
to cover its surface.   The number of threads which thus gyrate and
wind themselves round the steel vary in particular branches of the
manufacture, in some instances numbering twelve, in others running
up as high as thirty-two.   There are other varieties of the process;
but the one described is the most prominent, and the general result of

all of them is the same—the steel comes out securely covered with cotton. In the meantime the skirts are being prepared for the reception of the steel. Some are made a sort of skeleton-work, and the whole body of them is formed with the flexible steel hoops, covered as described. But others are much more elaborately finished. The material of the skirts varies, comprising calico, net, alpaca, mohair, &c. The material, whatever it may be, is first made up into the petticoat shape required. In the case of net, it is then finished by the steel (which is cut into the required lengths) being inserted, hoop-wise, through the apertures which exist in the net, and fastened together at the ends. But in the skirts of calico, alpaca, &c., another process has to be gone through. For this purpose sewing machines are brought into requisition. From sixty to seventy of these machines are in use at the Pond-hill works. The machine literally gallops with its ready stitches across the breadth of the skirt, the female who presides at each of them merely holding the material in its place. The object of the stitching is to fasten a breadth of tape round the circumference of the skirt, inside. When this is done, the cotton-covered steel is placed within the tape; and thus the skirt is ready to give to the ladies of the universe the amplest rotundity of figure to which the most ambitious of them can be desirous of aspiring. Some of the skirts are most beautifully finished, and are quite equal to the dresses ordinarily worn. From 500 to 800 persons—according to the demand for crinoline—are employed in the various branches of the manufacture at Messrs. Gray's, and almost all of them are females. The engraving on the preceding page represents one of the rooms at Messrs. Gray's, where steel is inserted in the skirts.

Messrs. Harry Holdsworth and Co., of the Spring works; New George-street, besides their general steel and tool trade, make up a large number of crinoline skirts. They are now preparing a room for the erection of new machinery, the dimensions of which are larger than those of any similar one in the town. Messrs. Clayton, Rourke, and Co., of Arundel Street, also do a large business in crinoline making.

ENGINEERING TOOLS, &c.

By many persons, Manchester and Leeds are thought to be the only places where the manufacture of machinery and engineers' tools is carried on to any great extent; and until the last few years this was the case. Latterly, however, in its rapid extension, Sheffield has taken up this branch of industry, and promises to be a formidable rival to the places mentioned, there being already a large and increasing demand for the productions of Sheffield in these departments. In former times any one would have taken the word "tool" to apply entirely to an instrument which could be worked with the hand; but, with the wonderful growth of machinery, this definition of the term has become obsolete. The tool now to a large extent takes the place of the workman, and may be of any size, weight, or degree of intricacy. To follow

INTERIOR OF MESSRS. DRURY BROTHERS AND WALKER'S FITTING AND ERECTING SHOP.

out the construction and uses of these complicated implements, is a very interesting task. One of the manufactories in which this may be fully done is the Don Tool Works, Mowbray-street, belonging to Messrs.

Drury Brothers and Walker. The great number of lathes and fixed machinery at work, moving in various directions, and the network of bands crossing on every hand, are quite bewildering to the eye on first entering the workshops. We have endeavoured to give an idea of the whole by an illustration of part of the works. The forging shops and smithies are on the opposite side of the premises. Almost everything is done by self-acting machinery. Thus in the manufacture of a lathe the bed is planed perfectly true and smooth on a planing-machine. The screw for it is cut in a screw-cutting lathe. The heads are bored true by a machine made for the purpose. All the holes are bored by drilling machines. The wheels and pulleys are turned in lathes. The key-gates are cut out by a slotting machine, and other parts of it squared by shaping machines. All these tools are manufactured by Messrs. Drury Brothers and Walker, together with many others, including punching and shearing machines, which cut iron and steel of an enormous thickness as though it were lead; cutting and grooving machines, bolt screwing machines, circular saw tables, upright saw frames, &c., &c. The other branch of trade carried on at these works is also a very important one. It includes all kinds of lifting-jacks for raising weights from 1 ton to 20 tons with ease, screwing tackle for cutting screws in iron, ratchet-braces for boring holes in iron, vices, cramps, flys, hammers, spanners, &c., &c.

Amongst the other large firms in the same line, we may mention Messrs. Easterbrook and Allcard, and the Messrs. Brookes.

STEEL WIRE.

An important manufacture of recent development, but which is growing rapidly, is carried on largely at the premises of Messrs. Cocker Brothers. Their wire mills and offices are situated in Nursery-street. They also manufacture steel on these premises, and at the Navigation Works and at Wardsend. The firm was originally established in 1752. The predecessors of Messrs. Cocker Brothers were the first manufacturers of cast steel wire, and they have obtained an extensive reputation for the quality of their goods. The value of cast steel wire over that made from iron is obviously very great, it being much lighter, more elastic, and more durable. The process of wire-drawing is a very delicate and beautiful operation. For the general kinds of wire, the steel is reduced by rolling to a quarter of an inch in thickness. It is then drawn through dies, graduating in size down to the fineness of hair. The wire is gradually reduced by being passed through these dies. Before being put into the die, the end of the wire is filed down till it fits the hole; and the power of the machinery, acting by steam, irresistibly draws the yielding metal through. But a preliminary process is necessary each time the steel wire is reduced, because in its state as it comes from the rolling mills it would be too hard, and would offer too great a resistance to the pressure of the die. It is therefore annealed, or softened. The old process of annealing consisted merely in baking

WORKS OF MESSRS. COCKER BROTHERS, MANUFACTURERS OF STEEL WIRE, FILES, ETC.

the wire for a certain time in heated ovens. Messrs. Cocker Brothers, however, have introduced a new process, which they have patented. The wire is taken red-hot out of the furnace and plunged into a bath of boiling water. When taken out it is cool enough to handle, and this operation makes the metal more soft and pliable, and removes all roughness from the surface. One of the most interesting processes carried on in these works is the making of pinion-wire. This wire is cut up into suitable lengths, and forms in that shape the cog-wheels used in watches and clocks. Of course, being employed for such delicate pieces of mechanism, the wire must necessarily be made most exact in size, and though it is drawn in many instances exceedingly small, none of it has less than six grooves, while some of it has twelve. The process does not essentially differ from that of ordinary wire-drawing, the only difference being that the dies are grooved instead of round. The watch motion-wire is made exquisitely fine—finer in fact than hair. Its price in weight is equal to that of gold; and one pound weight of it will produce a length of 552,960 inches. It is obvious that the dies through which these different kinds of wire have to be drawn must be very carefully made. Indeed, everything depends upon their precision of finish, especially in the pinion-wire, in which the minutest irregularity would altogether destroy the value of the finished article. Amongst the other productions which are sent out by Messrs. Cocker Brothers are needles, of which 5,000 may be seen wrapped up in a packet that will go comfortably in the waistcoat pocket. They manufacture large quantities of steel springs for watches, and steel ribs for the framework of umbrellas and parasols; and they roll steel into the shape required for making crinoline skirts. Another very important manufacture which is coming largely into use is the steel wire rope. This rope is of enormous strength, being formed of six strands twisted together, and each containing six pieces of wire. A rope thus composed of thirty-six thicknesses of the best steel must be evidently much stronger than almost any iron rope which could be made, in addition to which it is much easier to work, from its lightness and elasticity. All the pinion-wire, which used formerly to be made by hand, is now drawn by machinery; and the consequence is that a much greater quantity is used, and the price is reduced by more than one-half. This short sketch of their establishment is confined principally to steel wire, although they manufacture very largely steel in all its branches, files, edge tools, hackles, gills, and a great variety of articles too numerous to particularize in a work of this nature: they are also general merchants, and their predecessors, Samuel Cocker and Son, obtained three first-class prize medals at the Exhibition of 1851. Cocker Brothers were awarded a first-class medal at Paris in 1855; and a medal of honour by the Society of Arts in London, in 1856.

In this branch of manufacture there are other eminent houses, amongst which may be mentioned Messrs. James Cocker and Co., Messrs. Worrall, Hallam, and Co., and Messrs. Hadfield and Shipman. The last-mentioned firm shows some very beautiful specimens at the present Exhibition.

SURGICAL INSTRUMENTS.

The manufacture of surgical instruments is a branch of the Sheffield trade, though it is not generally known as such. This arises from the London shopkeepers claiming the credit of making the goods. The same as in general cutlery, the Metropolitan dealers are anxious to persuade their customers that all the best instruments are made by themselves; and so large is the consumption of their goods by means of the London shops, that the Sheffield makers did not in 1851 deem it advisable to take steps to remove the impression which prevails, by sending goods to the Exhibition of that year. At the International Exhibition of 1862 more spirit has been shown,

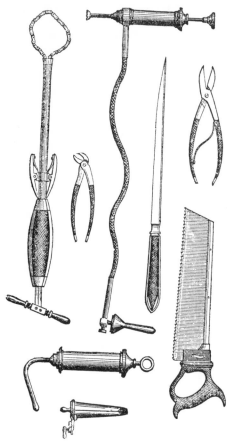

SURGICAL INSTRUMENTS. MR. W. SKIDMORE.   EYE DOUCHE.—MR. W. SKIDMORE.

and two firms have sent goods. The productions of the town are, however, shown there in abundance as the products of London houses with whose names they are stamped. A vast number of these formidable-looking yet very necessary instruments are manufactured here, and the precision and beautiful finish with which they are made are very great. One of the above engravings represents a group of a small number of the great variety made by Mr. William Skidmore, surgical, dental, and veterinary instrument maker, Cemetery-road and Pearl-street. The article to the left of the group is an *Ecraseur*, and is a French instrument, as its name imports. It is used instead of the knife for removing tumours, and prevents the effusion of blood. The other instruments are self-explanatory. The next engraving represents the eye douche, a most useful instrument for many affections of that organ, and one which can be used with the greatest ease by the patient himself. It consists of a syphon with elastic tube, to which is attached a glass cup, so adapted to the eye that no fluid can escape, except through a second tube into the waste basin. Mr. Skidmore also makes an ear douche of similar construction, the only difference being in the shape of the glass cup, at the bottom of which is a pipe passing into the orifice of the ear. The pipe is so constructed that it cannot pass too far and injure the interior of the ear, as is sometimes the case with the ordinary syringes, if they are not used with care. The *Medical Times and Gazette* says:—"The great advantage of these douches is, that the patient avoids the splashing and discomfort of having the fluid running down the neck or face, a great objection to the ordinary syringe ; and the patient never uses the same fluid twice." Some of the other principal houses in this trade are Messrs. W. and H. Hutchinson ; Lawson, Buxton, and Co. ; A. Green, Joseph Gray and Co., Joseph Ellis and Son, &c.

SILVER-PLATING, BRITANNIA METAL, &c.

These manufactures may be well illustrated in connection with the firm of Messrs. James Dixon and Sons, Cornish-place. The extent of their productions may be judged of by the fact that the works cover about four acres of land, and that more than 700 workpeople are employed in them.

The art of silver-plating is purely a Sheffield invention. The process was first discovered by Mr. Thomas Bolsover, in 1742. He was employed to repair the handle of a knife composed partly of silver and partly of copper, and was struck by the possibility of combining the two metals so as to present the appearance of silver. He began the manufacture, but did not carry it out to any very considerable extent. It was developed and brought into general use by Mr. Joseph Hancock. The original silver-plating process is carried out in the following manner :—An ingot of copper is cast, and is filed so as to give a perfect surface. A plate of silver is then fastened on it with wire. The ingot is put in a heated furnace until the silver is sufficiently melted to unite with the copper. The ingot is then rolled into sheets such as are required for the articles to be manufactured, the silver adhering to the copper so as to give a beautiful surface to the metal. Such was the method of silver-plating which for many years exclusively prevailed ; but it was materially interfered with by the discovery of the electro-plating process. This was invented by Mr. Wright, of Norton, near Sheffield. The process was purchased from him by a Birmingham firm, and has been carried out in that town to a large extent. Sheffield, however, is competing very successfully with Birmingham in electro-plating. The electro process is as follows:—A quantity of fine silver is dissolved in water with cyadine of potassium. In the vat containing this liquid are inserted sheets of silver, and the articles to be plated are suspended between these sheets. A galvanic battery, which is connected with the solution, is set at work ; and the silver is deposited on the articles from the sheets of silver, the solution acting as the guide. This process is very interesting to witness. Another process is in use by Messrs. Dixon, who for the last five or six years have abandoned copper as a basis for plating, using instead the modern metal, nickel silver. This is a composition of nickel, copper, and zinc. Nickel possesses the property of whitening the copper when mixed with it in proper proportions. The compound called *nickel silver* proves to be very valuable in use. It is employed not only as a substitute for copper in the old plating process, but also as a basis for electro-plating. Sheffield has never lost its reputation as the seat of the manufacture of first-class plated ware ; and " Sheffield plate" is still used as a term to designate first-class goods of this description.

Another industrial process which is largely carried on at Cornish-place is the manufacture of Britannia metal wares. This useful compound was first begun to be used to a considerable extent about 1770, by Messrs. Jessop and Hancock. Britannia metal is composed of block tin, copper, brass, and martial regulus of antimony. The tin is melted and raised to a red heat in a cast-iron trough. Into the liquid metal is poured the regulus of antimony, the copper, and brass, each of these having also been reduced to a melted state. While they are poured in, the compound is carefully stirred by the workman who has the management of it. When they are thoroughly mixed, the compound is transferred either to iron boxes, in which it cools in the shape of slabs, or into moulds, in which it takes the form of ingots. Britannia metal is most tractable to work, and has a very beautiful appearance when well finished. It is, indeed, so like silver that there was considerable difficulty, in the case of some of the articles exhibited in the Great Exhibition of 1851, in distinguishing the difference. So marked was this, for instance, in the case of the goods shown by Messrs. Dixon and Sons, that the authorities recommended them to inscribe the words " Britannia metal" on the cases, that the goods might not be mistaken for silver. Britannia metal has almost entirely thrown pewter wares into disuse. It is sometimes called " Prince's metal," and is commonly styled by the workmen " white metal." In addition to its ordinary use it is employed as a basis for electro-plating, for which it makes a cheap and durable material. There has been no material improvement or change in the composition of Britannia metal for the last forty years.

CORNISH PLACE.—MESSRS. JAMES DIXON AND SONS, MANUFACTURERS OF SILVER PLATE, BRITANNIA METAL GOODS, POWDER FLASKS, ETC.

CORNISH PLACE.—MESSRS. JAMES DIXON AND SONS, MANUFACTURERS OF SILVER PLATE, ETC.

Messrs. Dixon and Sons also carry on a very extensive trade in powder flasks and other shooting apparatus. Their show-rooms at Cornish-place contain numerous beautifully-finished specimens of all

M

their different branches of manufacture. The sight is a most interesting one to the stranger, the beauty of design and finished make of
the plated goods being of the very highest kind. A large collection of
powder flasks and other shooting apparatus, with Britannia metal wares,
are shown in one room, and silver and silver-plated goods in another. An
enormous number of powder-flasks are manufactured by the firm. For
these and other conveniences for sporting, " Messrs. Dixon and Sons,
of Sheffield, are a hundred to one against the world," says Frank For-
rester, the author of " Field Sports in the United States." The house
does a large business in silver goods, and has a special reputation
for its presentation plate. Mr. Alderman Fawcett, one of the members of the firm, had the honour of receiving, in 1855, as Mayor of
Sheffield, from the Emperor of the French, the gold medal awarded
to the town for its position in the Paris Exhibition of that year. This
mark of distinction is in the care of the Cutlers' Company. It has
been placed in a case, with the names of all the exhibitors engraved
on a silver plate accompanying it. At the Exhibition of 1851 two
medals were awarded to Messrs. Dixon and Sons, one for their Britannia metal and one for sporting articles. The firm also received a
first-class medal at the Paris Exhibition of 1855. This business was
established in 1806, and has gradually increased to its present magnitude.

Messrs. Walker and Hall, of the Electro Works, Howard-street, carry
on a large business in silver-plating and gilding for the trade. They
are also making special efforts in connection with electro-bronzing.
This beautiful process is little known to the general public. It is one
of the latest applications of electricity to the deposition of one metal
upon another. The general principle is the same as that already described in connection with electro-plating. The process is effected by
means of a galvanic battery brought to operate upon two metals
(zinc and copper) so as to form brass or bronze. A solution is made
from the oxides of these metals, by means of carbonate and cyanide of
potassium, combined with ammoniacal liquor. The article to be
bronzed is placed in this solution ; and the electric current, being
brought into play through the liquid, causes the particles of the metal to
be deposited upon the object till the whole surface is covered. Various
beautiful shades can be obtained by altering the proportions of the
compounds used. The process is particularly adapted to all ornamental iron and zinc work, such as stoves, fenders, balustrades,
lamps, figures, chandeliers, &c. Both modern and antique bronzes can
be imitated in almost every variety of shade and colour. Messrs.
Walker and Hall had for many years the right of patent, and they
have paid great attention to render the process thoroughly effective.
The great advantage of this process is, that it is cheap and durable,
while artistic finish of a high kind is given. Some large hat-stands,
&c., successfully bronzed in this way, are shown in the International
Exhibition. Messrs. Walker and Hall bronze for the trade by this

ELECTRO-PLATING WORKS.—MESSRS. WALKER AND HALL.

process. The great peculiarity of Messrs. Walker and Hall's productions in this department is that, by their perseverance and skill, they are enabled to carry out the process upon a larger scale and in a more perfect manner than has hitherto been accomplished.

Messrs. John Round and Son, of Tudor Works, carry on a large silver-plating and German silver trade, principally in the spoon and fork departments, more than 200 persons being employed in these branches. Some idea of the extent of the business may be gathered from the fact that in these two departments there are nearly 4,000 different kinds of goods, varying either in quality or pattern. Besides their Sheffield premises, Messrs. John Round and Son have a large establishment at Montreal, in Canada, where they also carry on business as general merchants.

Messrs. Henry Wilkinson and Co., of Norfolk-street, manufacture the best class of silver-plated goods upon a large scale; they have also introduced a very valuable process, the patent of which they hold, for preventing silver and silver-plated goods from tarnishing.

There are many other large houses in this trade, comprising Messrs. Hawksworth, Eyre, and Co.; Walker, Knowles, and Co.; Martin, Hall, and Co.; Atkin Brothers; R. Broadhead and Co.; Bradbury and Sons; J. Harrison; Roberts and Briggs; Roberts and Co.; W. Harrison and Co.; W. Hutton and Son; Padley, Staniforth, and Co.; Rhodes and Beardshaw; W. and G. Sissons; E. J. Buxton and Co.; Shaw and Fisher; Slater, Son, and Horton; Cutts, &c.

THE PARIS EXHIBITION OF 1855.

Sheffield took a very high position in the Paris Exhibition of 1855. The following honours were obtained by local manufacturers :—

Grand Medal of Honour awarded to Sheffield, which was received by the Mayor (Mr. William Fawcett,) from the hand of the Emperor. —FOR WROUGHT AND UNWROUGHT STEEL.—Medals of Honour to Spear and Jackson, T. Turton and Sons, G. Wostenholm, and H. E. Hoole, Sheffield. Decoration of the Legion of Honour to Mr. S. Jackson (Spear and Jackson.) *First-Class Medals :* J. Bedford, Cocker Brothers, J. Firth and Son, Hawcroft and Son, Ibbotson Brothers and Co., J. Kenyon and Co., Kirby, Beard, and Co.; J. Moss and Gamble Brothers; Naylor, Vickers, and Co.; J. Nowill, Sorby and Sons, Spencer and Sons, T. Wilkinson and Son, J. Wilson and Son, Sheffield. *Second-Class Medals :* R. Bagshaw, J. Bedford, Sheffield; Butterley, Hobson, and Co., Norton; Cocker and Son, Hathersage; T. Garfitt and Co., E. Greaves, Hoole, Staniforth, and Co.; J. Howarth, T. Jowitt, Saynor and Cooke, H. Taylor, and T. Ward , Sheffield. *Honourable Mention :* G. Beardshaw and Son, D. Flather and Son, Fox and Co., A. Green, W. Jackson and Co., J. S. Warner, and B. & J. Wilcock, Sheffield.—SILVERSMITHS' ART.—*First-Class Medals :* J. Dixon and Sons, Sheffield. *Second-Class Medals :* Shaw and Fisher, Sheffield; —HOUSE FURNITURE DECORATION.—*Medal of Honour :* H. E. Hoole, Sheffield. *First-Class Artizans' Medal :* Stevens, Sheffield.—GENERAL MACHINERY.—T. Walker, Sheffield, second-class medal.—APPLICATION OF HEAT, &c.—*Second-Class Medal :* H. E. Hoole, Sheffield. *Honourable Mention :* Thomas Walker, Sheffield.

ENTRANCE TO GREEN-LANE WORKS.—MESSRS. H. E. HOOLE AND CO.

STOVE GRATES, &c.

The manufacture of stove grates and fenders is a considerable branch of the Sheffield trade. Among the leading manufactories is the Green-lane Works, which were established in 1795, and have continued in the same family with little intermission. They were rebuilt in their present elegant style a few years ago by the proprietor, Alderman Henry E. Hoole, who has long been known as one of the principal manufacturers of stove grates, fenders, and fire irons. The productions of this house obtained the first Council medal at the International Exhibition in 1851, and the médaille d'honneur at the Paris Exhibition of 1855. The Society of Art and Industry also awarded Mr. Hoole the medal of honour for the works of utility and art which he exhibited in London and Paris. Mr. Hoole is a contributor to the present Exhibition of such works of refined taste and superior execution as cannot but extend his reputation as a manufacturer of stove grates and fenders suitable either for the palace or dwellings of more humble pretensions. Mr. Hoole, having consented to act as a juror, will be precluded from receiving any prizes in the particular class in which he exhibits. The

GREEN-LANE WORKS.—MESSRS. H. E. HOOLE AND CO., STOVE GRATE MANUFACTURERS.

jurors in this class have appointed Mr. Hoole as their chairman, a position which his well-known artistic discrimination, and his long experience as a manufacturer, qualify him to occupy. Mr. Hoole's manufactory is very spacious and complete, and will well repay the visits of strangers, who are always received with courtesy. They will there find works of the highest order of art, as well as those of a more unpretending class. The woodcuts on the preceding pages represent the entrance and the principal quadrangle.

Another of the principal firms in the stove grate trade is that of Messrs. Stuart and Smith, whose manufactory is called Roscoe-place. Besides the general round of useful goods, this house produces grates in the most finished and artistic style. One of the specimens they are showing in the present Exhibition may be taken as representing their enterprize. It is from a design by Mr. Thomas, the sculptor, many of whose works adorn the Houses of Parliament. The idea embodied is suggested by a scene in the "Midsummer Night's Dream"—the meeting of Oberon and Titania in the glades of a wood at night. On the front of the mantelpiece, which is of white marble, is represented the meeting of the fairies. It is evident that such a subject gives great scope for the imagination and taste of the artist; and the idea is carried out with much skill. The grate is finished in a manner worthy of the work of the artist. The poetical idea which runs throughout the whole composition is carried out in every detail of the ornamentation. Stars appear upon the front of the arch, and the rays of the moon are represented by a corona of bright steel, radiating from the dark ground of the inner surface of the arch. The front of the stove is supported by square pillars of polished steel. The hearth is formed of porcelain, upon which roses and bluebells are painted. The outer edge of the hearth is formed of a border of fern leaves, in ormolu. The appearance of the grate as a whole is exceedingly beautiful, for though there is an abundance of varying colours, they all harmonize with each other in the most tasteful manner. This firm received a Council medal at the Exhibition of 1851.

Messrs. Robertson and Carr, of Chantrey Works, have a large and growing reputation for the class of goods which they manufacture. They make every variety of stoves, register-grates, fenders, fire-irons, &c., suitable for every style of architecture. Their special aim is to produce effect without resorting to the aid of porcelain, glass, encaustic tiles, or other questionable devices for obtaining contrast of colour. They prefer to rely on a judicious and tasteful arrangement of metals; and in the stoves they have sent to the Exhibition they certainly have succeeded in showing how much can be done by the contrast of bright steel with jet-black surfaces, bronze, ormolu, &c. The combination of fire-grate and dogs shown in the engraving constitutes a design purposely made so that no particular style of architecture shall predominate. Features belonging both to Gothic and Italian architecture, as well as some appertaining to neither, have been used in producing this design, which may be considered suitable to the period when Elizabethan architecture became established in the sixteenth century. In some respects the present design, in other particulars besides the com-

STOVE.—MESSRS. ROBERTSON AND CARR.

bination mentioned, differs from fire-grates in general. It has not a particle of foliation about it, nor any vegetable or animal feature which could fairly be supposed incapable of standing fire, or which could be inconsistent with metal work for such use.

Among the other leading manufacturers are Messrs. Wright and Co., Longden & Son (who obtained a medal in 1851), J. M. Stanley & Co., Steel and Garland, &c.

CHANDELIERS, BRASS WORK, &c.

The manufacture of articles comprised under the above heading is no longer a Birmingham monopoly, but is pursued in this town with considerable energy and success. The Atlas Brass Works, situated in Saville-street East, and carried on under the style of Benjn. Vickers and Co., justly claim to be the representative house, upwards of 200 hands being here employed in the manufacture of an immense variety of articles, which may be enumerated as follows :—Amongst chandeliers and gas fittings may be seen specimens displaying artistic skill and beauty of workmanship of no mean order. One description of chandelier is worthy of particular mention, on account of its peculiar construction, and for which a patent has been obtained. The distinctive principle of this, the Atlas patent sliding chandelier, is one which gives security against the danger of explosion through the escape of gas, or accident through the breaking of the chains which support the balance-balls of ordinary chandeliers ; for, the counter-balance being on one ring, is not affected by the breaking of one chain,

ATLAS BRASS WORKS.—MESSRS. B. VICKERS AND CO.

and should all break, the weight would fall upon the body of the
chandelier, and instantly close a valve which would prevent an escape
of gas. Should a deficiency of water occur in the slides, a small

whistle connected with the water-cup emits a shrill sound, which is sustained until water is supplied, or the gas turned off. Thus, the most fertile source of explosion in private houses may be removed. In carriage, railway, table, and mining lamps a great variety is displayed; but the mining lamp deserves especial notice. The "Atlas Miners' Safety Lamp" has established itself over every other in present use by its self-extinction on the least appearance of explosive gas, and by the production of a more brilliant light than has previously been obtained. Plumbers' brass work, comprising steam and water cocks, railings, balustrades, cornices, water closets, baths, &c., constitutes another important branch in this establishment. In gas meters, also, considerable improvements have been made. The "Atlas Dry Meter" is secured to the firm by letters patent, the improvement being an arrangement peculiar to this meter alone, by which a more steady and correct measure is guaranteed to the public, whilst repairs may be executed by any ordinary gas-fitter. The wet meter is non-compensating, but the float is so arranged that irregularity of pressure does not affect it; and the drum is so constructed that the meter will stand to lose more water (within the range required by Lord Redesdale's Act) than almost any other meter made. The spacious front of the works is well shown in the annexed engraving.

OTHER MANUFACTURES.

We may mention, amongst other manufactures which are carried on largely in Sheffield, that of hair-seating and curled-hair. The principal firm in which, is that of Messrs. Saml. Laycock and Sons, Portobello street. There is a large trade done in ivory, tortoise shell, and horn combs. Brushmaking is also a branch of considerable importance. The trade in optical and mathematical instruments is a large and growing one. The leading firms are Messrs. Chadburn Brothers, who have show-rooms in Nursery-street, and Messrs. I. P. Cutts, Sutton, and Son, Division street. Messrs. Chadburn obtained, at the Exhibition of 1851, two medals for "good and cheap" instruments. The manufacture of cases for table cutlery, scissors, razors, strops, &c., is also finding employment for great numbers, and articles of great beauty are produced.

The manufacture of rolling stock for railways, hitherto carried on principally in the neighbourhoods of Birmingham, Manchester, and Leeds, has recently been introduced into Sheffield. Works of considerable magnitude have been erected on the Midland Railway (near the manufactory of Messrs. John Brown and Co.) They are termed the "West-Riding Railway Carriage Works." The buildings are furnished with machinery and every appliance specially adapted to the trade. The works are upwards of two acres in extent, have evidently been designed with a view of doing a large business, and their capabilities can be considerably augmented if necessary. The manufacture of leather is extensively carried on by Mr. Geo. Mills, and by several other firms.

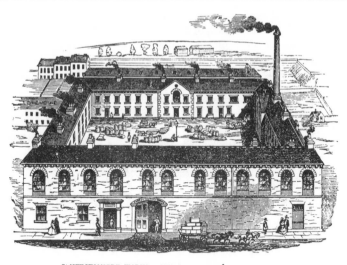

CONFECTIONERY WORKS.—MESSRS. GEORGE BASSETT AND CO.

The wholesale confectionery works of Messrs. G. Bassett and Co. in Portland-street, Infirmary-road, are on so large a scale that they are very interesting to inspect. Nearly one hundred and fifty persons are employed in them in the various processes of spice-making. In the lozenge department the lump sugar is ground in a steam mill, sifted through a dressing machine, and passed to the mixing-room. For plain peppermint lozenges, the ingredients used are oil of peppermint, sugar, and gum arabic, which are formed into a paste. In the case of lemon, rose, ginger, black currant, tamarind, ipecacuanha, opium, or other of the multifarious descriptions of lozenges, the difference is that the peppermint is omitted, and other ingredients, represented in the name of the lozenge, are substituted. The ingredients, having gone through the process of mixing, are rolled into sheets, which are passed to other workmen, who, with tube-shaped cutters made of steel, cut out the lozenge from the paste with wonderful rapidity. In the liquorice department a number of men are engaged in transforming the black extract of liquorice into the shapes in which it is presented in the windows of the confectioners' shops. The extract reaches the works in large black masses. After undergoing the process of boiling and purifying in a steam pan, in one of the rooms on the ground floor, it is hoisted to the rooms above by means of a crane. Portions of this mass, while in a soft state, are then weighed off, and rolled into Spanish juice sticks, or moulded into Pontefract cakes, or propelled through a brass cylinder with steam power into pipes. We next proceed to comfit-making. In the manufacture of the smaller sized comfits, a quantity of carraway seeds are placed in large rotary copper pans, and on these there falls very slowly

COMFIT ROOM.—MESSRS. GEORGE BASSETT AND CO.

a stream of liquid sugar. The pans are kept revolving with such rapidity that each seed gathers up only a small portion of the sugar, and this becomes solidified without the mass adhering. As fresh liquid sugar is added each seed receives its proportion and continues adding to its bulk till the requisite size is attained. In the large comfits, instead of carraway seeds almonds are used, but the process of manufacture is the same. The ordinary mode of comfit-making is by the pans being slung from a hook in the roof, and kept in motion by hand power. Messrs. G. Bassett & Co. were the first firm to introduce into this country the enormous pans, which are worked in a rotary motion by steam power, and at the present time are probably doing a larger trade in this branch of manufacture than any other firm in the world. The illustration of the comfit-room shows these large pans, which have a very curious appearance when seen in motion. Passing through the ju-jube and pastille rooms, we come to sugar candy, which is made in tin boxes. Each box is perforated at the ends with holes, through which a number of threads are passed. Liquid sugar is then poured in, and, the whole having been hermetically sealed on the outside, the boxes are placed in a stove, which is kept at a high temperature night and day. Through the application of this heat, the sugar crystallizes upon the threads, and at the end of a week, on the tin being opened, they present a series of sticks of pink, yellow, or white sugar candy, with a small portion of liquid at the bottom of each can. The candied lemon manufacture is a large department. Stored away and piled above one another we see about 3,000 boxes of lemons. These, as they are unpacked, are carried into a room where they are cut in two, and each half is placed between wooden machines, in the form of enormous nutcracks. Here they are pressed till the juice is extracted from them. The rinds are placed in casks, and preserved in a strong solution of salt and water till required for use. When that time arrives the rinds are washed in fresh water until the salt is entirely removed. They are then boiled in a steam pan until perfectly soft. The pulp is then removed, and the outer rinds are closely packed in a large vat, and boiling sugar and water is poured upon them. At intervals of three days this liquid is withdrawn, and is renewed in a boiling state, additional sugar having been added. This process is continued for three weeks, at the end of which time the lemon rinds, having become sufficiently saturated with sugar, are carried on trays into a stove, and, when dried, they undergo the process of being candied. For this purpose the rind is placed in a pan of boiling sugar.

CONFECTIONERY WAREHOUSE.—MESSRS. G. BASSETT AND CO.

Each separate piece is then carefully removed to the wire racks; and as soon as the sugar shall have become sufficiently set, the article is sent to the warehouse, ready to be packed-off in boxes to consumers. The manufacture of acid drops is very interesting. Over an intensely hot furnace at one end of a large room, and slightly elevated above the ground, are four copper pans, which are carefully watched. Each pan contains about 24 lbs. of sugar and a proportion of water. When the sugar has been boiled the requisite period, the workman carries the pan to a large stone table which has been previously prepared with butter, and on this he pours the seething liquid. The contact with the cold stone causes it gradually to set, and when it has slightly set, another man turns it into a heap. A quantity of tartaric acid is then added, and this, as it melts, is gradually worked into a mass, which is then, while in its soft state, cut into slices, and passed over to boys. One boy takes a slice weighing six or seven pounds, places it between a pair of brass rollers, which are kept revolving by steam power, and which are indented with holes the size and shape of the required drops, and as the machine is turned, there issues from the other side of the roller a long string of drops. These are received upon an iron tray, and the process is continued until the whole of the soft mass is converted into drops, In the course of two or three minutes the drops are sufficiently hardened or set to allow of their being separated from each other. In the case of barley sugar drops the only difference is that the tartaric acid is omitted. Jargonelle pear, orange, rose, raspberry, or other drops are obtained by the admixture of some chemical flavouring matter in lieu of the tartaric acid, and with the addition of a little cochineal or saffron for colouring. In addition to the above branches, Messrs. G. Bassett and Co. manufacture orange marmalade, which is boiled and cut up by steam power. They also do a large trade in those popular sweetmeats which are put up in penny packets in gelatine covers. The weight and constituent parts of a twelfth cake made to order by this firm are worth stating. It weighed 9,767 lbs.—namely, 1,364 lbs. sugar, 1,364 lbs. butter, 1,705 lbs. currants, 1,705 lbs. raisins, 2,046 lbs. flour, 1,024 lbs. candied lemon, 10,208 eggs, and 424 lbs. sugar for icing. The cost was £447 13s. 1d. Messrs. Bassett and Co. send confectionery all over the kingdom, and they also do a large export trade. It may be mentioned that in none of their productions are there any of those poisonous compounds which are so objectionable. To this fact the firm attribute the large and increasing business they are now carrying on.

THE SURROUNDING DISTRICT.

It now only remains for us to take up more in detail the subject briefly touched upon at the commencement of this work—the beautiful district surrounding the town. This portion of our task is almost inexhaustible ; and we might, without difficulty, occupy the whole limits assigned to this volume with a description of spots within easy reach of Sheffield. Indeed, though of course every resident is familiar with the general character of the scenery of the neighbourhood, comparatively few of those who live in Sheffield have explored the whole of the lovely haunts which are to be found within a very few miles of the town, so prolific has Nature been in her adornment of this locality.

The poetry of Elliott is everywhere tinged with the softening influence which the natural beauties of the neighbourhood must have had on his mind; and his fiercest political denunciations we find occasionally relieved by descriptive touches derived from the scenes among which he loved to linger. We shall, in our account of the neighbourhood, first deal with some of the spots made additionally interesting by an association with the poetry of Elliott.

THE RIVELIN, RIBBLEDIN, AND WYMING-BROOK.

It would be difficult to discover anywhere a more beautiful walk than that to be found along the valley of the Rivelin, one of five rivers previously mentioned as uniting in this locality. The "Ribbledin" is a tributary of the larger stream, and was so named by Elliott in one of his poems. The following description of a visit to these localities is from the pen of Mr. Christopher Thomson, whose pencil so tastefully illustrates his own words :—

In half an hour, starting from the monument to Ebenezer Elliott in the Market-place, we may reach the Rivelin valley, through Walkley. The eastern end of it has more of the town look than it had when the poet lived. But even in this part it is still very picturesque—sometimes sylvan in aspect, sometimes wild, romantic, or solemn. Along the stream, at intervals, buildings of gray and russetty stone arrest the eye. These are "grinding wheels," (described at page 136,) where the blades used in the cutlery have an edge put on them, &c. Originally all the grinding wheels were situated on the streams adjoining the

VIEW ON THE RIVELIN.—FROM A SKETCH BY MR. C. THOMSON.

town, in order that they might be worked by water power. Many of them still remain, and in some instances they considerably enhance the picturesque effect of the scenery. Close to the wheels are small lakes or dams of water, collected for the purpose of giving power to turn the grinding stones. These lakes, calm and silent, reflect the foliage and bank-sides around them, and make up lovely pictures. Far up the valley the little sheets of water sparkle out like sheets of silver, linking themselves to the dark time-stained buildings. The accompanying engraving gives a representation of one of the most beautiful and picturesque spots on this lovely river, and will enable the stranger to appreciate more fully the language in which Elliott (in his sadly-sweet lyrical poem, "Farewell to Rivelin,") addresses his favourite haunt:—

> "Beautiful river! goldenly shining
> Where, with the cistus, woodbines are twining,
> (Birklands around thee, mountains above thee,)
> Rivelin wildest! Do I not love thee?"

Between three and four miles from Elliott's monument lie those wild ravines of Ribbledin and Wyming, pictured in Elliott's verse. Let us visit the Ribbledin. If you enquire your way to "Ribbledin"

VIEW ON THE RIBBLEDIN,—FROM A SKETCH BY MR. C. THOMSON.

N

of any of the grinders in Rivelin Valley, they will probably tell you,
"There is no such place near here." It is generally called by them,
"Black-brook;" but we adopt the title given by the poet in his poem
of "The Christening." The name is more euphonious than the old
one, and it is now generally accepted by the townsfolk. If you desire
to learn whether it is truly named, sit down in silence when you reach
the stream. Listen awhile, and you will hear the jubilant river singing distinctly in a silver-toned voice, "Ribbledin," and you will be
ready to exclaim with this poet—

> " Would that I were a river,
>   To wander all alone,
>   Through some sweet Eden of the wild,
>   In music of my own.
>
> " And washed in bliss, and fed with dew,
>   Distilled o'er mountains hoary,
>   Return unto my home in heaven
>   On wings of joy and glory ! "

In the following stanza Elliott tells us why he christened this river :—

> " No name hast thou, lone streamlet,
>   That marriest Rivelin ;
>   Here if a bard may christen thee,
>   I'll call thee Ribbledin.
>   Here, where first murmuring from thine urn,
>   Thy voice deep joy expresses,
>   And down the rocks like music flows,
>   The wildness of thy tresses."

We will mark out the road to this glen so distinctly that the reader
will need no other guide. We proceed up the Glossop-road, pass the
Mount, and on through Broomhill bar. We can take the omnibus to
this spot. A few yards through the bar the road diverges on the right.
It was the great highway to Manchester in the old coaching days.
Once on this road, our route is straight before us. We pass the way-
side inn, " King Stephen," and, glancing over the stone walls on our
left, down in the valley, is the aquaduct along which the Water Company
brings the pure liquid from Redmires into the town. Here, too, we
may glance " o'er Hallam wide." We keep on a few hundred yards
further, and, passing through a little hamlet, make a gentle curve.
And now the purple hills of the moors and the wooded slopes of
Rivelin meet our eyes. Still forward, leaving all the lanes that
diverge from the high-road for the present neglected. Another
curve in the road, and through a little copse on our right, with high
quarries of many-tinted stone on the left, we come to the old and
well-known inn called " Bellhag." From the parlour of this inn and
the rocks beyond and in front of it, magnificent views of the Rivelin are
obtained. In the afternoon, when the westering sun shines on Keppel's Pillar, it may be seen from the Bellhag towering like a line of
light over Wentworth's halls. Leaving Bellhag we proceed towards
the moors, with the Coppice rocks on our left, and pass the third mile
stone ; and about three-quarters of a mile from the inn we find ourselves upon a bridge, under which the Ribbledin pours its flood to wed

with Rivelin. Should we cross the bridge we shall perceive an old
gray-walled cottage with twisted and knarled crab-stems and old thorn
trees belted around it. It is the first cottage on the road side since
leaving Bellhag. But we must stop on the Sheffield side of the bridge
in order to get to Ribbledin. On the left hand there is an old gray-
lichened gate. We must go through this gate, turn at once to the
right hand, and follow the track down to the river. We are now at the
Ribbledin; but at this part of it scarcely any indication is given of the
wild and glen-like character the spot will soon present if we continue
up the stream. We have to pick our way now over moist green rank
grass, intermingled with mosses and purple fox-gloves, now skip-
ping from stone to stone, and now over rush-bristled isles, masses of
fallen rock, and under arches of time-twisted and tempest-riven trees
that literally join shore to shore. It is a—

> " Dim world of weeping mosses!
>   A hundred years ago
> Yon hoary-headed holly tree
>   Beheld thy streamlet flow;
> See how he bends him down to hear,
>   The tune that ceases never!
> Old as the rocks, wild stream, he seems,
>   While thou art young for ever."

Still onward until we come to where this old, yet ever-young, streamlet
is issuing from its " urn." There we may climb the granite side and
sit. A more lovely spot for sweet contemplation of nature is hardly to
be found in England.

We may return by the mountain peaks over the Coppice rocks, or
retrace our steps to the old gray gate. The route over the Coppices

WYMING-BROOK.—FROM A SKETCH BY MR. C THOMSON.

will prolong the journey back for half an hour; but the glorious scene, particularly if the sun be declining, will well repay the labour.   The view of the Don, the Rivelin, and the Loxley, meandering through the picturesque and varied landscape, furnishes a scene of beauty which will remain "a joy for ever" in the mind of the visitor.

About a mile beyond the Ribbledin bridge on the Manchester road we may enter into the wild gorge of "headlong Wyming."   If we enter by the little Gothic lodge which is situated on the left hand of the turnpike road, and cross the head of the Compensation Reservoir, then turn again to the right hand, keeping along the edge of the water for about a quarter of a mile, we shall reach the foot of the brook.   This ravine is parallel with the Ribbledin.   We may follow up the stream from the foot of it.   It is more easy of access to ascend the river, for the masses of detached rock are often large and massive, and interspersed with fragments of granite, which in dry weather are very slippery, and often make the descent dangerous as well as laborious.   The tourist may, by the aid of fallen branches, twigs of trees, and the long grasses and brackens, make the ascent with safety and comparative ease.   For the student of nature, or the seeker after health and mental improvement, this wild glen teems with sermons.

On the opposite side of the valley of the Rivelin, and about four miles from Sheffield, in the district of Loxley Chase, is a beautiful spot called Little Matlock, from the resemblance of its scenery to that of the celebrated Matlock in Derbyshire.   Little Matlock may be reached by a half-hour's walk from Hillsbro', to which omnibuses run every hour.   Additional interest is imparted to this spot from the legend which is current, and which seems not unlikely to have a foundation of truth, that it was the birth-place of the famous outlaw, Robin Hood.   There is still a well which has been from time immemorial called "Robin Hood's well."

SHIRECLIFFE.

Shirecliffe is a spot as noted in the poetry of Elliott as the Valley of the Rivelin, and equally beautiful.   It is, indeed, peculiarly interesting to the admirers of Elliott, as the spot where was situated the "gospel tree," under which "the Ranter," in the poem of that title, went on Sundays to preach.   The peculiar title of "gospel tree," is not very appropriate, for the gospel preached in the poem consists principally of a denunciation of the Corn Laws and their supporters, mingled with sweet descriptive touches.   Elliott himself stated that he drew this picture from life; and it seems probable that the actual spot described in the poem was once used as a place for preaching.   The tree, which unfortunately no longer stands, was an ash; and Elliott drove a nail into it that his friends should be able to recognise it.

We shall endeavour to describe the scene as it exists at the present time.   First as to the road.   The visitor will find an omnibus that will convey him to the Pitsmoor toll-bar, from which it is not more

than ten minutes' walk to the spot where the "gospel tree" stood.
He turns up Shirecliffe-lane, at the top of which, on the left, are
the gates of Shirecliffe Hall, once the seat of the ancient family of the
Mounteneys, but now the residence of the Watsons.   A little beyond
the gates there is a fine view of the adjoining country, reaching out as
far as the villages of Handsworth and Laughton-en-le-Morthen.   A
little further on, to the left, we turn off into a quarry, and a pretty
steep ascent leads us to the scene we have set out to visit.   Formerly

SHIRECLIFFE.—FROM A SKETCH BY MR. C. THOMPSON

a view of the country on all sides could be obtained from one spot;
but the summit from which this was possible has been cut away in the
quarrying operations.   To see the whole district, therefore, it is necessary to go to places some little distance apart; and, passing from that
where may be seen an expanse of country which includes Hoober Stand
and Keppel's Pillar*, we come to the principal view, an outline of
which is given in the accompanying illustration.

It is scarcely possible to imagine a more magnificent sight than is
presented in the stretch of country laid out before the gaze.   Three
distinct ranges of hills undulate in the midst of the landscape, while these
again are backed by lofty prominences, which tower up in the far distance,
and mingle with their purple hues in the serene blue that is over all.
In the middle distance two rivers, bright in the golden sunbeams, gracefully meander through the green fertile earth.   Here a church spire

* Hoober Stand is a lofty tower near Wentworth; and Keppel's Pillar is an Ionic column at
Scholes, erected by the Marquis of Rockingham in memory of Admiral Keppel.

rises up through the surrounding foliage ; there a slender bridge spans the placid stream ; while yonder a chimney top peeps out through the green trees, the blue smoke curling lazily upwards. In the valley we see a fortress-like building of stone, extending over a wide range of ground; and this is backed by houses rising row above row on the hillside. At our very feet where we stand, a sea of green boughs stretches further than the eye can reach—its varying hues brought out in marked contrast by the bright sunshine, and the gentle, breezy rustling of the leaves mingling harmoniously with the sweet notes of the birds and the busy hum of the short-lived summer fly.

The visitor cannot mistake the spot from which this view is to be obtained, in consequence of the very prosaic notice—" No Road"—put up on the tree on the right that skirts the eminence on which it stands. Though the " gospel tree" no longer exists, the place thus marked cannot be far from the site where it originally stood. It is necessary to remark that the accompanying sketch of this magnificent view merely gives a general outline of its leading features, for the obvious reason that it is so crowded with objects that it was impossible to represent them within so limited a space. Following the panoramic scene before us, let us trace the objects somewhat in detail. The mass of foliage at our feet indicates that below runs the Old Park and Cook Woods, extending on our right for some two miles, and on the left for perhaps a mile—in fact into the suburbs close to the town, which year after year encroaches upon its limits and threatens before very long its entire destruction, in the resistless march of brick and mortar. Of the three large hills which front us, that on the left comprises the suburb of Walkley, and its rising sides are covered with the freehold-land allotments and building-society tenements which are such pleasing tokens of the thrift of our working men. The Walkley hill shelves down on one side to the valley of the Don, and on the other to the Rivelin, which runs hidden from our view at the back of Walkley. The eminence in the middle is the range on whose side stands Stannington, with its church ; and the third hill, on the right, gives local habitation to the villagers of Loxley. Between the verdant undulations of the Stannington and Loxley eminences and the brick-clad sides of Walkley hill, the Bradfield moors, clad in their purple heather, stretch across in the hazy background. Let us now come down to the comparatively level space between the foot of these eminences and the Old Park Wood at our feet. The hills surrounding the large valley below give it the shape of an amphitheatre, any great spectacle performed in which might be fully seen either from where we stand, or from any of the other eminences which are around it. The most prominent object is the vast pile of buildings on the left, which look as though they had been built in anticipation of a siege. These are the Barracks. In front of them winds the River Loxley. About the centre of the low land is the village of Hillsbro', where the Rivelin joins the Loxley, and both mingle with the waters of the Don, a short distance nearer

Sheffield. The St. Philip's burial-ground is visible amidst the trees at our feet, on the right; and the Manchester, Sheffield, and Lincoln-shire Railway runs close to the burial-ground. It is very curious every now and then to see a thin volume of steam ascend gracefully out of the trees at our feet, and steal along until the cover of the foliage is passed, when the train dashes into sight and hurries as with irresistible power into the far distance. A passing railway train is visible in the illustration, but there is no trace of a bridge over the river near the same spot, this having been constructed since the sketch was taken.

Elliott's description of the locality, taken from his poem " The Ranter," may be fitly introduced here, as giving a most vigorous sketch of the scene, and indicating other localities besides these we have mentioned :—

" Up! sluggards, up! the mountains, one by one
Ascend in light, and slow the mists retire
From vale and plain. The cloud on Stannington
Beholds a rocket.—No, 'tis Morthen spire.
The sun is risen! cries Stanedge, tipped with fire.
On Norwood's flowers the dew-drops shine and shake.
Up! sluggards, up! and drink the morning breeze;
The birds on cloud-left Osgathorpe awake,
And Wincobank is waving all his trees
O'er subject towns, and farms, snd villages,
And gleaming streams and woods, and waterfalls.
" Up! climb the oak-crowned summit! Hoober Stand
And Keppel's Pillar gaze on Wentworth's halls
And misty lakes that brighten and expand,
And distant hills that watch the western strand.
Up! trace God's footprints where they paint the mould
With heavenly green, and hues that blush and glow
Like angel's wings, while skies of blue and gold
Stoop to Miles Gordon on the mountain's brow.
Behold the Great Unpaid! the prophet. Lo!
Sublime he stands beneath the gospel tree,
And Edmund stands on Shirecliffe at his side!
Behind him sinks, and swells, and spreads a sea
Of hills and vales and groves. Before him glide
Don, Rivelin, Loxley, wandering in their pride
From heights that mix their azure with the cloud."

ENDCLIFFE WOOD, STANEDGE, &C.

A charming walk, in the immediate vicinity of the town, is to be found in Endcliffe wood. It can be reached in about five minutes from the Botanical Gardens. The character of the scenery is somewhat similar to that of the valley of the Rivelin. The Porter, a smaller stream, winds through it, and serves to keep at work seven or eight grinding wheels. The sketches of spots in this locality are by Mr. Walter Nicholson, who has drawn them on the wood. The first represents very accurately one of the dams where the water is kept for turning the machinery; on the further side the gable of the " wheel" is seen peeping up over the water. In order to increase the flow of the stream, there are weirs in connection with most of the dams, and some of the little waterfalls thus created have a very beautiful effect amongst the trees. There are also shuttles to stop the water and turn it in another direction when there is too much. These together

ENDCLIFFE WOOD AND DAM.—DRAWN BY MR. W. NICHOLSON.

with the variety of bridges, glens, dingles, &c., form a very delightful
walk of almost a mile and a half; the whole of the path is varied,
rustic, and beautiful. As the wood is very narrow in many places,

VIEW IN ENDCLIFFE WOOD.—DRAWN BY MR. W. NICHOLSON.

THE PORTER FALLS.—DRAWN BY MR. W. NICHOLSON.

peeps of cottages, churches, and green fields in the distance are
gained, which give a pleasing variety. Endcliffe wood perhaps presents on the whole a more sweet and varied walk than the Rivelin Valley, which excels in picturesque boldness. It is a great favourite with
artists, and sketches from its lovely precincts enrich many a portfolio.

Extending the walk still further, to the source of the Porter, the
visitor will be well repaid for his trouble. The stream runs through
the whole of the Endcliffe woods, and has its source much higher even
than Whiteley wood, another beautiful spot of a similar kind. The
Porter takes its rise in a small ravine between two hills, about three
miles from the town, at the straggling little village of Fulwood. After
flowing but a very short distance, it makes one of the most perfect
cascades that a lover of nature could wish to see. It is in a small
glen, a little way from the road, and unknown even to many who live
very near. The water falls some fifteen feet, and in a charming variety
of forms. The annexed sketch gives a spirited representation of this
beautiful fall.

REDMIRES RESERVOIRS.—FROM A SKETCH BY MR. W. IBBITT.

A convenient way of getting to this last-mentioned spot is by omnibus to Ranmoor, which is not far from Fulwood. There are some other places worth visiting in the same neighbourhood. From

STANEDGE.—FROM A SKETCH BY MR. W. IBBITT.

the church at Fulwood we proceed along a road which passes over Wyming-brook. This brings us to a magnificent stretch of country called Redmires, where are situated the three vast reservoirs (the largest seventy-five acres) which supply Sheffield with water. We give a sketch of this spot, by Mr. W. Ibbitt. A little above them is the commencement of an old causeway, probably either British or Roman, from which may be obtained a fine view of the reservoirs, Winco-hill, and the country extending from Sheffield to the Humber in the distance. The causeway passes up to Stanedge-pole, and, winding down the Edge, thence on to Castleton. Stanedge is part of that extensive range of rocks called the "backbone of England," which runs through the centre of the country. At this spot it is most picturesque. From its summit may be seen the giant mountains of the Peak, and at least two of its most fruitful valleys. There are in the rocks three interesting caves, which are well worth a visit. In one direction, looking into Derbyshire, may be seen Hope-dale, Winhill, Losehill, Mam Tor, the Wyniats, and that on which Peverel's Castle stands. The annexed sketch, by Mr. Ibbitt, shows Stanedge in one of its most striking aspects.

NORTON.

Norton is very interesting as the birth-place and burial-place of Chantrey. The tomb of Chantrey, which is in the churchyard, is quite plain, there being merely a large slab of stone covering the grave. A marble tablet to his memory in the church is also very simple, but it contains a good medallion likeness of the sculptor, executed by Mr.

NORTON CHURCH AND CHANTREY'S MONUMENT.

Heffernan.   A handsome granite obelisk has been erected in honour
of the sculptor, by public subscription.   This, with the exterior of the
church, is shown in the annexed engraving.   There are some other
monuments of interest in the church, including those of the Blythes,
two brothers, one of whom was Bishop of Lichfield and the other
of Salisbury.   Near to the church is Norton Hall, a fine mansion
with a spacious park, now the residence of Mr. Chas. Cammell, of the
Cyclops Works.

BEAUCHIEF.

Beauchief is an interesting and beautiful spot, about four miles from
Sheffield, and just within the confines of Derbyshire.   It is principally
noted on account of its having been the site of a fine old abbey.   This
structure is said to have been built in 1183, by Robert Fitz-Ranulph,
one of the four knights by whom Thomas à Beckett was killed.   The
legend states that Ranulph, feeling remorse for his share in the crime,
strove to expiate it by building and endowing this abbey, which he
dedicated to the archbishop whom he had assisted in murdering.
There are no traces of the old structure left, with the exception of
a small church at the west end.   Though this building possesses no
particular architectural merits, it makes a very pleasing object, combined with the adjoining churchyard and the picturesque scenery which
surrounds it.   Wild flowers are peculiarly plentiful in the woods surrounding Beauchief.

ECCLESFIELD.

Ecclesfield, a large village about five miles from Sheffield, is worthy
of mention here on account of its fine church, which used to be called
"the Minster of the Moors."   It is supposed to have been built about
the end of the eleventh century.   It is in the perpendicular style, with
nave, aisles, transept, and chancel, and a square tower in the middle,
opening from four massive piers where the transept crosses the body
of the church.   Two hundred years ago Dodsworth wrote of this edifice,
"This church is called (and that deservedly) by the vulgar the Mynster
of the Moores, being the fairest church for stone, wood, glasse, and neat
keeping that ever I came in of country church."   The building had
become much dilapidated, but, under the incumbency of the Rev. Dr.
Gatty, the present vicar, it has been restored and beautified, and might
now again challenge the admiration of old Dodsworth, could he behold
it.   In the churchyard at Ecclesfield lie the remains of Mr. Hunter,
the author of the "History of Hallamshire;" and a monument, with
a suitable inscription in Latin, has been erected to his memory.

WHARNCLIFFE

Is a favourite place of excursion from Sheffield, and very easy of
access by means of the Manchester, Sheffield, and Lincolnshire
Railway.   Wortley Hall, the seat of Lord Wharncliffe, is situated here.
There is a magnificent range of forest, hill, and dale; and a day may
be most delightfully spent in exploring the beauties of the neighbour-

WHARNCLIFFE, FROM THE TABLE ROCK.—FROM A SKETCH BY MR. W. IBBITT.

hood. The railway passes directly through the wood, which is open to the public on Mondays and Wednesdays. Wharncliffe Crags are a series of rocks which are remarkably fine. Elliott, describing the wild and rugged scene, with the river at its base, says :—

" Where Don's dark waters bathe the rugged feet
Of billowy mountains—silent, motionless,
As if the Almighty's hand had stilled and fixed
The waves of chaos in their wildest swell."

The above engraving shows a point at the summit, called the Table Rock, situated over what is known as "the Dragon's Den." From this spot a most commanding view may be obtained, including, it is said, on a very clear day, the dim outlines of the cathedrals at York and Lincoln. "The Dragon's Den" is a cavity in the face of the rock, about four yards long and two yards wide. It is so called from the legend which is preserved in the old ballad of "The Dragon of Wantley." The scene of which is undoubtedly Wharncliffe. The ballad begins—

" In Yorkshire, near fair Rotherham,
The place, I know it well,
Some two or three miles, or thereabouts,
I vow I cannot tell ;
But there is a hedge, just on the hill side,
And Matthew's house hard by it,
O there and then was the dragon's den,
You would not choose but spy it."

The song proceeds to describe More of More Hall as the champion who undertakes to encounter the monster. This directly connects the affair with the neighbourhood of Wharncliffe. The Table Rock mentioned is directly opposite the valley where More Hall stands, and which formerly the residence of the More family.   The ballad, after describing the hero, relates how he went to Sheffield for a suit of armour :—

> " But first he went new armour to
>   Bespeak at Sheffield town ;
> The spikes all about, not within but without,
>   Of steel so sharp and strong,
> Both behind and before, arms, legs, and all o'er,
>   Some five or six inches long."

The description of the dragon's deeds is sufficiently grotesque :—

> " Devoured he poor children three,
> That could not with him grapple,
> And at one sup he ate them up,
> As one would eat an apple.
> All sorts of cattle this dragon did eat;
> Some say he ate up trees,
> And that the forests sure he would
> Devour up by degrees;
> For houses and churches to him were geese and turkeys,
> He ate all and left none behind,
> But some stones, dear Jack, that he could not crack,
> Which on the hill you will find."

Of course the brave More, with the help of his Sheffield armour, destroyed the dragon.   There have been many attempts to explain the

WHARNCLIFFE CRAGS AND DRAGON'S DEN.—FROM A SKETCH BY MR. W. IBBITT.

allusions in the ballad, which is universally believed to be a caricature of some local occurrence.   Dr. Percy suggests that it "alludes to a contest at law between an overgrown Yorkshire attorney and a neighbouring gentleman.   The former, it seems, had stripped three orphans of their inheritance, and by his encroachments and rapaciousness was become a nuisance to the whole country, when the latter generously espoused the cause of the oppressed, and gained a complete victory over his antagonist, who with mere spite and vexation broke his heart." Another conjecture is that the song referred to some local dispute about tithes. The engraving represents the face of the rocks where the cave called " The Dragon's Den" is situated.

On one of the highest of the rocky eminences is built a small residence called the Lodge. Here the celebrated Lady Mary Wortley Montague once lived ; and her judgment of the scenery in the locality is shown in a letter she wrote subsequently from Avignon. A delightful spot near that place she describes as "the most beautiful land prospect I ever saw, *except Wharncliffe*." Attached to this dwelling there is the following interesting inscription showing that the Lodge was built in the time of Henry VIII. by Sir Thomas Wortley :—

> Pray for the Saule of
> Thomas Wyttelay Knyght
> for the Kyngys bode to Edward
> the forthe Richard third Hare the vii. & Hare viii,
> bows Saules God perdon wyche
> Thomas caused a loge to be made
> hon this crag in mydys of
> Wanclife for his plesor to her the
> hartes bel in the pere of our
> Lord a thousand ccccc x

The words are difficult to decipher, having been cut in the face of the rock and left to the action of the elements for many years. They are however, preserved from further destruction, being now enclosed in a room and covered over with moveable woodwork.

ROTHERHAM.

Rotherham is a manufacturing town of rising importance, about six miles from Sheffield. At the census of 1861, the population of Rotherham and Kimberworth (which latter includes Masbro',) was 18,922.

The iron trade, waggon building, brass work, stove grate manufacture, &c., are carried on in the town. The chief object of interest to visitors is the fine old Parish Church, erected in the reign of Edward IV., on the site of an old Saxon place of worship. At the entrance to the chancel there still stands a font believed to be a relic of the Saxon edifice. Hunter describes the church as "one of the most beautiful in the diocese," and as presenting " a complete model of the Ecclesiastical Architecture of England in its purest age." Amongst the monuments is an interesting one to the memory of fifty young persons who were accidentally drowned at Masbro', at the launch of a vessel, in May, 1841. The Rev. R. Mosley, M.A., is Vicar.

Rotherham was the birth-place of Thomas Scott, usually called Thomas of Rotherham, who was created Archbishop of York in 1480. He founded a college at Rotherham, which was destroyed at the Reformation. There is a Grammar School, founded in 1584 by Laurence Woodrett and Anthony Collens, two London merchants. A handsome building was erected for the purposes of this institution in 1857. It is under the management of the Feoffees, a body somewhat similar to the Town Trustees at Sheffield, and who have an income of about

£700 a year, which is expended in charitable and other uses in connection with the inhabitants. There are a Mechanics' Institute, a Savings' Bank, and a Dispensary. The town's meetings are usually held in the Court House, where room is provided for the business of the Quarter and Petty Sessions, &c. On the outside of the town, at Masbro', is situated Rotherham College for the training of ministers in the Independent body. There are several Dissenting places of worship in Rotherham. The market (Monday) for corn and cattle, the latter especially, is largely attended, and is noted throughout the county.

EXCURSIONS FROM SHEFFIELD.

Not only is Sheffield situated in the midst of a most beautiful locality, but it is a centre from which a number of picturesque and celebrated spots may easily be reached. Buxton, the beautiful watering place in Derbyshire, is about 28 miles from Sheffield, and coaches run there two or three times a day. Six miles from Sheffield, and near to Longshaw, the shooting box of the Duke of Rutland, is Fox House, to which omnibuses run during the summer. Hathersage, Eyam, &c., are within easy walking distance of this place; and in the immediate neighbourhood are Froggatt Edge and other points from which are obtained some of the most beautiful and extensive views of Derbyshire scenery. Castleton, another interesting spot in Derbyshire, is only about 16 miles from the town. Still more attractive is Chatsworth (about 13 miles from Sheffield), the magnificent seat of the Duke of Devonshire, where the beauties of nature and art are combined in so surpassing a degree. There are many other places in Derbyshire, such as Matlock, Darley-dale, &c., to which delight ful excursions may be made; but the favourite one, next to Chatsworth, is Haddon Hall, on account of its architectural beauty, its picturesque location, and the pleasant reminiscences which are connected with it. Wentworth House, the seat of Earl Fitzwilliam, is very easy of access. It is only about eight miles from Sheffield, and the Rotherham Railway will convey the visitor to within about three miles of the place. Roche Abbey, near Maltby, about thirteen miles from Sheffield, is an interesting place for excursionists. It was founded about the middle of the twelfth century, and was occupied by Cistertian monks. The ruins of Conisbro' Castle are about twelve miles from Sheffield, and can be reached by railway. They are very interesting, and are rendered additionally so on account of their having been made by Sir Walter Scott one of the principal scenes in his "Ivanhoe." Adjoining the town of Worksop, which is accessible by railway (18 miles from Sheffield), is Clumber House, the beautiful residence of the Duke of Newcastle. The parks of Clumber, Worksop, and Thoresby, which adjoin each other, have obtained for this outlying portion of Sherwood Forest the title of the Dukery. At Shireoaks, near Worksop, is a church, built by the Duke of Newcastle, of which his Royal Highness the Prince of Wales laid the foundation stone in 1861.

JOSEPH RODGERS & SONS,

CUTLERS,

BY SPECIAL APPOINTMENT TO HER MAJESTY,

No. 6, NORFOLK-STREET,

SHEFFIELD,

AND

No. 4, CULLUM-ST., FENCHURCH-ST., LONDON, E.C.,

MERCHANTS

AND MANUFACTURERS OF

CUTLERY OF EVERY DESCRIPTION

Silber and Plated Desserts, &c.,

DEALERS IN

SILVER, BEST SHEFFIELD ELECTRO-PLATED WARES,

AND MOST OTHER ARTICLES OF

SHEFFIELD MANUFACTURE,

(CORPORATE ✳ ✠ MARK.)

J. R. & Sons beg to caution the public against spurious goods, offered by unprincipled Belgian and German houses, bearing their marks, and made to imitate their genuine manufactures; a considerable quantity has been recently seized in the port of London, and condemned by the officers of Her Majesty's Customs.

To distinguish Articles of Joseph Rodgers & Sons' manufacture, please to see that they bear the Corporate Mark as above.

WM. JESSOP & SON,

STEEL MANUFACTURERS,

SHEFFIELD.

Manufactories:

BRIGHTSIDE WORKS, **SHEFFIELD.**

PARK WORKS, **SHEFFIELD.**

SOHO WORKS, **SHEFFIELD.**

Depots:

55, DALE STREET, **MANCHESTER.**

8, RUE DE LANCRY, **PARIS.**

91, JOHN STREET, **NEW YORK, U.S.**

147, MILK STREET, **BOSTON, U.S.**

MARKET STREET, **PHILADELPHIA, U.S.**

MAIN STREET, **ST. LOUIS, U.S.**

WEST SECOND ST., **CINCINNATTI, U.S.**

PROVIDENCE, **RHODE ISLAND, U.S.**

COCKER BROTHERS,

(Successors to Samuel Cocker and Son,)

SHEFFIELD.

ESTABLISHED 1752.

MANUFACTURERS OF

STEEL, FILES, WIRE, TOOLS,
SAWS,
STEEL WIRE ROPES,

CRINOLINE STEEL, & SPRINGS, &c.

ALSO,

GENERAL MERCHANTS.

The only Firm honoured with THREE PRIZE MEDALS at the
Exhibition of London, 1851;

FIRST CLASS PRIZE MEDAL at the Exhibition of Paris, 1855;

MEDAL of HONOUR of the Society of Arts, London, 1856;

AWARDED FOR THE SUPERIOR QUALITY OF THEIR

STEEL, FILES, WIRE, TOOLS, &c.

E. LUCAS & SON,

Steel Converters

AND REFINERS,

MANUFACTURERS OF

SPINDLES AND FLYERS

OF ALL DESCRIPTIONS,

FILES, EDGE TOOLS,

Cast Steel Spades and Shovels,

AGRICULTURAL IMPLEMENTS

MALLEABLE IRON FOUNDERS.

THE ORIGINAL PATENTEES OF MALLEABLE CAST IRON,

AND

GENERAL MERCHANTS,

DRONFIELD FOUNDRY,

NEAR SHEFFIELD.

THOMAS TURNER & CO.,

SUFFOLK WORKS, SHEFFIELD,

MANUFACTURERS OF

TABLE KNIVES

AND FORKS,

Silber and Plated Table Knibes and Forks,

DESSERTS, FISH CARVERS, FRUIT KNIVES

AND SCISSORS,

PEN AND POCKET KNIVES,

GARDENERS' KNIVES,

AND RAZOR; also,

SAW FILES, EDGE TOOLS,

AND STEEL.

A CAUTION.—WHEREAS, certain parties have of late assumed the title of "TURNER & Co.," we deem it advisable, in justification to ourselves, to notice the matter by public advertisement, and otherwise to caution our friends, lest they be imposed upon by the deception thus practised. All parties will therefore kindly observe, that our address be written in full, and that goods be marked with our corporate mark.

THOMAS TURNER & Co., SUFFOLK WORKS.

We beg further to observe that we shall commence the usual proceedings against any person infringing upon any of our Trade Marks.

MESSRS. BIRKS'S
TEA, COFFEE, AND GROCERY
ESTABLISHMENT.

(From the Sheffield and Rotherham Independent of December 22, 1860.)

THE enormous development of some of our large manufacturing establishments, is the subject of every-day remark; but not a wit less surprising is the development of some of our principal retail establishments. Prominent among these is that of Messrs. BIRKS, of 69, Market-place, which has just been greatly enlarged by the addition of the whole of the back, and nearly the whole of the upper front premises, attached to the adjoining shop of Mr. Bach,—an enlargement which has enabled Messrs. BIRKS to make a wide and convenient entrance from the Hartshead passage for general access to the wholesale, and access to the rear retail shop during the busier periods of the week. Capacious as is the front shop of Messrs. BIRKS, it forms but an insignificant part of the whole establishment, the retail sale room, which has just been added in the rear, with *all the stories above it, being of even larger dimensions.* The establishment including the cellaring, which, during the last few weeks, has been far more than doubled, embraces five stories, comprising no less than nineteen rooms, many of them of the largest size. It contains machinery of the completest character for the grinding and roasting of coffee, the grinding of pepper, mace, and spices; for the dressing of fruit, the cutting of lump sugar, and the hoisting of heavy packages, &c. The sale rooms are fitted up with every appliance for the prompt despatch of business. Every shopman has a pair of scales suspended over the counter at his own position; every two have a till between them; while on shelves under and behind the counter are stowed various sized packages, ready

MESSRS. BIRKS'S FRONT SHOP—51 FEET LONG.

weighed, of all the articles most in request. Immense as is the establishment, there is not a corner, niche, or recess, however small, from the cellar to the roof, but is filled with stock, weighed or unweighed, in addition to the immense numbers of small packages piled upon the shelving behind, and in the recesses beneath the long counters. Indeed, the quantity of goods weighed and packed, in anticipation of Saturday's and Monday's demand, is something enormous, looking more like a full year's provision than the supply for a couple of days. One ton of candied lemon; upwards of a ton of coffee: two tons of tea, in packages varying from an ounce to one pound and upwards; and fifteen tons of currants and raisins; such are the quantities weighed and packed of some of the lighter and more costly articles. From these figures, and from the fact that no less than 45 persons are employed, some idea may be formed of the amount of business transacted at this widely known and extensive establishment.

MESSRS. BIRKS'S BACK SHOP—79 FEET LONG.
Entrance either through the Front Shop or from Hartshead passage.

S. S. BRITTAIN & Co.,

ST. GEORGE'S WORKS.

SHEFFIELD.

MANUFACTURERS OF

SAWS, FILES,

EDGE TOOLS, &c.,

ALSO OF

BLISTER, SHEAR, CAST, SPRING,

AND ALL OTHER DESCRIPTIONS OF

STEEL.

S. S. B. & Co.'s SUPERIOR

CIRCULAR, MILL, & SEGMENT

SAWS

Are universally approved, and can be Manufactured to any given Specification.

N.B.--First-rate Workmen employed, & none but the best Material used.

Sierras de Acero Fundido Garantizado de la Fabrica de
S. S. BRITTAIN Y Co.

Limas Garantidas de Acero Fundido Superior de la Fabrica
de S. S. BRITTAIN Y Cia.

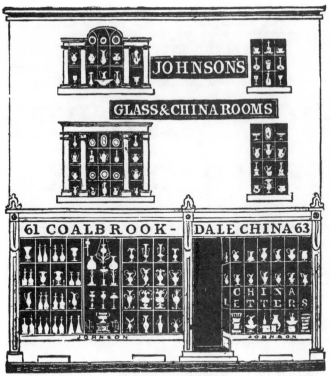

ESTABLISHED 1797.

JOSEPH JOHNSON,
GLASS, CHINA, and LAMP ROOMS,

61. & 63. FARGATE,
SHEFFIELD.

In these rooms are displayed one of the largest stocks in the
Provinces of

GLASS, CHINA, EARTHENWARE, LAMPS,
BOHEMIAN & FRENCH VASES, PARIAN STATUETTES, &c.,

Manufactured by Minton, Copeland, Wedgewood, and other First
class Makers; also from the Coalbrook-dale and Worcester China
Works. CRYSTAL TABLE GLASS from the *best Makers in
the Kingdom.*

J. J. is the Manufacturer of the IMPROVED WATER FILTER, at
8s.6d. & upwards.

DEALER IN FRENCH COLZA OIL, AND YOUNG'S PARAFFIN OIL.

SAMUEL OSBORN,

CLYDE STEEL WORKS,

SHEFFIELD,

CONVERTER

AND

REFINER OF STEEL,

AND MANUFACTURER OF

BEST CAST STEEL

FOR

TOOLS, CHISELS, TAPS, AND DIES,

SINGLE & DOUBLE SHEAR STEEL,

BLISTER, COACH, AND RAILWAY SPRING STEEL,

AND

ALL KINDS OF STEEL FOR MINING PURPOSES, &c.

FILES MADE OF THE BEST REFINED CAST STEEL,

AND IN EVERY VARIETY, FOR ENGINEERS,' MACHINISTS,' & SMITHS' PURPOSES.

SOLID CAST STEEL HAMMERS,

SAWS & TOOLS of SUPERIOR QUALITY

MERCHANT, AND IMPORTER OF

SWEDISH, RUSSIAN, AND OTHER FOREIGN IRONS.

SAMUEL OSBORN,

FABRICANT

D'ACIER, DE LIMES, DE SCIES, ET D'OUTILS,

EN TOUT GENRE,

CLYDE STEEL WORKS, SHEFFIELD

ANGLETERRE.

COPPER-PLATE
AND
LITHOGRAPHIC PRINTING,
PLAIN AND ORNAMENTAL.

PAWSON & BRAILSFORD,

CHURCH GATES,

HIGH STREET, SHEFFIELD,

Gratefully acknowledge the liberal support which has been given to them in these departments of their business, and respectfully announce that they have been thereby enabled to make such extension of Premises, Mechanical Improvements, and additions to their Staff, as qualify them to execute economically and in the best style, every variety of

ENGRAVING AND LITHOGRAPHY,

Whether Plain, Tinted, Coloured or Embossed

ILLUSTRATED LISTS.	SHOW CARDS.
MANUFACTURERS' DRAWINGS.	NOTE & LETTER HEADINGS.
PATTERN BOOKS.	PLANS OF ESTATES, &C.
BUSINESS ADDRESS CARDS.	VIEWS OF BUILDINGS, *(Coloured or Plain.)*
LABELS OF ALL KINDS.	ORNAMENTAL CIRCULARS,
BANKERS' CHEQUES.	CARDS, &C.
BILLS OF EXCHANGE.	CRESTS, CYPHERS, LAW
INVOICES.	FORMS, &C.

Every process executed on the premises by Artists and Workmen of first-rate ability.

Mechanical and Ornamental Drawings furnished of any Objects intended to be Engraved or Lithographed.

Estimates supplied and samples exhibited. Periodical Contracts made with Public Companies and other large consumers.

STATIONERY.

Possessing special advantages in the purchase of Papers, Pawson and Brailsford are able to supply Account Books, Letter and Note Papers, Envelopes, &c., at very low prices. All Ledgers and other Account Books being made on their own premises, they can warrant them in all respects the best that can be produced.

PRINTING EXECUTED BY STEAM POWER.

MOSES EADON & SONS,

MANUFACTURERS OF

STEEL, FILES, SAWS,

BY ROYAL LETTERS PATENT, No. 1628,

INVENTORS AND PATENTEES OF THE

Solid Endless Belt or Band Saw,

PATENT PLANE IRONS, IMPROVED TOBACCO KNIVES,

MOULDING & GROOVING SAWS & IRONS,

AND OTHER MACHINE KNIVES,

CAST STEEL ENGINEER HAMMERS,

RATCHET BRACES, &c., &c.,

SOLID TILLER BUCKLES, WEDGES, &c.,

Machine - Ground Circular Saws,
Mill Webs,

CONVERTERS & REFINERS OF STEEL,

PRESIDENT STEEL WORKS,

SHEFFIELD.

N.B. Mark,—"MOSES EADON."

CASTLE WORKS,

105, EDWARD-ST., SHEFFIELD.

CORPORATE | ACUTE | MARK.

Granted according to Act of Parliament by the Cutlers' Company, 1770.

F. G. PEARSON,

(Formerly Manager to MESSRS. SPEAR AND JACKSON, and late Manager at MESSRS. SORBY AND SONS,)

MERCHANT, AND MANUFACTURER

OF EVERY DESCRIPTION OF

LIGHT AND HEAVY EDGE TOOLS,

AUGERS, GIMBLETS, AWLS;

JOINERS' TOOLS,

AND OF THE CELEBRATED

CAST STEEL BRIGHT ELASTIC HAY, MANURE, AND DIGGING FORKS;

CAST STEEL REAPING KNIVES,

CHAFF KNIVES, GARDEN HOES,

Turnip Cutters, &c., made to Order at Reasonable Prices.

LONGDEN & CO.,

MANUFACTURERS OF

ORNAMENTAL FIRE GRATES

APPARATUS FOR COOKING

By open or close Fires, by Steam or by Gas;

WARM AIR STOVES,

VENTILATING HOT WATER APPARATUS,

STAIRBALUSTERS, PALISADES, TOMB RAILINGS, &C.

ALSO OF

CASE-HARDENED AND GRAIN ROLLS,

AND CASTINGS FOR HEAVY MILL WORK,

PHŒNIX FOUNDRY, FURNACE HILL,

SHEFFIELD.

CORPORATE  **MARK.**

Granted according to Act of Parliament by the Cutlers' Company, 1770.

PEACE BROTHERS,

GARDEN-STREET STEEL & FILE WORKS,

SHEFFIELD,

GENERAL MERCHANTS,

AND MANUFACTURERS OF ALL KINDS OF

CAST, SHEAR, AND BLISTER

STEEL,

FILES, SAWS, EDGE TOOLS,

MACHINE KNIVES, &c.

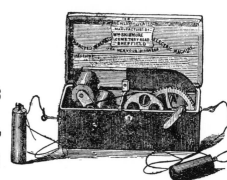

JOHN WALTERS & CO.,

GLOBE WORKS,

SHEFFIELD,

Prize Medal, Great Exhibition, 1851, awarded to
J. WALTERS & Co., for the superiority
of their Goods.

CORPORATE  MARKS.

MANUFACTURERS OF EVERY DESCRIPTION OF

TABLE AND SPRING CUTLERY,

RAZORS & SCISSORS;

WARRANTED CAST STEEL FILES,

FOR ENGINEERS AND BRASS FOUNDERS.

SOLE MANUFACTURERS OF J. WALTERS & CO.'S

Patent Adjustable Vice.

LONG AND SHORT SAWS.

LIGHT AND HEAVY EDGE TOOLS.

48, SNIG HILL, SHEFFIELD.

THOMAS Mc GIVERN,

MERCHANT, AND MANUFACTURER

OF EVERY DESCRIPTION OF

CUTLERY, EDGE TOOLS, FILES, &c.,

FOR HOME TRADE AND EXPORTATION.

A LARGE STOCK ALWAYS ON HAND.

☞ *No connection with any other House in Sheffield.*

STEEL & GARLAND,

STOVE GRATE

AND

FENDER MANUFACTURERS,

WHARNCLIFFE WORKS,

SHEFFIELD.

HOT-AIR STOVES, ASHES PANS, AND FIRE IRONS.

J. GIBBINS & SONS,

MANUFACTURERS OF

SCISSORS

OF EVERY DESCRIPTION,

NAIL & CHAMPAGNE NIPPERS,

Slide Pruning Shears, &c., &c.; also,

PEN, POCKET, AND SPORTSMEN'S KNIVES,

HEADFORD STREET,

SHEFFIELD.

SPEAR & JACKSON

CONVERTERS

AND

REFINERS OF STEEL,

MANUFACTURERS OF

SAWS, FILES, EDGE TOOLS,

CURRIERS'

AND

TANNERS' TOOLS,

LEDGER BLADES AND SPIRAL CUTTERS,

PATENT SOLID CAST STEEL,

SPADES & SHOVELS,

HAY, MANURE, & DIGGING FORKS.

Contractors for Mining and Trenching Tools to
Her Majesty's War Department.

ÆTNA WORKS, SHEFFIELD.

No. 3131.

No. 3130½.

By Special

Appointment.

THOMAS WILKINSON AND SON,

No. 17,

NEW CHURCH STREET,

SHEFFIELD,

MANUFACTURERS OF SCISSORS TO HER MAJESTY.

CUTLERS TO HIS LATE R. H. PRINCE ALBERT.

Manufacturers of the Celebrated Tailors' Shears, with Brass and German Silver Handles.

First Class Prize Medals awarded to Thomas Wilkinson and Son at the Great Exhibition, 1851, and the Paris Exhibition, 1855.

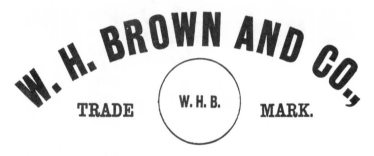

W. H. BROWN AND CO.,

TRADE W. H. B. MARK.

ALBION IRON AND STEEL WORKS,

SHEFFIELD,

MANUFACTURERS OF

INDIAN, SPANISH, AND SWEDISH

BAR IRON AND STEEL;

Cast Steel, for Wire, in Rods or Coils; for Needles, Hackle Pins, Umbrella Ribs, Fish Hooks, Spiral Springs, Telegraphs, Pit Ropes, Marine Cables, and other purposes;

CAST STEEL IN RODS,

For Spindles, Razors, Scissors, Table, Pen & Pocket Knives, Hammers, Chisels, Edge Tools, and Bars for Railway Carriage and Locomotive Engine Springs, &c., &c.

ALSO, MANUFACTURERS OF

CRINOLINE STEEL,

In Sheets, flattened Wire, or cut into Strips, Hardened, and Tempered, ready for the covering process, and any other purpose to which Steel may be applied.

WALKER AND HALL,

Electro - Platers

AND GILDERS,

AND

ELECTRO-BRONZERS,

MANUFACTURERS OF

ELECTRO-PLATED

SPOONS & FORKS,

DESSERT,

BUTTER AND FISH KNIVES

&c., IN EVERY VARIETY,

ELECTRO WORKS,

HOWARD-STREET,

SHEFFIELD.

CORPORATE MARK.

JAMES CHESTERMAN & CO.,

(LATE CUTTS, CHESTERMAN, AND BEDINGTON,)

BOW WORKS, NURSERY STREET,

SHEFFIELD,

AND 5, EYRE STREET HILL, HATTON GARDEN,

LONDON,

SOLE MANUFACTURERS OF

CHESTERMAN'S PATENT

SPRING, METALLIC, STEEL,

AND OTHER TAPE MEASURES,

STEEL RULES, SQUARES, & STRAIGHT EDGES

IRON & HARDENED & TEMPERED STEEL LAND CHAINS.

ENGINEERS' TOOLS, SCISSORS, BUSKS,

CAP SPRINGS,

CRINOLINE STEEL, &c., &c.

MANUFACTURERS OF THE

PATENT SPRING JOINT SCISSORS,

AND THE

PATENT PORTABLE TENT.

CORPORATE   J C   MARK.

DODDS AND SON,

HOLMES ENGINE & RAILWAY WORKS,

ROTHERHAM,

ENGINEERS AND MILLWRIGHTS,

MANUFACTURERS OF THE

PATENT WEDGE EXPANSIVE MOTION,

Locomotive, Portable, Stationary, and other Steam Engines;

PATENT STEAM HAMMERS AND TILTS,

WITH ADJUSTING ANVILS;

TURN-TABLES, POINTS, & CROSSINGS;

BOILERS of every Description,

PROOF AGAINST BURSTING;

T. W. DODDS' PATENT WHEEL AND AXLE,

Wrought Iron Girders, Castings, Railway Bar Straightening Presses, and every kind of Railway Rolling Stock;

ANVILS, SCREW JACKS,

&c.;

Spades and Shovels Steeled by T. W. Dodds' Patent;

ALSO HIS

PATENT UNOXYDIZING STEEL FOR BOILER PLATES,

PATENT STEEL TYRES, AXLES, & RAILS,

MANUFACTURERS AND LICENSERS OF

DODDS' PATENT FILES,

Which for Quality and Price are unequalled; Testimonials from the most eminent Engineers of the day.

Sole Provincial Agents for Baillie's Patent Volute Springs for General Railway Purposes. Patentees and Manufacturers of every kind of Steel and Case-Hardening Material.

LOCOMOTIVE ENGINES AND ROLLING STOCK, RAILS, CHAIRS, &c.,

Inspected or Valued for Home or Exportation.

MOROCCO & CABINET WORKS,

10, ST. THOMAS STREET, SHEFFIELD.

JAMES DEWSNAP,

MANUFACTURER OF

Table & Dessert Knife Cases,

PLATE CHESTS & CABINETS,

Military Canteens,

FISH CARVER CASES,

KNIFE, FORK, AND SPOON CASES,

Ladies' and Gentlemen's

TRAVELLING DRESSING BAGS,

DRESSING CASES & WRITING DESKS.

LADIES' AND GENTLEMEN'S ETUI CASE,

IN SOLID IVORY,

Mother-o-Pearl, Tortoise Shell, all kinds of Fancy Wood,
Russia, and every description of Fancy
Leather, &c., &c., &c.

RAZOR CASES AND STROPS.

ALL DESCRIPTIONS OF PATTERN CARDS.

ALMA FILE & STEEL WORKS,
SHEFFIELD.

WILLIAM HALL
CONVERTER

AND

Cast Steel Refiner,

MERCHANT,

AND MANUFACTURER OF

FILES, EDGE TOOLS,
SAWS,
TABLE CUTLERY,

&c., &c.

None are Genuine unless Stamped } W. HALL,
with the Corporate Mark, } 2865.

WILLIAM OWEN,

(LATE SANDFORD AND OWEN,)

PHŒNIX IRONWORKS, FORGE & FOUNDRY,

ROTHERHAM,

Manufacturer of Arbel's Patent Stamped Solid Wrought Iron Engine, Tender, Carriage, and Waggon Wheels. Owen's Patent & other Axles, Best Best Solid Weldless Tyres, finished by Owen's Patent Rolling Process, so that turning or boring is rendered unnecessary. Hammered Shafts, Uses and best bar iron of every description. Engine, Carriage, Waggon and general Ironwork, Buffers, Axleboxes, and every other description of Castings.

STEER'S HOTEL

AND

DINING ROOMS,

OLD HAYMARKET,

(CORNER OF DIXON LANE,)

SHEFFIELD.

ANTHONY ROTHERAM,

CORPORATE MARK.

FOR MANY YEARS IN THE EMPLOY OF

J. RODGERS AND SONS, CUTLERS TO HER MAJESTY,

MANUFACTURER OF

TABLE KNIVES,

PEN, POCKET,

AND

SPORTMEN'S KNIVES, RAZORS, &c.,

OLD ROCKINGHAM WORKS,

ROCKINGHAM STREET, SHEFFIELD.

A. R. has had the honour of supplying all the Cutlery required for the Refreshment Stalls at the Great Exhibition of 1862.

MACHEN, MILLER & MACHEN

Steel Converters

AND REFINERS,

MANUFACTURERS OF EVERY DESCRIPTION OF

FILES & RASPS,

AND

GENERAL MERCHANTS,

WADSLEY BRIDGE

FILE & STEEL WORKS,

Near SHEFFIELD.

IMPORTANT TO BREWERS.

COOPER'S REFRIGERATOR.

GEORGE COOPER,

ELECTRIC WORKS, WICKER LANE, SHEFFIELD,

Begs respectfully to call the attention of Brewers to the important advantages of this REFRIGERATOR, the principle of which is explained in the accompanying Engravings.

This Invention, besides preventing the great loss from evaporation which arises in cooling under the old process—a saving of fully three per cent. will enable the Brewer TO COOL IN ONE HOUR 30 BARRELS, or 1,080 gallons of wort, a quantity which, under the ordinary process of cooling with fans, &c., would take during the summer no less than *eight hours* and during winter *five or six hours.*

In addition to the great saving realized by the rapidity with which the cooling of the wort is carried on, Cooper's Refrigerator has also effected a saving of one barrel in every forty from evaporation alone!

COOPER'S REFRIGERATOR, Figure 1.

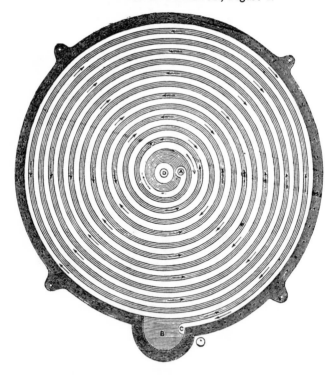

Figure 1 represents the interior. The hot wort enters at the receiver B, being then at a temperature of 140. Passing along the channels shown by the shaded lines in the engraving, it comes in contact with a continuous body of cold water flowing through the channels shown white, the effect of which is that by the time the wort leaves the Refrigerator at the tap D, its temperature has been reduced to 60. The letter A shows the point at which the continuous stream of cold water enters from the cistern, and C the overflow pipe by which, after accomplishing its purpose of cooling the malt wort, it leaves the Refrigerator.

COOPER'S REFRIGERATOR, Fig. 2.

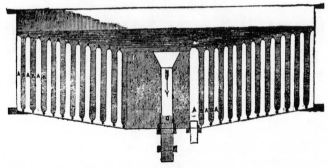

This engraving shows a cross section of the Refrigerator. A represents the water inlet pipe and channels, and B the wort channels. C shows the outlet for the wort.

COOPER'S REFRIGERATOR, Fig. 3.

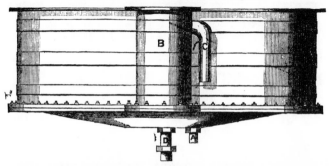

This gives the exterior view. A is the water inlet pipe, and C is its outlet. B is the receiver whence the hot wort enters from the hopbecks, and D the tap at which the wort leaves the Refrigerator. The bottom of the Refrigerator is fastened by the screws shewn in the engraving, and can be detached when required for the purpose of cleansing the watercourse. This Refrigerator takes two barrels of water to one of wort.

TESTIMONIAL.

Pond Street Brewery, Sheffield, May, 1862.

MR. GEORGE COOPER,—SIR,—The Refrigerator made by you has been in constant work for upwards of eighteen months, and we have pleasure in bearing testimony to its durability, simplicity, and large amount of cooling surface; it has fully answered our expectations.

We are, Sir, yours truly,   THOS. RAWSON & CO.

GEORGE COOPER,

Coppersmith, Tinner, Brazier, Sheet Iron, and Zinc Worker, Whitesmith, Locksmith, Gas-Fitter, Bell-Hanger, &c.

PATENTEE & MANUFACTURER OF THE NEWLY-INVENTED SAFETY LAMP FOR COLLIERS,

BY HER MAJESTY'S ROYAL LETTERS PATENT.

Manufacturer of Spargers, Refrigerators, Cooking Apparatus, Copper Boilers, Piping, Balls, Stove Piping, Wrought-Iron Gates, Palisading, Tomb Railing, Hurdles, Fancy Park Fencing, Wind Vanes, Water Tue Irons, and all kinds of Furnace Work; Patent and Registered Chimney Tops, Patent and Galvanized Iron and Zinc Eaves, made to any design; Guttering, Fall-Pipes, Sausage Machines, &c. Packing Cases and Casks lined on the shortest notice. Fire Engines, Garden Engines, and Baths of every description, Wholesale and Retail. Shower, Hip, and Slipper Baths Let Out. Sole Manufacturer of Thomas Restell's Louvre, Venetian and Invisible Ventilators, by Her Majesty's Royal Letters Patent.

ORNAMENTAL ART.

Theophilus Smith, Sculptor and Ornamentalist,

16, CEMETERY ROAD, SHEFFIELD,

Designer, Modeller, and Decorator

In connection with the various branches of Ornamental Manufacture, viz., PLATE in GOLD, SILVER, and ELECTRO BRONZE, STOVE GRATES, and all kinds of ORNAMENTAL CASTINGS in Iron.

CHANDELIERS and every description of Ornamental Castings in Brass and Bronze.

MEMORIAL BRASSES, &c.

CARVING (Ornamental or Ecclesiastical) in Stone, Alabastar, Marble, &c.

DESIGNS for POLYCHROMIC DECORATIONS for Civil and Ecclesiastical purposes.

BERNARD SEALE,

27, CHURCH ST., & ATTERCLIFFE BRIDGE,

PLUMBER, GLAZIER,

AND

GAS FITTER.

AGENT TO THE BIRMINGHAM PLATE GLASS COMPANY.

JAMES COCKER,

(LATE JOHN COCKER & SON,)

CAST STEEL WIRE DRAWER,

STEEL REFINER,

MANUFACTURER OF SPIRAL SPRINGS,

PATENT DOOR SPRINGS,

HACKLE AND GILL SPRINGS, &c., &c.,

WICKER WIRE AND STEEL WORKS,

BLONK STREET, SHEFFIELD.

SIDNEY STREET, BOTTOM OF FURNIVAL STREET AND DUKE STREET, SHEFFIELD.

JOSEPH SMITH.

ENGLISH AND FOREIGN TIMBER MERCHANT,

IVORY, BONE, & WOOD TURNER, &c.,

MANUFACTURER of Tea Pot Handles; Ivory, Ebony, Fancy Wood, and Japanned DRAWER and DOOR KNOBS
of every description;

Dealer in all kinds of WHEELWRIGHTS' TIMBER, cut out & Seasoned for present use; also, DEAL BOARDS, TIMBER, &c.

SAW MILLS FOR CUTTING DEALS, LATHS, BENT-WORK, &c.

CONTRACTOR FOR OAK TIMBER, CUT OUT FOR RAILWAY AND COLLIERY PURPOSES.

ALWAYS ON HAND A LARGE QUANTITY OF WHEELBARROWS.

JOHN HARRISON,

MANUFACTURER OF

EVERY DESCRIPTION OF

SILVER, SILVER - PLATED

AND

BRITANNIA METAL GOODS,

COMPRISING

THE NEWEST AND MOST CHASTE DESIGNS

IN

DISHES, DISH COVERS,

DINNER SERVICES,

TEA AND COFFEE SETS,

CRUET AND LIQUOR FRAMES,

CAKE AND CARD BASKETS,

WAITERS, VASES, EPERGNES,

Communion Services, &c., &c.;

SPOONS, FORKS, LADLES, FISH CARVERS,

ASPARAGUS TONGS, ETC.;

DESSERT KNIVES AND FORKS

With Pearl, Ivory, Silver, and Plated Handles.

NORFOLK WORKS, SHEFFIELD.

N.B.—A large assortment of Silver Goods and Presentation Plate always in Stock.

MOULSON BROTHERS,

Merchants and Manufacturers of

SAWS, EDGE TOOLS,

JOINERS' TOOLS,

STEEL, FILES, & CUTLERY,

UNION WORKS,

SHEFFIELD.

BROOKES AND CROOKES,

ATLANTIC WORKS, ST. PHILIP'S ROAD,

SHEFFIELD,

MANUFACTURERS OF

FINE PENKNIVES, RAZORS, SCISSORS,

AND SPORTSMAN'S KNIVES;

ALSO MANUFACTURERS OF

Button Hooks, Nail Files, Tweezers, Stilettoes, and every description
of Pearl, Ivory, & Steel Instruments, suitable for Dressing Cases.

AGENTS FOR SAUNDER'S TABLET RAZOR STROPS.

CORPORATE MARK.

ESTABLISHED 1824.

JOSEPH PICKERING,

(Successor to the late J. Needham,)

MANUFACTURER OF

POLISHING PASTE,

FURNITURE POLISH,

PLATE POWDER, &c.

N.B.—As there are many
Imitations of NEEDHAM'S
POLISHING PASTE, see
that the Signature is on the
Label, as shown in the above
cut.

MANUFACTORY:—

22, MOWBRAY-ST., SHEFFIELD.

Sold retail by the principal Ironmongers, Druggists, Grocers, and
Brush Dealers in the United Kingdom.

SHEFFIELD FIRE OFFICE,

ESTABLISHED A.D. 1808.

Trustees.

WILLIAM FREDERICK DIXON, Esq., Page Hall, Sheffield.
WILLIAM SMITH, Esq., Dam House, Sheffield.
FRANCIS HUNTSMAN, Esq., Loversall, Doncaster.
JAMES WILSON, Esq., Brincliffe, Sheffield.

Directors.

WILLIAM FREDERICK DIXON, Esq., J.P., Chairman.

ELIAS LOWE, Esq.	WM. HOWARD, Esq.	EDWD. BINGHAM, Esq.
EDWIN SORBY, Esq.	WILLIAM JARVIS, Esq.	EDMUND J. READ, Esq.
SAML. MITCHELL, Esq.	FRANCIS WHITE, Esq.	SAMUEL BARKER, Esq.
JOHN BOOTH, Esq.	WM. JENKINSON, Esq,	JOHN WILSON, Esq.
WM. FAWCETT, Esq.	JAS. SANDERSON, Esq.	REV. H. BARLOW.
J. HOULT DIXON, Esq.	EDWD. HUDSON, Esq.	

Auditor.—SAMUEL MITCHELL, Esq.

Bankers.

THE SHEFFIELD BANKING COMPANY, AND THE SHEFFIELD
AND ROTHERHAM BANKING COMPANY.

Solicitors.—MESSRS. W. & B. WAKE.

Secretary.—MR. CHARLES ESAM.

The Directors beg to call the attention of their *Shareholders* as well as their *Townsmen* and the Inhabitants of this neighbourhood generally, to the *special claims* which it is believed this *long-established Local Office* has for their patronage and support.

1. It was the first Office established in the town of Sheffield.

2. It is the only Insurance establishment whose head office is in Sheffield or the neighbourhood,

3. It has been in operation for fifty-four years.

4. The Shareholders are principally inhabitants of the town and neighbourhood of Sheffield.

5. The Directors are all resident in or near that town, which greatly conduces to, and has hitherto resulted in, a prompt and liberal adjustment of all claims.

6. No expense attends the transfer of Policies from other offices, and all alterations are made free from charge.

7. From the extent and character of the Company's business it is enabled to effect Insurances at rates as low as those of any substantial and safely conducted office, and parties insuring in it possess the advantage of having, free of all charge, the use of the Company's powerful and efficient engines whenever required.

8. Farming Stock insured at 5s. per cent. premium without, and 4s. per cent. with, the average clause, and Steam thrashing Machines allowed.

9. Compensation for losses arising from lightning and explosions of gas.

Any further information may be obtained on application to

Mr. CHARLES ESAM, Secretary.

W. K. & C. PEACE,

(LATE IBBOTSON, PEACE, & Co.,)

EAGLE WORKS, MOWBRAY ST.,

MERCHANTS & MANUFACTURERS OF

STEEL, FILES, SAWS,

EDGE TOOLS,

PATENT SCYTHES, STRAW KNIVES,

MACHINE KNIVES, &c.,

Manufacturers of the Goods Stamped { "IBBOTSON, PEACE, and Co." and "R. IBBOTSON."

JOSEPH PEACE & CO.

STEEL CONVERTERS AND REFINERS,

FORGERS, TILTERS & ROLLERS

MANUFACTURERS OF

SAWS, FILES, BUSKS,

Doctors', Machine, Cork, and Tobacco Knives,

LOOM, TRUSS, LEGGING, TRUNK, & OTHER SPRINGS,

CRINOLINE ROLLERS & MANUFACTURERS.

INVENTORS OF THE

REGISTERED PLATES FOR SAW HANDLES, ORNAMENTED SAWS, AND COLD ROLLED SAWS.

MERCHANT WORKS, NEEPSEND LANE,

SHEFFIELD.

Prize Medal awarded for SAWS, at the Exhibition, 1851.

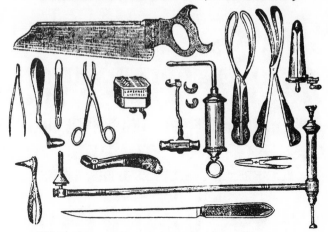

ESTABLISHED 1750,

THE
Only Prize Medal
AT THE
GREAT EXHIBITION,
1851,
FOR
Sheep and Other Shears,

WAS AWARDED TO

WILLIAM WILKINSON & SONS

GRIMESTHORPE, NEAR SHEFFIELD,

MANUFACTURERS AND INVENTORS OF THE NEW

PATENT SHEEP SHEARS,

AND EVERY DESCRIPTION OF

SHEEP, HORSE, GLOVERS', THATCHERS', AND WEAVERS' SHEARS;

SHOE, BUTCHERS', COOK, PALLETTE, BREAD KNIVES,

&c., &c.

Observe that the Address be written in full and that the Goods
are marked with our Corporate Mark.

And on the
reverse blade the
CORPORATE MARK.

WILLIAM WILKINSON & SONS,

GRIMESTHORPE, NEAR SHEFFIELD.

SEE INTERNATIONAL E HIBITION, 1862, CLASS 32.

ARGUS
LIFE ASSURANCE COMPANY,
39, THROGMORTON STREET, BANK, LONDON.

Chairman—WILLIAM LEAF, Esq.
Deputy Chairman—JOHN HUMPHERY, Esq., Alderman.

Accumulated fund, £510,000 ; income, upwards of £85,000 per annum ; subscribed capital, £300,000.

PREMIUM TO ASSURE £100.

Age.	One Year.	Seven Years.	Whole Term.	
			With Profits.	Without Profits.
20	0 17 8	0 19 1	1 15 10	1 11 10
30	1 1 8	1 2 7	2 5 5	2 0 7
35	1 3 3	1 4 2	2 12 1	2 6 8
40	1 5 0	1 6 9	3 0 7	2 14 10
50	1 14 1	1 19 10	4 6 8	4 0 11

Advantages of Assuring with this Company.

The premiums are on the lowest scale consistent with security.
Half or one third credit allowed on whole-life policies.
No charge for the volunteer rifle or artillery corps, on home service.
Claims paid one month after satisfactory proof of death.

MEDICAL REFEREES FOR SHEFFIELD :
WILSON OVEREND, Esq., and EDWARD JACKSON, Esq.
AGENTS :
Messrs. MILNER, BURBEARY, and SMITH, 8, Campo Lane,
AND
Mr. CHARLES ESAM, Sheffield Fire Office, George Street.

RALPH SKELTON,
CHURCH STREET, ATTERCLIFFE, NEAR SHEFFIELD,
ORIGINAL MAKER OF THE
SOLID STEEL SPADES AND SHOVELS, WARRANTED,
AND MANUFACTURER OF
SPADES AND SHOVELS,
DRAINING AND GRAFTING TOOLS,
HAY & PARING SPADES, LOCOMOTIVE & SOCKET SPADES, SHOVELS,
GRIPES, &c., of superior quality.

S. & C. WARDLOW,
STEEL MANUFACTURERS
SHEFFIELD.

MANUFACTORIES:
PORTOBELLO STEEL WORKS, SHEFFIELD.
CONGRESS STEEL WORKS, OUGHTIBRIDGE.

BRANCH OFFICE & STORES:
20, CLIFF-STREET, NEW YORK, U.S.

ALFRED UNWIN,
STEEL MANUFACTURER,
&c.,

WHITELEY WOOD & BLONK STREET
STEEL WORKS,
SHEFFIELD.

HENRY WILLIS,
MANUFACTURER OF ALL KINDS OF

CAST, SHEAR, SPRING, AND CRINOLINE
STEEL,
CARLTON STEEL WORKS,
ATTERCLIFFE,
SHEFFIELD.

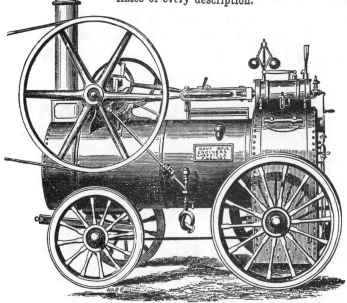

H. CUTLER, SON, AND CHAMBERS,

MERCHANTS & MANUFACTURERS OF

STEEL, TOOLS, FILES,

SAWS, CUTLERY, &c.,

CASTLE HILL WORKS,

SHEFFIELD.

ESTABLISHED BY THOMAS WELDON, in 1780.

CORPORATE MARKS. ☩ **F. WELDON. A.1.**

(To Imitate which is Felony.)

W. T. L. SMITHIES,

(LATE CUTLERY MANAGER TO MESSRS. HY. WILKINSON & Co., 20, NORFOLK ST.)

MANUFACTURER OF

Silber & Plated Dessert Knives & Forks,

FISH CARVERS, FISH EATING KNIVES & FORKS,

Melon & Cake Carvers, Butter Knives, Pickle Forks,

FINE TABLE CUTLERY,

BREAD KNIVES, CHEESE CARVERS, &C.,

NO. 62, UPPER ST. PHILIP'S ROAD,

SHEFFIELD.

T. REDMAYNE & CO.,

STOVE GRATE & FENDER

MANUFACTURERS,

WHEATHILL FOUNDRY,

ROTHERHAM.

HOT AIR STOVES, ASHES PANS, AND FIRE IRONS.

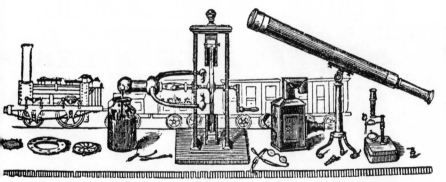

Exhibiting in the International Exhibition of 1862, Class 13, Case 2875, also Water and Steam Gauge in Eastern Annex and Patent Steam Gauges in Western Annex.

CHADBURN BROTHERS,

Opticians to his late R.H. the Prince Consort,

ALBION WORKS,

NURSERY, SHEFFIELD;

THE GREAT EXHIBITION JURY AWARD TO CHADBURN BROTHERS WAS FOR

GOOD & CHEAP INSTRUMENTS,

Shewn in the Exhibition, especially in reference to their light Elastic Steel SPECTACLES.

MANUFACTURERS OF

SPECTACLES, TELESCOPES, MICROSCOPES, STEREOSCOPES,

AND ALL KINDS OF

OPTICAL AND MATHEMATICAL INSTRUMENTS,

BAROMETERS, THERMOMETERS, RULES;

GALVANIC, ELECTRIC, AND OTHER APPARATUS.

Visitors are invited to inspect C.B.'s EXHIBITION ROOM, Nursery street, Sheffield, which contains a great variety of the above Instruments, MODELS of STEAM ENGINES, the EYE, &c.; and an extensive assortment of other interesting objects. C.B. adapt with the *greatest care* their SPECTACLES of the *most* APPROVED *construction and* QUALITY, to the *various defects of* VISION, or for its *Preservation*, at the most reasonable Prices. Articles purchased of C.B. if not approved may be exchanged.

PATENT METALLIC STEAM OR WATER PRESSURE GAUGES.

PHOTOGRAPHIC CHEMICALS AND APPARATUS.

Instruments by Celebrated London & Continental Makers.

CHADBURNS' OBSERVATIONS ON THE CHOICE OF SPECTACLES AND WHOLESALE AND RETAIL LISTS OF PRICES, ON APPLICATION, GRATIS; WITH COPPER-PLATE ENGRAVINGS, ONE SHILLING EACH.

BRANCH ESTABLISHMENT, 17, LORD ST., LIVERPOOL.

JAMES HOWARTH,

BROOMSPRING WORKS,

BATH-ST., FITZWILLIAM-ST.,

SHEFFIELD,

MERCHANT, & MANUFACTURER OE EVERY DESCRIPTION OF

EDGE TOOLS and JOINERS' TOOLS,

SAWS & FIES, WARRANTED OF SUPERIOR QUALITY AND TEMPER.

Corporate Mark.

JAMES HOWARTH had the first-class Prize Medal awarded to him for the Superior Quality of his Tools, at the Exhibition of 1851. J. H. had the honour of receiving the Prize Medal at the Paris Exhibition, 1855.

JAMES HOWARTH has also been presented with the Special Medal of Honour by the Universal Society of Arts and Industry, London, for the superiority of his goods, as exhibited in Paris, 1855.

SLACK, SELLARS, and Co.,

CORPORATE

MARK.

SPEED

TOWNHEAD STREET, SHEFFIELD,

MERCHANTS,

MANUFACTURERS OF IMPROVED

SAWS, FILES, EDGE TOOLS,

LEDGER BLADES, SPIRAL CUTTERS, SPRING BEDS,

AND EVERY DESCRIPTION OF SAWS,

TO WORK BY POWER,

MACHINE KNIVES OF ALL KINDS,

STEEL CONVERTERS AND REFINERS.

S. S. and Co. were honoured with Prize Medals of the Exhibition of 1851.

SHORTRIDGE, HOWELL & Co.,

MERCHANTS,

STEEL CONVERTERS & REFINERS,

FORGE, TILT, AND ROLLING MILLS,

HARTFORD STEEL WORKS,

WICKER, SHEFFIELD,

39, BEDFORD STREET, STRAND, LONDON,

AND

24, CLIFFE STREET, NEW YORK.

MANUFACTURERS OF EVERY KIND OF CAST STEEL FOR

TAPS, DIES, CHISELS, AND TURNING TOOLS,

IMPROVED SOFT CENTRED STEEL FOR TAPS

WARRANTED NOT TO FLY IN HARDENING.   THIS ARTICLE IS INVALUABLE FOR LARGE TAPS.

IMPROVED HARD CENTRED STEEL FOR MINT DIES, LATHE
HARBORS, &c.   ALSO, IMPROVED

CAST STEEL FILES FOR ENGINEERS' & MACHINISTS' PURPOSES.

CORPORATE MARK. | SHOT |

SOLE MANUFACTURERS OF

HOWELL'S PATENT HOMOGENEOUS METAL,

Combining the strength of Steel with the malleability of Copper,

FOR PLATES, ANGLES, AND RIVETS FOR BOILERS,

ALSO PLATES FOR SHIP BUILDING, BREWING VATS,
AND LOCOMOTIVE FIRE BOXES.

SOLID AXLES, and CRANKS and PINS for MARINE and LOCOMO-
TIVE ENGINES, and PISTON RODS.

RUSSELL AND HOWELL'S PATENT HOMOGENEOUS

AND CAST STEEL TUBES.

Also, HOWELL'S PATENT CHAINS for Couplings for
Railway Carriages, Chain Cables, &c.,

As exhibiting in the International Exhibition, 1862, Class 32.

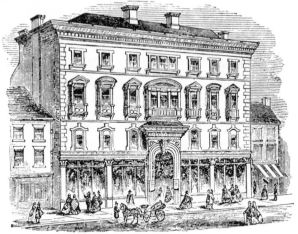

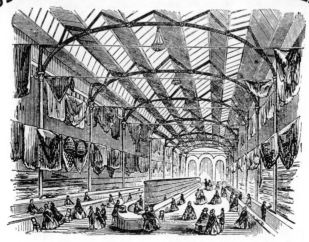

IMPORTANT TO HOUSEKEEPERS.

VICTORIA PARK

J. ADAMS'

UNIVERSALLY-APPROVED

PATENT FURNITURE POLISH,

*For Cleaning and Polishing Cabinet Furniture, Piano-fortes, Papier Mache,
Japanned and Varnished Goods, Carriage Bodies, &c.*

J. A. cautions the public against spurious Imitations, offered under the allurement
of cheapness, and got up to resemble the genuine article.

J. ADAMS'

IMPROVED

POLISHING PASTE,

For Brass, Copper, Britannia Metal, &c. Warranted a superior Article.

J. ADAMS'

HIGHLY-APPROVED PLATE POWDER,

Warranted free from Mercury.

PREPARED SOLELY BY THE INVENTOR,

J. ADAMS, CHEMIST,

VICTORIA PARK, (late Hanover-st.,) SHEFFIELD,

And sold Retail by Druggists, Grocers, Ironmongers, Cabinet Makers, &c.

*Shopkeepers supplied Wholesale, on liberal terms, by the Manufacturer, and the
Wholesale Houses in the above Trades throughout the Kingdom.*

See Exhibition, 1862, No. 118, Class 2.

ESTABLISHED 1817.

THOMAS COCKING,

CABINET MAKER,

UPHOLSTERER, & UNDERTAKER,

Nos. 15 & 17, WATSON'S WALK,

SHEFFIELD.

☞ Every description of Walnut, Mahogany, and Painted Furniture, kept in Stock, or made to order.
Shops Fitted up, and all kinds of Show Cases made.

York Family & Commercial Hotel,

BROOMHILL,  **SHEFFIELD,**

JOSEPH HIELD, Proprietor.

J.H. takes the present opportunity of returning his sincere thanks to the numerous Friends who have so kindly and liberally honoured him with their support during his occupation of the above Hotel.

The York Hotel is situated in a healthy locality, about twenty minutes' ride from the Railway Stations, and will be found to possess all the comforts of a private home. It has an excellent Commercial Room, Smoking Room, cheerful Sitting Rooms, and Comfortable Bed Rooms. The strictest attention is paid to cleanliness.

The Proprietor hopes to secure a continuance of the patronage and recommendation of his Friends, and begs to say that every article he supplies is of the best description, and on the most reasonable terms.

OMNIBUSES ARE CONSTANTLY RUNNING TO AND FROM THE TOWN,
A CAB STAND ADJOINING.

BRADLEY'S
SUPERIOR
SHEFFIELD ALES
INDIA PALE ALE,
HIGHLY PATRONISED PORTERS,
MADE OF PATENT CRYSTALISED MALT.

MESSRS. BRADLEY AND Co. beg to call the attention of the Public and Exporters to their

EAST INDIA PALE AND MILD ALES
AND MUCH PATRONISED PORTERS,

Which may be had in Casks of Eighteen Gallons and upwards, either singly or in any quantity, by application direct to

SOHO BREWERY, SHEFFIELD,

Or at their respective Stores, 60, High-street, Hull ; White Horse Yard, Chesterfield ; and Marsh Gate, Doncaster.

VICTORIA PARK HOTEL,

(OPPOSITE THE BOTANICAL GARDENS,)

Commercial & Family Boarding House,

SHEFFIELD.

JOHN LAW, PROPRIETOR.

WINES, &c., OF THE PUREST AND BEST QUALITY.

BOWLING GREEN & AMERICAN BOWLING ALLEY.

DINNER & TEA PARTIES will find excellent accommodation.

JOHN LAW,

LANDSCAPE GARDENER,

VICTORIA PARK, SHEFFIELD.

Plans and Estimates furnished for Villa Residences or Greenhouses.

OMNIBUSES pass hourly to and from the Station.

ESTABLISHED 1832.

WILLIAM JOHNSON,

CABINET MAKER

AND

UPHOLSTERER,

CARPET

AND

GENERAL FURNISHING

SHOW ROOMS,

82 and 84, FARGATE,

SHEFFIELD.

ESTIMATES GIVEN FOR COMPLETE HOUSE
FURNISHING.

Special Designs for Furniture, &c.
made to order.

THE SHEFFIELD UNITED
GAS LIGHT COMPANY.

INCORPORATED BY ACT OF PARLIAMENT, 1855.

GAS FITTERS,

AND MANUFACTURERS OF ALL KINDS OF

GAS BURNERS.

Dwelling-houses, Manufactories, and Public Buildings supplied
and fitted-up with

CHANDELIERS,

LAMPS, PENDANTS, BRACKETS, BURNERS,

AND

COOKING AND HEATING APPARATUS

OF EVERY DESCRIPTION.

THE SHEFFIELD UNITED
GAS LIGHT COMPANY'S
SHOW ROOMS & MANUFACTORY,
19, SHUDE HILL,
SHEFFIELD,

WHERE A LARGE AND VALUABLE ASSORTMENT OF

FITTINGS

Are constantly kept ready to be put up on the Shortest Notice,
and upon the most Reasonable Terms.

CONTRACTS

For a specified sum of money will be entered into by the Company,
if required, before the work is commenced.

W. H. STAFFORD,

For the guidance of his numerous Patrons, begs to apprise them of the various branches of Business executed at his

WEST END PAINTING ESTABLISHMENT.

House and Furniture Painting,

From its Plainest and Cheapest form, to its most highly-finished and durable style.

IMITATION OF WOODS AND MARBLES,

In their Cheapest form, upwards, to the most faithful resemblance of polished nature.

SIGN PAINTING & WRITING

Of every description on the most impressive principles.

WRITING & GILDING ON GLASS

For Shop Fronts and other Exhibitory Purposes.

ILLUMINATED OR MEDIÆVAL WRITING

For Ecclesiastical Purposes, &c.

WRITING AND ORNAMENTING

On Coloured Glass for Lamps, Fanlights, and Staircase Windows, with Arms, Crests, Monograms, &c.

Plate Glass, embossed and ornamented,

To exclude or confuse vision and improve light for Entrance Hall Doors, Offices, and lower parts of Windows.

PLATE GLASS FURNITURE PANELS,

DRAFT AND OTHER TABLE TOPS,

In Gold and Colours, Flat or Embossed.

Flags and Banners for Sunday Schools & Public Demonstrations.

W. H. STAFFORD'S,

WEST END PAINTING ESTABLISHMENT,

81½, WEST-STREET, SHEFFIELD.

THE

BLACK SWAN

Commercial & Family Hotel,

SHEFFIELD.

THOMAS S. MORRIS, PROPRIETOR

WINES, &c.,

OF THE PUREST AND BEST QUALITY.

LION HOTEL

Commercial, Family, & Posting House

WORKSOP, NOTTS.

Richard M. Morris, Proprietor.

EVERY CONVENIENCE HAS BEEN STUDIED IN THE POSTING AND CARRIAGE DEPARTMENT FOR EXCURSIONISTS VISITING THE EXTENSIVE AND BEAUTIFUL PARKS OF

Worksop Manor, Clumber, Welbeck, Thoresby, and Sherwood Forest.

P.S.—A LETTER BY POST WILL ENSURE PARTIES BEING MET AT THE STATION.

JOSEPH HADFIELD,

NORFOLK-LANE MARBLE WORKS,

NEAR THE FREE LIBRARY,

SURREY-STREET, SHEFFIELD,

AND No. 10, EARL-STREET, WESTMINSTER, S.W.

𝔙. ℜ.

POST OFFICE, DIVISION-ST.

C. K. JARVIS,

BOOKBINDER, PRINTER, BOOKSELLER, STATIONER,

AND NEWS AGENT.

BOOKBINDING in every variety of style, in Morocco, Russia, Calf, Vellum, Cloth, &c. or in the PUBLISHER'S OWN CASES IF REQUIRED, in the most secure and splendid style of Workmanship.

PRINTING.—Bill heads, Circulars, Advice Notes, Price Lists, Address Cards. and every description of Plain and Ornamental Printing.

STATIONERY.—Account Books of every description made to open perfectly flat. Day Books, Ledgers, Journals, Cash Books, and Tradesmen's Account Books; Wallets; Pocket, Metallic, and every variety of Memorandum Books; Copying and other Inks, Steel and Quill Pens; WRITING PAPERS and ENVELOPES in Extensive Assortment.

BOOKS.—Bibles, Prayer Books, Church Services and Hymn Books; and a great variety of Books suitable for Presents, &c.

NEWS AGENT.—C. K. J. engages to supply all the Daily and Weekly Newspapers, and Weekly, Monthly, and Quarterly Periodicals and Magazines, as early as they are out; Odd Books, and Back Numbers. Parcels from London Daily.

MUSIC.—New Music at Half-price. Many Thousands of Pieces of Cheap Music, Musical Instruction Books; Music Folios and Rolls; Violin Strings, Rosin, Pegs, Bridges, &c.

SCHCOL BOOKS of every ¡kind.

Schools and the Trade Supplied on the best Terms, at the POST OFFICE, DIVISION STREET.

TENNANT BROTHERS,

ALE, PORTER,

AND

BITTER BEER

BREWERS,

EXCHANGE BREWERY,

BRIDGE STREET,

S H E F F I E L D.

GEORGE MILLS,

Wool Stapler,

FELLMONGER

AND

Leather Dresser,

MANUFACTURER OF

SHUMAC SKIVERS,

OIL LEATHER, ROANS,

PLASTER SKINS,

Roller Leather, White Aprons & Strains,

GLUE, NEATS FOOT OIL, TALLOW, &C.

N.B. VELLUM & PARCHMENT.

FELLMONGERS WORKS,
NEEPSEND LANE, SHEFFIELD.

LEATHER MILLS,
TWELVE O'CLOCK, SHEFFIELD.

WAREHOUSE,
8, DIXON LANE, SHEFFIELD.

COMPLETE IMMUNITY FROM FIRE, THIEVES, & GUNPOWDER.

COTTERILL'S
IMPROVED PATENT WROUGHT-IRON
FIRE-PROOF SAFES, CHESTS, DEED, & BULLION BOXES,
Warranted in every way perfectly Fire-proof, Thief-proof, Powder-proof, and Drill-proof.

FITTED WITH THE "ROYAL CLIMAX DETECTOR LOCKS;"
The only Unpickable and Powder-proof Locks extant,
The Keys of which can neither be Copied, nor Impressions taken from them in Wax.
The only Keys possessing this great security.

DOUBLE CHAMBERED,
Fitted with the Royal Climax Detector Lock, and Hardened Steel Plates.
No. 50.

DOUBLE CHAMBERED.
Fitted with the Royal Climax Detector Lock, and Hardened Steel Plates.
No. 51.

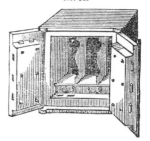

PRICES.

Inches High.	wide.	deep.	With Drawers. £ s. d.	Without Drawers. £ s. d.
24	18	18	9 0 0	8 0 0
26	20	20	10 0 0	9 0 0
28	22	22	11 10 0	10 10 0
30	24	24	13 0 0	11 10 0
32	26	26	15 0 0	13 10 0
34	26	26	17 10 0	16 0 0
36	26	26	20 0 0	18 10 0

Outside Measure.

PRICES.

Inches High.	wide.	deep.	With Drawers. £ s. d.	Without Drawers. £ s. d.
27	27	20	18 12 0	17 2 0
30	30	32	20 0 0	18 10 0
33	33	24	23 8 0	21 18 0
36	34	27	25 4 0	23 4 0

Outside Measure.

TREBLE CHAMBERED HOLD-FAST SAFE,
Fitted with the Royal Climax Detector Lock, and Hardened Steel Plates.
No. 53.

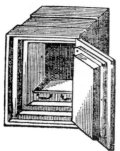

TREBLE CHAMBERED HOLDFAST SAFE,
Fitted with the Royal Climax Detector Lock, and Hardened Steel Plates.
No. 52.

PRICES.

Inches High.	wide.	deep.	With Drawers. £ s. d.	Without Drawers. £ s. d.
24	18	18	14 7 6	12 17 6
26	20	20	16 0 0	14 10 0
28	22	22	18 10 0	17 0 0
30	24	24	21 10 0	19 10 0
32	26	26	25 0 0	23 0 0

Outside Measure.

PRICES.

Inches High.	wide.	deep.	With Drawers. £ s. d.	Without Drawers. £ s. d.
30	30	24	30 0 0	28 10 0
33	33	27	35 0 0	33 10 0
36	36	30	40 0 0	38 0 0
40	36	30	47 0 0	45 0 0
48	38	30	55 0 0	53 0 0
54	38	30	65 0 0	63 0 0
60	40	30	80 0 0	77 0 0

Outside Measure.

Sole Agents, PAWSON & BRAILSFORD, Church Gates.

COTTERILL'S FIRE-PROOF DOORS, DEED BOXES, &C.

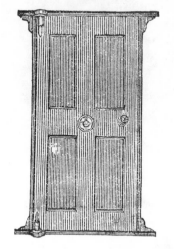

ADELAIDE WORKS,
SHEFFIELD.

TAYLOR BROTHERS,
MANUFACTURERS OF
SAWS,
STEEL, FILES, EDGE TOOLS, MACHINE KNIVES, &c.,

And General Merchants,

MANUFACTURERS OF THE GOODS STAMPED

TAYLOR BROTHERS.	J. TAYLOR & SON.
JOSEPH TAYLOR.	J. & I. TAYLOR.

J. & J. STEVENSON,
SHELL, INDIA RUBBER, AND HORN COMB
MANUFACTURERS,
No, 44, ARUNDEL STREET,
SHEFFIELD.

London Warehouse :—
9, Cripplegate Buildings, Wood-St.

CHARLES BRINDLEY,

ORGAN BUILDER

CARVER STREET,

SHEFFIELD.

The Instruments by C. B. are **CONSTRUCTED THROUGHOUT**
upon the most approved plan of

GERMAN

ORGAN BUILDING,

AND ARE FAR

CHEAPER AND BETTER IN MATERIALS

THAN THOSE OF ANY ENGLISH BUILDER.

ESTIMATES & TESTIMONIALS

OF THE HIGHEST CHARACTER,

FORWARDED FREE ON APPLICATION.

Tuning in any part of the Kingdom, by Contract or otherwise.

A WELL MADE
SILVER LEVER WATCH
FOR FIVE GUINEAS.

The above is offered to the Public with the greatest confidence as a most efficient and useful article. On Personal application, or receipt of Stamped envelope, references will be given to a great number of parties to whom these Watches have been sold.

A WELL ASSORTED
STOCK OF GOLD AND SILVER WATCHES
ALWAYS ON HAND.

GILT FRENCH CLOCKS WITH SHADES,
ALSO IN BRONZE AND MARBLE, FOR PRESENTATION, &c.

JOSEPH WILKINSON,
77, SOUTH-STREET, SHEFFIELD-MOOR.

F. J. MERCER,
LATE A. JESSOP,
Cabinet Maker,
UPHOLSTERER, &c.,
24 & 26, FARGATE, SHEFFIELD,

Respectfully calls the attention of his Friends and the Public to his Extensive

STOCK of FURNITURE
OF HIS OWN MANUFACTURE,

Comprising endless variety for Dining and Drawing Rooms, Libraries, Bed Rooms, &c., at VERY LOW PRICES.

DAMASKS, SATINS, CHINTZES, FRINGES,
And every description of Upholstery Trimmings.

AGENT FOR THE PATENT KAMPTULICON OR INDIA-RUBBER FLOOR COVERING.

STEAM PRINTING.

PAWSON & BRAILSFORD,

STEAM PRINTERS,

BRITANNIA PRINTING OFFICE, CASTLE STREET,

(AND AT CHURCH GATES, HIGH STREET,)

Have two unique Printing Machines, worked by Steam Power, which with all the other adjuncts of a well-appointed Printing Office, enable them to print with the greatest possible expedition, and at low prices—

BOOK WORK	POSTING BILLS
PAMPHLETS	HAND BILLS
SERMONS	CIRCULARS
CLUB RULES	CARDS
COLLIERY RULES	INVOICES, &c., &c.

ACCOUNT BOOKS.

PAWSON and BRAILSFORD

MANUFACTURE

LEDGERS, CASH BOOKS, JOURNALS, &c.,

In every style of Binding, the quality of which cannot in any way be surpassed. Every Book made to open well, and warranted quite firm and durable. In proof of the excellence of their work, P. and B. are able to refer to several eminent Firms whose Account Books they make. Orders executed with promtitude. Charges strictly moderate.

PAWSON and BRAILSFORD,

CHURCH GATES & CASTLE STREET.

DESPATCH BOXES, STATIONERY CASES,

WRITING DESKS, INK TRAYS, BOOK SLIDES, &c.,

IN

WALNUT, ROSEWOOD, OAK, EBONY,

With or without Gilt Mountings: also,

RUSSIA & MOROCCO TRAVELLING WRITING-CASES,

POCKET-BOOKS, WALLETS, BILL-CASES, PURSES, &c.,

OF THE BEST, MOST TASTEFUL, AND NOVEL DESCRIPTIONS,

TO BE HAD AT

PAWSON AND BRAILSFORD'S,

CHURCH GATES, HIGH STREET.